The Work
of the Counselor

Second Edition

LEONA E. TYLER

University of Oregon

APPLETON-CENTURY-CROFTS, INC.

New York

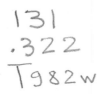

Preface to the First Edition

We might paraphrase a famous quotation and say, "Some are born counselors; some achieve counseling; and some have counseling thrust upon them." In a single educational system we may have all three kinds of workers. Some counselors are former teachers whose natural sympathy for the joys and struggles of students seems to fit them uniquely for this work. Some have undergone a carefully planned series of courses designed to equip them for it. Others are listed on the school records as part-time counselors only because they have a willing spirit and a vacant period. In other settings where counseling occurs—in industry, religious institutions, and social agencies—we find the same diversity in background and training.

I have had all these kinds of counselors more or less in mind as I wrote this book. Primarily it is for psychology students, a text for a first course in counseling procedures, and primarily it is for persons expecting to work in colleges or high schools. However, I have tried to make it broad enough to meet at least some of the needs of high school teachers who enroll for summer courses and workshops in order to obtain help with work they are already doing as best they can, and of men and women from many other walks of life who find that counseling makes up some part of their daily tasks. The book is written from the point of view of the general counselor who attempts to help clients with a variety of different problems rather than from that of the specialist in vocational guidance, marriage counseling, or psychotherapy. I have tried to stress common principles underlying many types of counseling activity rather than to outline special methods for each.

What these basic principles are can be briefly stated here. First, counseling is more a matter of what one perceives or comprehends than it is of what one says or does. No book can give one this sensitivity, but it can help one practice it by telling him something about what to look for, how to listen, and how to make use of all available aids to understanding. Second, success in counseling depends more upon personal qualities in the counselor than upon correct use of specified techniques. Warmth, responsiveness, and sincerity are essential. No book can give one these things, but it can help him to know how to express and manifest them. Third, there are individual differences in what counselors do and in how clients respond, so that every interview is actually a unique experience. We cannot really standardize procedures, and we can never be sure either that two counselors are using the same methods or that two clients are being treated in the same way.

By organizing my thinking around the twin ideas of unity of attitude and aim and diversity of word and action, I hope I have avoided the necessity for controversy over the directive/non-directive issue. To me the principal value of the non-directive movement has been to make us all very much more aware of the subtle psychological realities in each counseling situation. This awareness is as important in all other kinds of counseling as it is in psychotherapy and should be stressed in training men and women for such work regardless of what their specific duties are to be.

The illustrations and case material I have used are to be taken as *samples* of ways of meeting certain situations rather than as models to be followed. I have used free adaptations of cases drawn from my experience rather than verbatim records. This was partly in order to sidestep difficulties relating to the publication of confidential material and partly in order to achieve precision in illustrating points under discussion. Enough verbatim case material is now available in other books so that it did not seem necessary to include more of it here. It is assumed that the student in the course of his training will have access to such published material as well as to recorded interviews. In this book examples are to be read as *fiction,* but fiction bearing the same sort of relationship to fact as an autobiographical novel bears to the writer's life. Any of my clients who recognize some of their lives in these cases will know that the resemblance is not merely coincidental but also that the person described is not really any one single individual. Obviously such material cannot be used as evidence in connection with any theoretical issue.

A further word needs to be said in explanation of the research summaries. Since counseling is still to a large extent an art, dependent more on shared experience than on reported experiments, it was more natural and seemed somehow more honest to organize the body of each chapter in terms of what we have come to think and do rather than in terms of research evidence, scanty as it is in many areas. Our counseling practices do not in fact rest primarily on this evidence but on other bases entirely. But it seems to me very important that we do shift over as rapidly as we can to the use of dependable evidence rather than custom and intuition as a basis for judgments as to how counseling should be done. Therefore I have tried at the end of each chapter to summarize all the research material I could find and to evaluate its significance. I attempted to make a thorough survey of the literature of the last thiry years in this and related areas and then to sift out just those reports that presented *data* giving evidence for something rather than just an idea or a point of view. The project was perhaps somewhat overambitious, and I am not at all certain that I found all relevant material. The coverage is most satisfactory on those topics most directly tied in with counseling. On such subjects, for example, as the evaluation of non-directive psychotherapy and the contribution of tests to vocational guidance, I am confident that practically everything published through 1952 has been included. On topics intermediate between counseling and other fields such as psychiatric diagnosis and therapy, general interview methods, and the uses of cumulative records, I have probably missed some things which might well have been included. Trying to put together these summaries has made me realize the many directions in which counseling spreads out and the vagueness of some of its boundaries. In spite of these limitations I still hope that the research summaries and bibliography will be a help to students desiring to do research on counseling problems and to practicing counselors trying to distinguish between things we do simply because they seem to work well and things we do because of some definite research evidence.

It would be impossible to list all the people to whom I am indebted for ideas expressed in this book. Names that stand out are those of Donald G. Paterson and John G. Darley who started me out on this fascinating pursuit and saw me through the development of the basic concepts to which all later ideas have been grafted. My University of Oregon colleagues, especially Howard R. Taylor and Robert Leeper in the Psychology Department and Spencer Carlson in the Counseling Center, have discussed many of these ideas with me again and again. It will be apparent that I owe much to the published work of Carl R. Rogers and his associates in the non-directive movement. Above all, I should like to thank my clients over the years. Their willingness to share their lives with me has been one of the major sources of whatever wisdom I possess.

L. E. T.

Preface to the Second Edition

The principal reason that the task of revising this book presented itself to me with increasing urgency was that the research summaries were getting more and more out of date; anyone who undertakes to summarize research and evaluate its significance for those who practice an art takes on a responsibility to keep his readers in touch with the times. As I proceeded to sift the material published since 1952 in the field of counseling and the fields adjacent to it, I became increasingly convinced that this job must be done by someone. It was heartening to find that there had been more papers in which actual research data of some sort were presented published during this eight-year period than had been published altogether during the previous thirty years. Some issues are now settled or nearly settled. Many large questions have been analyzed into smaller questions upon which research is possible.

As in the previous edition, I tried to include all published papers that presented data or evidence. As before, I am not at all certain, now that I have finished the job, that I found everything. I did not attempt to read all doctoral dissertations in the counseling area but relied on *Dissertation Abstracts* for what they contained, and my search for relevant material in the journals of related areas, such as education and social work, was less thorough than it was in psychology. But I offer what is here without apology, except to those whose contributions may have inadvertently been overlooked. I tried to make the survey complete.

As I proceeded, I found myself revising the bodies of the chapters themselves more than I had expected to do. Partly these changes in organization and emphasis grew out of the research findings themselves. Partly they represent thinking I have done during the eight-year interval in preparing papers for professional meetings and in teaching courses in counseling. (Large parts of several of these previously published papers are imbedded in the appropriate chapters.) Partly they are related to general changes in the *Zeitgeist* that are difficult to analyze but very real in their effects.

Perhaps the most basic change is that a unified conceptual or theoretical approach has been made much more explicit. I have more definite ideas than I had in 1952 as to what counseling is and what counselors can contribute to the society in which they live. For me it has become more clearly differentiated from psychotherapy on the one hand, education on the other. The key words in this formulation are *choice, decision, plans*. This point of view is presented in the first chapter, woven into the fabric of the following chapters, and recapitulated at the end.

One other kind of modification of the previous edition has been attempted. As I wrote I have tried to keep in mind counselors in many types of setting besides the college counseling centers in which most of my own experience has been obtained. My aim has been to stress the things that school counselors, marriage counselors, rehabilitation counselors, and those in many other positions have in common. This means that not every reader will wish to read all the chapters. Those whose work involves no vocational guidance, for example, can omit Chapters 6, 7, and 8, moving directly from 5 to 9, without missing essential ideas about the use of information in counseling. Those whose work involves no counseling with regard to personal problems can omit Chapter 11. The other chapters are designed for all.

As before, I wish it were possible for me to thank individually all the writers and speakers whose ideas have influenced my thinking and all the clients who have given me so much to think about. I am indebted to the *Personnel and Guidance Journal* for permission to reprint large portions of "The Initial Interview" and "Minimum-Change Therapy" and to the *Journal of Counseling Psychology* for the use of parts of "Theoretical Principles Underlying the Counseling Process." I am particularly indebted to my friend and neighbor, Mrs. Lu Downey, whose comments on ideas expressed and sensitivity to discrepancies and errors in the text made her secretarial contribution most significant.

L. E. T.

Table of Contents

Preface to the First Edition   v

Preface to the Second Edition   ix

1. What Counseling Is   1

Definition; The Complexity of the Occupational World; Rapid Social Change and the Individual; The Loss of Old Certainties; Scarcity of Informal Counseling; Historical Origins—Vocational Guidance; Historical Origins—Mental Health Movement; Distinction between Counseling and Psychotherapy; Essentials of the Counseling Process

Research Summary   18

Evidence of Need for Counseling; Types of Problems in College Counseling Centers; Definition of Counseling; Different Perceptions of Counselor's Role; *Evaluation*

2. Essential Qualities of Counseling Interviews   24

Basic Attitudes—Acceptance and Understanding; Basic Skill —Communication; Dealing with Silent Intervals

Research Summary   34

What Aspects of the Interview Are Most Important? Differences in Counselor Style; Differences Related to Topic of Discussion; Counselor Differences and Counseling Outcomes; Voluntary Versus Referred Cases; *Evaluation*

3. The Initial Interview   40

Special Importance of Initial Interviews; How to Get Started; Client Expectations and the Counseling Relationship; Counselor Attitudes and the Counseling Relationship; The Goals of the Initial Interview

4. Diagnostic Activity in the Initial Stage of Counseling   59

Different Points of View about Diagnosis; Objections to Diagnosis as a Central Concept; Diagnosis as Comprehensive Picture or Working Image; Varieties of Decisions: Whether to Continue the Relationship; Varieties of Decisions: What Kind of Treatment? Varieties of Decision: Is Consultation Necessary?

Research Summary   78

Diagnostic Categories for Counseling; The Diagnostic Process; *Evaluation*

5. The Use of Background Information and Case Records in Counseling   82

Nature of Filed Information; Objections to the Use of Case Records; The Values of Case Records; How to Study a Case Record; Obtaining Case Information; Records of the Counseling Process; Professional Use of School Cumulative Records; Problems with Regard to Confidentiality

6. The Use of Tests in Educational and Vocational Counseling: General Considerations   102

The Purposes Tests Serve; Specific Questions Tests Help to Answer; Counseling Uses of Tests Distinguished from Other Uses; Principal Types of Counseling Tests; Personality Tests —Special Considerations; Validity Concepts in Counseling; Counseling Uses of Test Norms; Reliability Concepts in Counseling

Research Summary   116

Evidence That Tests Contribute to Counseling Success; Evidence with Regard to What Vocational Tests Predict; Aptitude Batteries Based on Factor Analysis; Personality Tests in Counseling; Miscellaneous Work on Tests; *Evaluation*

7. The Use of Tests in Educational and Vocational Counseling: Integration with Counseling   124

Planning the Testing Program for an Individual; The Organization of Test Information into a Pattern; Communicating Test Information in the Interview

Research Summary 146

Effects of Counseling, Including Testing, on Self-Knowledge; Effects of Client-Centered Techniques of Test Selection and Interpretation; *Evaluation*

8. The Use of Occupational Information in Vocational Counseling 153

The Importance of Occupational Information; Purposes for Which Occupational Information Is Used in Counseling; Kinds of Occupational Information

Research Summary 169

Evaluation of Published Materials; The Functional Occupational Classification; Occupational Information Related to Social Roles; Personality Differences Between Occupational Groups; Occupational Choice and Early Childhood Experiences; *Evaluation*

9. General Use of Information in Counseling 177

Information a Vital Part of Counseling; Information Does Not Mean Advice; Essential Characteristics of Information; Problems of Communication

10. Decision-Making Interviews 189

Examples of the Decision Process; Counseling Skills Facilitating Decision-Making; Indecision Versus Indecisiveness; Criterion for Evaluating Decisions

Research Summary 205

Inadequacy of Counselor Prognoses as Basis for Decisions; Research on Vocational Development; Other Research on Vocational Choice; *Evaluation*

11. Counseling for Personal Adjustment 211

The Counselor's Responsibility in This Area; General Features of Minimum-Change Therapy; First Stage: General Exploration; Second Stage: Clarification; Third Stage: Reinforcement; The Use of Limits in Personality Counseling; The Use of the Counseling Relationship as Therapy

Research Summary   233

How Effective Is Therapy? What Kind of Personality
Change Does Therapy Produce? How Different Are Thera-
pies Based on Different Theoretical Systems? *Evaluation*

12. The Counselor as a Person   239

Reasons for Concern with This Topic; The Training of Professional Counselors; Problems of Selection; Professional
Responsibilities; Relationships to Other Workers

Research Summary   255

Characteristics of Counselors; Effects of Training; Professional Ethics; *Evaluation*

13. The Evaluation of Counseling Effectiveness   260

Evaluation Research as a Basis for Counseling Progress;
Difficulties and Pitfalls in Evaluation Research; Evaluation
of Guidance Programs; Client Attitudes toward Counseling;
Effects of Counseling on School Achievements; Effects of
Counseling on Vocational Adjustment; Effects of Counseling
on Personal Adjustment; Counseling in Rehabilitation Settings; The Relative Effectiveness of Different Kinds of Counseling; Implications of Evaluation Research

14. A Conceptual Framework for Counselors   287

The General Process of Development; The Transformation
of Potentialities into Actualities: Two Different Processes;
The Place of Counseling in Development; Limits and Communication

Appendix A   297

Appendix B   301

References   303

Index   321

The Work
of the Counselor

CHAPTER ONE

What Counseling Is

DEFINITION

Counseling is one of those words that everybody understands but no two people seem to understand in precisely the same way. The term was not invented by psychologists, educators, or social workers. It is a part of our everyday language, and the activity it represents is a part of our everyday life. But during the last half century there has been an ever-increasing amount of *professional* counseling carried on, and an increasing number of people who see themselves *primarily* as counselors. It is their concept of the counseling function that will concern us particularly in this book.

One way of formulating a definition of counseling, for the professional or for the man in the street, is to say that it is a process designed to help a person answer the question, "What shall I do?" One of the most fundamental activities of human beings is the making of choices. Philosophers and mythmakers, artists and moralists have thought deeply about this basic truth. A man does not have any built-in repertory of responses to the world in which he lives, as many animals do. The outer world of his natural surroundings and his culture and the inner world of his unique individual capacities and emotions are both incredibly complex. Yet he must somehow manage to steer his own course through these labyrinthine channels. It is not too speculative to assume that over the centuries counseling developed as a means by which people could help each other to meet this challenge. The knowledge we have acquired during the twentieth century, based on professional counseling practice and research, can then be seen as a continuation of this long-term trend.

THE COMPLEXITY OF THE
OCCUPATIONAL WORLD

It is probably true also that the need for counseling is greater in our era than it has ever been before. Each person growing up in our modern society faces a far more complex situation than his grandfather did. It is obvious that a young person who tries to choose intelligently among the 40,000 or more separate occupations that have been identified faces no easy task. Of course no one individual ever considers all 40,000, counseling or no counseling, but if he is left to his own devices he will probably make his choice from among the three or four that are most familiar or most convenient, and there are more and more men and women who have come to feel that the results of choices made in this way are not satisfactory. Bill Penfield, for example, gets a job in a men's clothing store after he graduates from high school. It is the easiest thing to do, since he has been working there part time during his last two school years and the manager is a friend of his family. Twenty years later, with financial responsibilities that now rule out any possibility of a drastic change of plans, he is still doubtful as to whether he might not have been happier as a surveyor or geologist. He adapts himself without too much discontent to the pattern his life has taken, but he wishes to be sure that his son has broader opportunities than he had. Peter Jensen goes to a good college and eventually takes his expected place in his father's law office, but he never quite frees himself from a feeling that he has missed something along the way—that this is not really the role in life he would have chosen had he thought the matter through. Consequently he uses his influence on the school board to make sure that adequate vocational counseling facilities are made available to the boys and girls of the community.

It is the combination of an extremely diversified industrial society with democratic ideals and attitudes that makes counseling necessary. Although often denied in practice, the principle that any individual has a right to fill any position for which he can qualify is a basic premise in our democratic thinking. The most reactionary of us would hardly be willing to advocate that only the children of professional men be admitted to professional schools or that children of unskilled laborers should invariably be shunted into unskilled jobs. We believe that it is the individual's right, or even his duty, to improve his position and achieve as much as possible. These attitudes are a part of the cultural heritage that each child internalizes, automatically adopts as his own set of values. They constitute subtle but strong determiners of his vocational ambitions. It is because the complexity is a matter of attitudes as well as situations that no simple means of disseminating occupational information and giving aptitude tests can possibly meet the need for counseling. A boy of sixteen may be handed a test profile that makes perfectly clear what his pattern of abilities is like, be informed about occupations in which such abilities are most applicable, and yet be totally unable to grasp the significance of these facts because of the network of ambitions, family expectations, and self-doubts in which he is enmeshed. It is more than information that he needs; it is wise counseling.

We see the effects of these American attitudes and the problems they create for American adolescents especially in our high schools and colleges. The tremendous increase in enrollment at these institutions during the last fifty years is a matter of common knowledge. Many factors have combined to channel such a large proportion of our boys and girls, young men and young women, through educational institutions. Compulsory education laws now in force in most states require attendance until the age of sixteen, in some places even until eighteen. These laws, in turn, reflect various social factors—the wish to keep young people off the labor market, the conviction that democratic government requires an intelligent body of voters, the faith in education as a vehicle for social and individual advancement.

Whatever the reasons, the presence of so many young people from such diverse backgrounds in our schools and colleges has made the need for counseling very apparent. The individual must find his way around in a complicated curriculum and somehow select those courses that will be of most value for his particular life pattern. But to do this he must *have* a life pattern, and many things make it difficult for him to develop one. Conflicts between the attitudes and standards of his home and those he encounters in classmates from very different types of families make it hard for him to know just where he himself stands. The necessity for making his place in the social and extracurricular life of his school and at the same time keeping up with its intellectual activities often causes him trouble. Deficiencies he finds in himself, in reading or mathematics, social skills or personal appearance, must either be remedied directly or hedged in by those elaborate and often curious systems of defenses which make them tolerable.

Thus it seems reasonable to suppose that the development of a counseling profession has come about partly as a result of the sheer complexity of modern life, especially as it confronts the adolescent boy and girl. A parent, teacher, or friend finds it less easy to realize this complexity and its impact on the individual than does the counselor, whose special training and experience has accustomed him to look at the whole picture.

RAPID SOCIAL CHANGE AND THE INDIVIDUAL

There is another feature of present-day society which seems to be leading to the development of a counseling profession. It is the instability generated by the rapid changes that have been occurring in our ways of life. Sociologists as well as poets have labeled this an "age of anxiety." Various writers have called attention to factors creating insecurity in the individual, factors ranging all the way from broken homes to the threat of atomic annihilation. It is true that it would be very difficult to prove that this age is more anxious than previous periods. There are no statistics which permit us to compare the incidence of even the major psychoses from century to century, and it is even more impossible to gauge the comparative frequencies of neuroses and the lesser varieties of disequilibrium. Nevertheless, in the books we write and the pictures we paint there is much to suggest that the prevailing mood of our time is one of uncertainty and apprehension.

The most serious of the social instabilities for the individual, if the conclusions of psychiatrists and other mental health workers are sound, is the threat to the family. Among the clients who come to a counselor with personal problems a very considerable proportion are children of divorced parents. Sometime during their childhood, long before emotional growth was completed, they have been confronted with problems of conflicting loyalties that would have strained even the capacities of maturity. The counseling process constitutes for them a new opportunity to think the whole thing through and assimilate the experience and its consequences in their later development.

If divorce itself were the only problem, however, our task would be considerably easier than it is. It is the emotional conflicts that lie back of the break-up rather than the separation itself which unsettle children. Naturally not all persons seeking psychotherapy are the products of divorce, but most if not all of them reflect in their attitudes the strains to which their childhood homes were subject. For every marriage that ends in the divorce courts there are probably several more which generate tensions almost as severe. Children in these homes have had to learn to cope with bitterness, hatred, neglect, and confusion and to put up some sort of defenses against the anxiety such attitudes bring.

It goes without saying that social problems are not to be solved by counseling alone. Many agencies and organizations are concerned with the family and are attempting to improve an unsatisfactory situation there. To the extent that long-range educational programs aimed at improving family relations succeed, counseling to ameliorate the effects of bad family situations will become less necessary. For the present, however, home difficulties are a major source of problems for workers in three types of setting. Child guidance clinics are attempting to help the children themselves at the time when their problems are most acute. Marriage counselors have developed a specialized service for men and women who wish to try to salvage their relationship rather than to break it off. General counseling agencies in schools, even when their principal function is to help students make good educational and vocational choices, also help individuals to understand and modify emotional attitudes that have grown out of home environments.

Many other social problems growing out of the conditions of our times are reflected in the insecurity felt by individuals. There is the ever-present threat of war and the possibility of ever-more-serious consequences that accompany technological improvements in weapons. The cold war with its necessity for constant vigilance against dangers that are never too clearly defined brings its own strains. There is always the threat of unemployment in an economic system where a man has no control over his own job. There are the anxieties that arise from the necessity for competition and the emphasis on success in our society.

It is, however, the lesser threats and uncertainties arising from these social problems, rather than the problems themselves, which are most disturbing. The possibility of sudden death and destruction does not seem to produce as much anxiety as do the minor worries about one's own immediate future. Will I be drafted this year or not? Shall I enlist now or wait? What good will it do me to study this term if I am not going to be allowed to finish my education anyway? It is in such questions that the troubled international situation makes its impact on the individual. Will I ever be able to get my grades up high enough so that I will be admitted to medical school? How can we keep up our country club membership and the social activities that go with it unless I can make more money? How can I ever face mother if her sorority doesn't pledge me? How can I get over my inferiority complex? Wherever I go I never feel as good as other people. It is such problems that our competitive economic and social system raises for each person. They may seem trivial by comparison with the larger social issues, but they are the stuff of individual human experience.

THE LOSS OF OLD CERTAINTIES

Still another element in the growing need for counseling services in our time is the crumbling of the old certainties. A great many people no longer have the religious anchors that used to hold them steady in times of crisis. Various political and economic theories compete for men's loyalties. The development of communication to its present level has made it harder for a man to retreat into some little shell of orthodoxy which can shield him from conflicting winds of doctrine. This is more than a superficial state of affairs. A century ago Matthew Arnold wrote the famous lines[1] delineating a feeling that was to grow ever more widespread as time passed:

Ah, love, let us be true
To one another! for the world, which seems
To lie before us like a land of dreams,
So various, so beautiful, so new,
Hath really neither joy, nor love nor light,

[1] Matthew Arnold, "Dover Beach" (In Van Doren, 1928).

Nor certitude, nor peace, nor help for pain;
And we are here as on a darkling plain
Swept with confused alarms of struggle and flight,
Where ignorant armies clash by night.

In our own time, Robinson Jeffers[2] expresses the same realization of lost certainty:

Have men's minds changed
Or the rock hidden in the deep of the waters of the soul
Broken the surface? A few centuries
Gone by, was none dared not to people
The darkness beyond the stars with harps and habitations.
But now, dear is the truth. Life is grown sweeter and lonelier
And death is no evil.

Many more passages from poems, plays, and novels of our century could be assembled, describing a feeling that counselors will have encountered in many of their clients. Not all, it is true, react to the prevailing uncertainty in this way. Many try to lay hold of something which they will almost arbitrarily accept as true. Witness the proliferation of fundamentalist religious sects, the fanatical loyalty of Communist party members, and the rigid and intolerant varieties of patriotism and nationalism which flourish in our time. What we can easily lose sight of is the psychological fact that a faith desperately grasped and maintained as a way out of chaos and a simple faith that has never been threatened are really very different things. There is a defensiveness about these rigid, last-stand orthodoxies that enables us to recognize them as symptoms of the underlying anxiety rather than as genuine solutions.

Whether an individual is troubled by uncertainty or trying to defend himself against it, he may want the help which counseling may bring. It is in the relatively calm, non-threatening counseling atmosphere that such a person is most likely to be able to face confusions courageously, to sort out from the ideals and values he has been exposed to the ones which are valid for him, and thus to come out with a workable philosophy of life. It is a significant fact that churchmen sensitive to the needs of their congregations are beginning to stress counseling as a supplement to preaching,

[2] Robinson Jeffers, "Night" (In Van Doren, 1928).

which has hitherto been their principal method for dispelling
doubt and confusion. Pastoral counseling is a flourishing new field
of specialization and each year many ministers are being trained
in psychological techniques to enable them to serve in this way.

Whether or not he has specialized in this area, any counselor
is often confronted with the ferment produced by conflicting
values and beliefs. Problems of vocational choice, simple on the
surface, often turn out to be rooted in just such conflicts. A boy
with all his aptitudes pointing toward a successful career in
accounting may be unable to settle on this objective because he
is in revolt against his conception of the businessman's philosophy.
A girl's determination to be an artist, although she has been
repeatedly discouraged and told that she has only mediocre
talents, may represent an attempt to achieve a way of life in
harmony with her philosophy. Since these are highly individual
problems, only the individualized techniques of counseling are
adequate to deal with them. Listening to lectures and sermons or
reading books about other people's philosophies does not accomplish the same purpose.

It might be noted in passing that the very fact that he wit-
nesses the resolution of such difficulties and the working out of
strong, satisfying patterns of faith and conduct makes the counselor less pessimistic than many writers and thinkers are about
the chaos in our values and our lack of a unifying philosophy. He
knows that human individuals have the capacity to face confusion
and organize it in meaningful ways. That, after all, is the most
important consideration.

SCARCITY OF INFORMAL COUNSELING

These, then, are some of the social trends that create a need
for counseling services: the complexity of our social and economic
system, our democratic ideals, the anxiety that arises from rapid
changes in basic institutions, and the loss of a unifying religion
or philosophy. At the same time that these changes have been
occurring, other changes in our ways of living have been making
it less and less likely that non-scheduled, informal counseling will
take care of the needs. We have been increasingly becoming an
urban people. In a large city there is very little of the genuine
interest in neighbors' affairs that we find in small towns. Many

young men and women have moved to the city primarily to free themselves from undue prying into their affairs. Once there, however, they find that they have shifted from one extreme to the other, and that to have no one taking any interest whatever in one's thoughts and problems is fully as uncomfortable as to have someone taking too much interest in them. Urban life is less likely than village life to supply an individual with an understanding old uncle, a family doctor or minister, or a teacher who has known him from boyhood. The sort of influence such people represent is seldom noticed while it is present, but its complete absence leaves a basic need unmet.

Similarly, the shift toward small families makes incidental counseling harder to obtain. In the case of an adolescent boy or girl, there is no longer likely to be in his immediate vicinity a person whose relationship has the right combination of sincere interest and neutral objectivity to make for good counseling. His father or mother, or his brother or sister only slightly older than himself, is too close to him, too emotionally involved in his behavior, to serve in this particular capacity. No longer does the typical household include grandfathers and grandmothers, relatives, guests, trusted servants, and other miscellaneous persons. The outer circle has disappeared, and no matter how well-intentioned those in the inner circle may be they cannot carry out the counseling function very successfully. The reasons for this will become more apparent in later chapters as we describe the counseling function in more detail.

HISTORICAL ORIGINS—VOCATIONAL GUIDANCE

Professional counseling as we know it today is a product of two kinds of historical development. The first of these is the vocational guidance movement. The publication in 1906 of the book *Choosing a Vocation,* by Frank Parsons, is usually pointed to as the beginning of this movement. Parsons was impressed with the great need in an industrial society for helping young people find suitable places in the world of work. As he thought through the problem, it took on a clear structure for him, and this structure has dominated vocational counseling ever since. What a person must have in order to make a good choice is dependable information about: (1) the characteristics of different occupations, and

(2) his own talents and limitations. The task of the vocational counselor is to make both these kinds of information available to the counselee and to help him comprehend and utilize it.

As the years passed, a technology built on these basic principles gradually developed. It was realized that the kind of information about an occupation one could gain by watching a person work or by asking him what his work was like was not at all satisfactory. Scientific methods of studying an occupation were worked out so that its demands could be formulated in precise language or even in quantitative terms. Systems of classification of occupations were formulated, tested, and revised. Books and pamphlets setting forth information about specific occupations or general occupational areas were written and published. Courses in occupational information were introduced into the high school curriculum. Field trips, movies, lectures, interviews, and many other devices were added to the resources placed at the counselor's disposal.

Beginning not long after World War I, the technical developments designed to facilitate the understanding of individual talents and limitations were even more conspicuous. The group intelligence-testing program carried out during the war demonstrated that it is possible to obtain in a few minutes information about a man's capacity that may be used to predict with a reasonable degree of accuracy whether or not he will succeed in certain situations. There was an immediate public demand for such tests in industry and in education, and within a few years literally hundreds of them became available.

Vocational counselors were quick to see that to have many tests of specific vocational aptitudes would be an advantage in carrying out the second part of their task as it had been formulated by Parsons—the analysis of the individual. Large-scale research projects such as the Minnesota study of mechanical aptitude and individual "free-enterprise" attempts to construct aptitude tests that would sell were prominent features of the landscape in the applied psychology of the 1920's and the 1930's. The statistical and methodological tools needed to standardize and validate such tests became sharper and more precise. Ways of educating counselors and other test users so that they might distinguish between reputable and disreputable tests became essential, and standards for counselor training were raised. The vocational counselor envisaged by Parsons was becoming more and more of a specialist.

HISTORICAL ORIGINS—MENTAL HEALTH MOVEMENT

The second of the two historical streams that merged with vocational guidance to form our present counseling profession was the mental health movement. Here, too, an influential book forms a convenient landmark from which we can chart its beginning. Clifford Beers, in *The Mind That Found Itself*, published in 1908, called public attention to mental illness as an individual experience and a social problem. Organizations were formed. Books were written. Lectures were given. People began to be concerned about prevention as well as cure, about the less serious as well as the more serious emotional difficulties.

It was during this same period that psychoanalysis began to catch the attention of the literate public, both as a method of treatment for the emotionally disabled and as a way of thinking about human motivation and behavior. Persons who in previous eras would have accepted anxiety and frustration as inevitable, or blamed it on their circumstances and associates, began to look within themselves for its sources. The emotional roots of delinquency and the kinds of illness that were now being labeled "psychosomatic" were sought. The magic wand that it was hoped would dissolve these stubborn ills was psychotherapy, the treatment which attempts to enable a person to get rid of his difficulties by talking about them.

This development did not reach its peak until the 1940's. As World War I had convinced people that mental abilities were measurable, so World War II convinced them that emotional difficulties were curable. The profession of psychiatry expanded rapidly, and more and more psychiatrists embarked upon the practice of psychotherapy rather than the administration of hospitals for the mentally ill. The profession of clinical psychology, until then only a minor part of psychology as a whole, showed an even more spectacular development and entered upon a long struggle with the medical profession, a struggle not yet ended, for the right to practice psychotherapy.

Those who participated in the mental health movement and

had no connection with vocational guidance used the term *counseling* to refer to what others were calling *therapy*. Although the vocational guidance emphasis tended to be dominant in schools, the mental health emphasis was dominant in clinics and social agencies. But the force of circumstances tended to bring these two disparate meanings of the term together. So-called "vocational counselors" repeatedly encountered personal, social, and emotional problems in the clients they interviewed. So-called "counselors" in mental health agencies found that they needed to concern themselves with their clients' outer circumstances as well as their inner conflicts. Thus the two kinds of service—helping people to make wise choices and helping them to improve their emotional health and well-being—have increasingly been offered by the same professional person.

DISTINCTION BETWEEN COUNSELING AND PSYCHOTHERAPY

There is still a great deal of ambiguity and confusion in the helping professions, and we must expect that in any discussion of counseling the participants will attach somewhat different meanings to the term. But a synthesis is beginning to emerge in a clear enough form that it can be used at least for the purposes of all later discussions in this book. Instead of using the term *counseling* as a rough synonym, perhaps in some instances even a euphemism, for *psychotherapy*, we shall make a clear distinction. The aim of therapy is generally considered to be personality *change* of some sort. Let us use *counseling* to refer to a helping process the aim of which is not to change the person but to enable him to utilize the resources he now has for coping with life. The outcome we would then expect from counseling is that the client *do* something, take some constructive action on his own behalf. Whether the need that brings him to counseling grows out of his arrival at a point in his life where an important decision must be made or out an emotional conflict that is paralyzing his ability to act, the counselor will attempt to make forward movement possible.

This distinction could be elaborated in much detail, but to do so at this point is unnecessary, since clarification of the counseling process in all of its ramifications is the purpose of the book as a whole. But it might be well at this point to head off some possible misunderstandings of what has been said and to counteract some ideas that seem to me to be misconceptions.

When one says that a counselor helps a client decide what to do, it does not mean that the counselor gives him advice or tells him what he *should* do. There may be occasions when this is the best way to proceed, but generally speaking a person facing a choice where he must take responsibility for the consequences needs to be given an opportunity to do his own thinking rather than to have someone do it for him. This is where the professionally trained counselor differs most from the man in the street. To the average person counseling is practically synonymous with advising. To the counselor it is quite a different procedure.

Another inadequate formulation fairly common among psychologically trained persons is that counseling is essentially a somewhat superficial kind of therapy applicable only to relatively normal persons with minor personality handicaps. Events of the past twenty years have made this way of defining what counseling essentially is increasingly inappropriate. The thriving Veterans Administration program in counseling psychology has demonstrated that even hospitalized psychotic patients, persons who as a group show more extreme personality deviations than any other with which psychologists have worked, can benefit from counseling. Analysis of objectives has shown that superficiality *vs.* depth is *not* the dimension upon which various techniques differ. The ways a person sees his work, his religious beliefs, or his relationships to his wife and children are as deep and fundamental a part of him as are his anxieties over sexual or aggressive motivation. It is well for psychologists and prospective psychologists to try to avoid this inadequate formulation because of its consequences. It leads to a relative *neglect* of a very useful kind of treatment in favor of "deeper" methods—in psychology *deep* is a good word, a carrier of prestige.

If we are willing to define counseling as the process through which individuals are enabled to make good choices and thus improve their relationships to the world and to their fellow men, as they set the pattern for their own unique patterns of development, we shall have a framework within which we can fit most of the things counselors are doing, whether their clients are old or young, sick or well. We will also be concentrating our efforts on goals that are achievable rather than those that are illusory. Various kinds of follow-up research, summarized in some detail in Chapters 11 and 13, have produced almost no evidence that measurable personality change *occurs* as an outcome of counseling. What does happen is that limited problems are solved, workable decisions are made, the client moves forward with more assurance than before. If we take a long-range view of individual development, each such step forward is a significant factor in the growth of a person. Counselors must get their satisfaction not from making people over but from helping each person to become more truly himself.

ESSENTIALS OF THE COUNSELING PROCESS

If we think of the counseling process in this way, what do we see as its real essentials? We shall be returning to these ideas throughout the book, but perhaps it will be useful to summarize them here. The foundation of the whole enterprise is the relationship between counselor and client. In some ways it is misleading to speak of *the* counseling relationship, because it varies from case to case. A counselor's relationship with Mr. Christie, a mature graduate student in his own field, is of necessity quite different from his relationship with Jane Julian, an 18-year-old first-term freshman. But in his attempt to create a solid, fruitful relationship with each person, a counselor proceeds according to certain principles or guidelines, and these can be specified. First, he must have a genuine, sincere interest in each client, *as he now is.* As Rogers has put it, the client must feel that he is *received.* Such an interest is communicated to the client in many ways—by promptness in meeting appointments, by sensitiveness to doubts and misgivings the client may express at the beginning, by posture and facial expression, as well as by verbal responses to what the client says. Such an interest cannot be faked or simulated. If a counselor finds a client boring or distasteful to him, it is far better that he try to put the person in touch with some other service than that he continue a relationship almost certain to be unproductive.

Secondly, the client must be able to have confidence in the counselor, to feel safe with him. It is this requirement that makes what is called *confidentiality* so important. If a person is going to relax his defenses and think out loud about weaknesses as well as strengths, he needs to be sure that these weaknesses will never under any circumstances be held against him because he has revealed them here. But there is more to a feeling of confidence than this. It includes respect for the counselor's competence, liking for him as an individual, perhaps favorable impressions of the field he represents, such as psychology, social work, or the ministry. There is no simple technique for winning or communicating such confidence. It is rather an ongoing process of becoming the kind of person in whom confidence can reasonably be placed and demonstrating this constantly by what one says, what one does, and what one refrains from doing.

The third defining characteristic of counseling relationships is that they are *limited* in many ways, and these limits themselves are used to promote development. Interviews are held at definite times, by appointment, and unless there are unusual reasons, a client is not permitted to overstay his allotted time. There are limits to the services the counselor is willing to give. He does not ordinarily intercede for a client with outside agencies or authorities, although on occasion he may make some recommendation about minor matters like permitting a student to drop a course or move out of a dormitory. There are limits to the intimacy or closeness of the relationship. The counselor does not express his own views in interviews as he would in conversations with friends. He may encounter his clients socially, but he avoids close friendships with them. He also avoids being cast in the roles of other significant persons in the client's life—father, brother, lover—the kind of phenomenon psychoanalysts call transference. Some of this inevitably occurs, because people generally try out new persons they meet in the roles they know best. But a counselor discourages the continuation of such transference ties by the kinds of response he gives—consistent, realistic, matter-of-fact. The purpose of all these kinds of limits is to make it clear at all times that responsibility is in the hands of the client. What is to be done he must do. He cannot depend upon someone else to decide things for him or to protect him from the consequences of his actions.

It is in such relationships that the real power of counseling lies—relationships that are warm, sincere, dependable, but not close in the ordinary sense of the word. It is the setting up of such a relationship with each unique individual person that mainly constitutes counseling skill. It is this relationship that furnishes the psychological environment in which a person is able to make the choices and decisions through which his own distinctive personality takes shape. In practice, training programs for counselors have not paid enough attention to it. Teachers still tend to think that it is counseling *techniques* they need to acquire. Employment service counselors and juvenile court counselors are likely to be technique-oriented. If we are really to make use of the potential counseling resources in our society, we must find ways of making prospective counselors aware of the subtleties of these relationships between people instead of simply trying to tell them what to *do* or not to do.

Counseling can be distinguished from many other varieties of psychological treatment by the way in which information of many varieties is used. Under the broad term *information* we include background facts about the person's school and work experiences, psychological test results, and facts about occupations and social organizations, as well as a multitude of other specific things that may come up in connection with specific cases. It is evident that such facts can have a bearing on any kind of psychological treatment. What gives counseling its specific emphasis is that information is treated as a resource to be used by the *client* rather than as background for the therapist.

This *client-centered* approach to information has a number of implications. For one thing, the emphasis must always be on things the client wants to know. Therefore the relevance of any series of questions he is expected to answer or any set of tests he is asked to take should always be explained to him. This does not always mean that the assessment process must be confined to questions the client raises when he comes in. Part of a counselor's skill consists in reformulating questions in more answerable terms. Furthermore, it is quite possible to add some questions of his own to those the client brings. If, for example, he has doubts about the general soundness of the client's personality that would lead him to question whether counseling is the preferred form of treatment, it is quite possible for him to say without alarming the client, "It might be a good idea if you took a few general tests to start with to give us a preliminary idea of what sort of person you are. That would make it easier for me to help you decide the best way of going at this problem." In other instances where the counselor is carrying out some research project that necessitates obtaining certain kinds of test information from all clients, he can state frankly at the outset that tests are being given for this purpose and explain how the results are to be handled.

Aside from such exceptions that are explained to him ahead of time, a client in a counseling situation is a "partner in the firm." He himself analyzes the significance of his past experience for his present attitudes. If he takes tests, the meaning of the scores he obtains is explained to him as clearly as possible. (This does not mean, however, that the scores themselves with all the complications related to inadequate reliability, complicated validity, and diverse norm groups, will necessarily be placed before him.) If friends, relatives, or teachers are interviewed, he knows about such contacts and concurs in their purpose. He is encouraged to seek out for himself the facts he needs about occupations, hobbies, clubs, or religious beliefs, though the counselor may help put him in touch with the sources of such information.

The reason for stressing this point is that it is important for the success of the whole counseling enterprise that the client keep the responsibility for his own life firmly in his own hands. Decisions must be *his* decisions, and he must know on what basis he made them, or he will not have taken the step toward maturity which is the chief aim of the counseling process.

We can sum up by saying that the psychological purpose of counseling is to facilitate *development*. Thus it can be considered a part of the whole broad educational process that extends from the earliest months of infancy to the declining years of old age. One way of defining development is to think of it as *patterned change*. Moment by moment, year by year, the process continues. A person is continually being transformed, but there is order and a measure of predictability in the transformations themselves. The more a person becomes aware of the structures that he has built up through previous development—abilities and talents, social assets and liabilities, emotional strengths and weaknesses, wishes, values, and aspirations—the more he is able to influence his own subsequent development by the choices he makes. The main purposes of counseling are to promote this kind of awareness, to facilitate this kind of choice.

Research Summary

EVIDENCE OF NEED FOR COUNSELING

We do not really have a clear picture of the total need for counseling services in our society. Occasionally some information about the numbers of people who wish some kind of help is obtained almost by accident. A paper by Ginsburg (1948) is one striking example. He reports what happened when in 1947 a man wrote to Mary Haworth, the author of a syndicated newspaper column, asking where he could get psychiatric help. Her reply was a rather hasty and ill-advised diagnosis along with the suggestion that he write to Dr. George S. Stevenson, Medical Director of the National Committee for Mental Hygiene. The significant thing about the incident was that following the newspaper publication of this advice the National Committee for Mental Hygiene received more than 2,000 letters. They came from forty-four of the forty-eight states and from Puerto Rico, Newfoundland, Nova Scotia, and Hawaii. Their writers included persons with all sorts of neurotic and psychotic symptoms, pregnant unmarried girls, unhappily married couples, and individuals with educational and vocational problems.

Where students in colleges have been asked what counseling services they would like to have available, the majority have indicated need for some such services. Stump (1942) asked entering freshmen at Keuka College to fill out a questionnaire. Each of the ten items listed as possible counseling services was checked frequently, and 50 per cent of the group were interested in all of them. Sageser (1951) reports a similar study on a much larger number of students. He sent a questionnaire to 1,212 students in eight institutions. Only 4 out of the total number expressed no need for counseling. Three fourths of them desired help with academic problems, one half with vocational problems, and one tenth with psychological or psychiatric problems. The fact that he obtained only a 41 per cent return of questionnaires leaves some doubt about non-respondents, but the proportions cited for those who did reply constitute a considerable fraction even of the total group.

There have been several studies analyzing the problems and characteristics of students who do make use of a counseling service. Williamson and Bordin (1941c) examined case records of 2,053 students who received counseling at the University Testing Bureau, University of Minnesota, during the period 1932-1935. About two thirds of the problems presented were vocational or educational. Problems of the social-emotional-personal variety were next most frequent. Students who sought counseling on their own initiative averaged higher in school achievement and college aptitude test score than those who were referred by members of the university staff. In another University of Minnesota study Schneidler and Berdie (1942) showed that counseled students did not differ from the student body as a whole in high school scholarship, college aptitude test scores, and achievement and personality test scores. Baller (1944) reports some figures for 1942-1943 from the University of Nebraska which show that freshmen who consulted the guidance office were above average in ability. For those with educational-vocational problems, grades for the year did not fall below what would have been predicted from their aptitude tests. For the personal problem group, grades were slightly low. What these studies all show is that counseling is needed and utilized by students at all ability levels, not just by the inadequate.

In fact, several studies indicate that good students are particularly likely to see the value of counseling. Kirk (1955) found that 28 per cent of the 1955 Phi Beta Kappas at the University of California had been clients of the Counseling Center, as compared with 22 per cent of the total student body, and that their reaction to the experience was generally positive. A smaller proportion of graduate students, 7.1 per cent in 1955-1956 and 6.3 per cent in 1956-1957, were included in the clientele of this center according to another report by Kirk (1959), but it is interesting to observe that even this fraction of the highly selected graduate student group sought counseling.

Dement (1957) reports some evidence as to the need for counseling obtained as a by-product of a ten-year follow-up study of 70 men who graduated from a highly selective university. In answer to the general question, "How might the University have prepared you better for the demands of the last ten years?" one third mentioned counseling. These spontaneous remarks appeared with approximately equal frequency in the replies of respondents classified as *A*, *B*, or *C* men on the basis of their college records.

TYPES OF PROBLEM IN COLLEGE COUNSELING CENTERS

What type of problem predominates seems to vary from place to place, depending perhaps on how the program is organized. The University of Minnesota studies, as indicated above, show that vocational and educational problems turn up most frequently. Another study at the same institution reported by Darley and Williams (1939) analyzed case records from the General College, a two-year college primarily for low-ability students. Educational problems ranked highest for both men and women, but there were sex differences as to what came next. For men vocational problems were second and personal-social-emotional problems third. For women this order was reversed. McKinney (1945), reporting from the University of Missouri where counseling is given by a personality clinic, stated that the majority of the problems with which students came were social, motivational, or emotional, only 12 per cent falling in the academic classification. About two thirds of the clients had more than one problem. This report, like those from Minnesota, indicates that the counseled group included all kinds of students and was average in academic ability. They were somewhat more likely than the average to be young, to be women, and to be from cities rather than small towns.

Abrahamson (1954), analyzing a sample of 526 cases constituting one fourth of the total case load at the University of Washington over a three-year period (1948-1951) found that vocational-educational problems made up 78 per cent of the total, with a scattering of many others. W. L. Stone (1955) classified problems presented by students in an Indiana college in terms of the socializing process in its various aspects. The categories and the percentages of the total they represented were as follows: I. Family relationship, 23 per cent; II. College situation, 17 per cent; III. Scholastic situation, 20 per cent; IV. Social adjustment, 15 per cent; V. Sex adjustment, 25 per cent. Here the emphasis seems to have fallen on personal problems.

Some studies have attempted to find out whether or not students have confidence in their counseling services so that they would consult them if need arose. Form (1953) developed a scale for measuring student attitude and found that 84 per cent of the Michigan State students strongly endorsed the Counseling Center. Koile and Bird (1956) asked freshmen at East Texas State Teachers College to fill out the Mooney Problem Check List and then to indicate to whom they would go for help with each problem. Although 40 per cent of these respondents indicated that they would not seek help from anybody, 14 per cent named counselor or psychologists and 11 per cent mentioned faculty counselors. Other kinds of person received fewer votes.

DEFINITION OF COUNSELING

Attempts to distinguish between counseling and therapy have given rise to a good deal of discussion and stimulated some provocative research. Among the discussions one of the most influential is that of Perry (1955) speaking for a commission in counseling and guidance that met prior to and during a conference on these issues. He sets up a continuum ranging from problems of intrapersonal conflict at one end to role problems at the other. Any individual helping person covers a range of this continuum, but counselors are more concerned with the role problems, therapists with the intrapsychic conflicts. In an official statement defining counseling psychology (Div. Couns. Psy., 1956) a committee of Division 17 of the American Psychological Association lists as distinctive counseling emphases personal growth and development, achievement of harmony with the environment, influencing society to recognize individual differences and encourage development of individuals. They consider the distinctive features of the counselor's activity to be the wide range of clients and social settings in which he works and his collaboration with other groups in his agency and community.

DIFFERENT PERCEPTIONS OF COUNSELOR'S ROLE

Several research studies have suggested that students perceive the counselor's role primarily as one of helping with vocational and educational problems. Jenson (1955) asked a 20 per cent random sample of the 8,000 boys and girls in Phoenix high schools to answer five questions about ways in which counseling was helpful. Counselors received about as many votes as parents for helpfulness with personal problems, but considerably more for helpfulness with vocational-educational planning. Grant (1954a) asked students in nine high schools in central New York State to register first, second, and third choices for persons to whom they would turn for help in situations of three kinds representing vocational planning, educational planning, and personal-emotional problems. There was fairly clear evidence that counselors were seen as operating in the first two of these areas but not in the third. In another paper, Grant (1954b) reports that school administrators and teachers also see educational and vocational but not personal problems as the counselor's responsibility, but that 56 per cent of the counselors themselves consider social and personal problems within their area of operation.

At the college level there is also some evidence of a discrepancy between the way others perceive the counselor's role and the way he himself perceives it. Thrush (1957) found that between 1952 and 1956 the staff of the Ohio State center had shifted away from an emphasis on vocational counseling toward an emphasis on personal adjustment. King and Matteson (1959) discovered that at Michigan State two kinds of perception showed up in the questionnaire responses of 390 randomly selected students. Some saw the counseling center as a place to take vocational and educational problems, others as a place to take personal and social problems. Warman (1960) constructed an attitude scale upon which respondents could indicate how appropriate they considered three kinds of student problems to be for consideration by counselors at the college counseling center. Responses were obtained from counseling center staff members, other student personnel workers, faculty members, and students before and after counseling. Vocational Choice ranked first in appropriateness for all the groups. For all groups except counseling center staff, College Routine ranked second, and Adjustment to Self and Others lowest. Counselors themselves ranked the Adjustment category second, giving it a much higher rating than any of the other respondents did.

That high school students do interpret need for counseling in terms of seriousness of problem behavior rather than in terms of stimulation of satisfactory students would seem to be indicated by Heilfron's report (1960). In this study students were asked to indicate the degree of counseling needed in each of 14 cases, briefly described. On the basis of their ranks, the cases fell into five groups. Only those with rather serious academic or personal problems were generally rated as needing as high a degree of counseling as the one designated by "possibly one conference each quarter in addition to programming." Since the only higher degree is referral to an outside agency, there is some question as to what these results mean. None of the alternatives subjects were given to choose from with regard to "degree of counseling" clearly designated the *kind* of counseling relationship that would be of much use to the student who was not seriously maladjusted.

Evaluation

We have at least some evidence that counseling services in the schools are needed and used. How great the unmet need is in the rest of society we cannot determine from any research available. There seems to be some ambiguity about what counselors should be doing. The most clear-cut distinction is between vocational and educational planning, on the one hand, and facilitating personal and social adjustment, on the other. There is some indication that although counselors are perceived in terms of the first of these kinds of duty, they increasingly *prefer* to be cast in the other role.

CHAPTER TWO

Essential Qualities
of Counseling Interviews

BASIC ATTITUDES—ACCEPTANCE
AND UNDERSTANDING

At the very heart of the counseling process is the interview. Whether it is fifteen or ninety minutes long, whether the participants explore feelings or discuss facts and schedules, whether or not it is supplemented by test scores and information from the files—whatever influence counseling has is related most closely to the way this time is spent. The would-be counselor should direct his attention first to this most indispensable skill. He cannot begin too soon to develop it, yet he will find that its development is never complete. After a lifetime of experience he will still be sharpening his perceptions of what occurs during an interview and increasing his capacity to communicate what he perceives.

The essential foundations upon which interviewing rests are the *attitudes* of understanding and acceptance, and the *skill* of communication. The three aspects, understanding, acceptance, and communication, are so inextricably bound up together in the counseling process that it is only for the purpose of talking about them that we can single out one at a time. They cannot be separately practiced or learned, and it is unlikely that a competent counselor will be rated high on one and low on the others. Let us then consider these basic qualities.

There is no simple way to make clear just what the term *acceptance* means. The capacity for accepting others is far broader than any skill developed by specific training in counseling. The counselor's basic attitudes toward human beings are involved, and such basic attitudes are not the product of a year's cultivation or of specific educational experiences. They grow from the responses a person makes to all the experiences of his life. We know only a little about the kinds of experience that produce the accepting attitude. Thorough grounding in psychology probably helps to the extent that it enables one to be interested in the mental processes behind another's behavior instead of passing judgment on the behavior itself. Reading novels, poetry, and plays seems to deepen one's respect for human personality. Dealing with all kinds of people in everyday life helps one to feel at home with them. Fortunately there seems to be no single road to the attitude of acceptance. Most men and women who are preparing for counseling careers have already developed this attitude to a considerable degree, or else they would not have been attracted by this profession. What they need is a deepening and enriching of what is there, and the enriching process need not be confined to the period of undergraduate and graduate education but can go on throughout life. Indeed, a benign circle begins when the counselor takes up his work: The basic regard for the worth of human individuals that undergirds his work from the beginning inevitably is strengthened as he gets more experience. As it increases he becomes a better counselor and thus better able to stimulate the kind of achievement in his clients that adds still more depth and solidity to his acceptance of them and of others.

Acceptance involves primarily two things—first, a willingness to allow individuals to differ from one another in all sorts of ways, and second, a realization that the ongoing experience of each person is a complex pattern of striving, thinking, and feeling. The accepting counselor has no standard measuring rod against which he sizes up all comers. Whatever measuring devices he does use are to help him understand the *pattern* of the individual personality, not to determine the worth of it. To him the ambitious boy with the 90 IQ—or the lazy boy, for that matter—naturally commands just as much interest and respect as his classmate with an IQ of 150. In either case the individual's goals, values, plans, beliefs, and feelings are of absorbing interest. If the counselor has this genuine interest in the person, respect and liking will probably follow as a natural consequence. The accepting attitude is the opposite of contempt. Cynicism about human nature has no part in it. And it is a feeling about the *individual*, not about man-

kind in the abstract. Lofty generalizations about the dignity of
personality are irrelevant to it. Respect for the individual may or
may not accompany optimistic philosophical or religious beliefs
about man as a species. Because acceptance is so closely tied to
understanding the person as an individual, the two qualities we
have stressed cannot be separated, in counseling or anywhere else.

Acceptance does not involve either approval or disapproval
of the particular aspects of a client's personality or conduct upon
which he happens to be reporting at any given time. It is the
personality as a whole, not any one facet of it, that the counselor
accepts. It is easy to see that disapproval of something he has
done or thought may give a client the feeling that he is not liked
or that his difficulties are beyond help. It is not so obvious, but
just as true, that commendation for something which looks ad-
mirable may also retard the development of sound attitudes. We
must never jump to conclusions in counseling. What looks like a
minor fault may be a necessary concomitant of one of the person's
most valuable traits. What looks like a sterling virtue may be a
defense against anxiety destined to change its shape as anxiety
diminishes.

The importance of not letting approval or disapproval deflect
the counseling process from its course can be illustrated more
easily than it can be explained. Dick McDonald has been referred
to a counselor by a faculty member, who recognizes his high
ability and is concerned about his poor scholarship. The appointment is made through the usual procedures. On the morning of
his first scheduled interview Mr. McDonald shows up ten minutes
late, his hair disheveled and a 24-hour growth of beard on his
good-looking face. The counselor of course says nothing about
either the tardiness or the untidiness but invites him to sit down
and make himself comfortable. He begins the conversation by
mentioning what Mr. Larson, the faculty member, has said about
Dick's capacity for doing better work than his record shows so
far and asks the young man to tell him a little more about himself—such as where he has gone to school and what his future
plans are. The boy outlines some bare facts about himself without
any clues as to his real interests and motives. The counselor tries
without much success to find some point of departure for more
productive conversation. McDonald answers each question with
a single word or phrase and then sits back and waits for the next.

He does not appear unfriendly or uninterested, but it is plain that nothing much is being communicated. The interview seems to be bogging down. Suddenly with a wry smile the young man says, "I'm sorry. I'm just not on the ball this morning. I was out celebrating with some of the boys at the house last night and we didn't get in until five o'clock this morning. I set the alarm for eight o'clock because I didn't want to miss this appointment, but I just can't think. My head feels as if it were about the size of a watermelon."

What should the counselor do? The habits represented by this incident are in all probability quite closely related to the poor scholarship. But would any useful purpose be served by pointing this out and delivering a litle lecture on the evils of alcohol? Quite obviously the answer is "No." Mr. McDonald knows these facts as well as the counselor does—or better. The only effect of such a procedure would be to leave him feeling that one more person is disappointed in him. In doing this the counselor would also risk identification with others who have taken reproving or punishing roles toward him in the past, his father, for example. If this happened, Mr. McDonald would be likely simply to repeat the reactions he had made to this person in the past rather than to learn something new.

On the other hand, for the counselor to smile in a jovial way and say something like "We all need a little fun occasionally" would be just as unfortunate. Mr. McDonald needs to do some thinking about the pattern his life is taking. He has shown that he wishes to do this by making an extra effort to keep his appointment and by explaining candidly why he is inadequate. To treat the drinking bout as a bit of natural and unimportant play activity is to defeat his efforts, to gloss over the struggle going on in his inner self instead of helping him carry it through.

If he can show the right kindness of accent and expression, perhaps the best move for the counselor is to say, "All right. Would you like to come back tomorrow at this hour?" By such a reply he recognizes both the feeling of not being able to think and the real desire to do the thinking. By setting the time in the very near future he shows that he is not trying to punish the boy but is really eager to help him. No comment whatever need be made about the problem behavior itself. To show acceptance of the person with all his shortcomings and his strivings but avoid being sidetracked into expressions of opinion about the things he does—this is the counselor's aim.

Keeping in mind what has been said about the accepting attitude as a first essential, let us turn next to a consideration of *understanding* as it functions in good counseling. Let us be clear from the beginning that this quality we are thinking about is a strictly limited thing. It is not any magical power, any intuitive wisdom, or any X-ray eye that enables a psychologist to see through to a person's innermost nature. To understand is simply to grasp clearly and completely the meaning the client is trying to convey. Probably no human being ever fully understands another and certainly the good counselor never feels that his client's whole personality is like an open book. Furthermore, it is neither necessary nor desirable that the counselor understand the individual better than he understands himself. In the productive interview, communication of thoughts and feelings is at a maximum; thus understanding is a sharing process. Whether the topic under discussion is the meaning of a set of objective-test scores, the facts underlying an occupational choice, or a puzzling aspect of the counselee's relationship to his wife, what the person says gives the counselor a sense of the meaning of this bit of experience, a meaning which he then attempts to put into words which will clarify it for both of them.

In order to understand in this way it is not enough that one find out the facts of the individual's life. It is the attitudes growing out of these facts that matter, the way the person sees them and reacts to them. It is necessary that the counselor, as he listens, constantly and automatically put himself in the client's place and try to see the circumstances as he sees them, not as they look to an outsider. Simple as this is to say, it is the skill which seems hardest to learn. When a child tells us how hard his parents are on him, how often and how severely he is punished for trivial offenses, our first impulse is to check up on the facts. Are these parents in fact cruel? No one would deny that it is often necessary to make such an investigation, but the checking up is not counseling. There are other professional workers whose business it is to look into situations like this. The counselor's task is to see this family as the child sees it. Whether it would look the same to someone else or even whether it looks this way to him in all moods at all times is at the moment irrelevant.

If we think of a human life as a large, very complex, somewhat blurred and ambiguous tapestry, it may help make tangible what we are trying to do. We need to see the pattern of this tapestry as clearly as possible. This cannot be done at a glance, and there is no way of doing it without effort. It may be necessary to scrutinize for a considerable time each of several small details before we begin to see how they fit into the large design. Where parts do not seem to fit together we must trace the connecting threads. The analogy carries us only a part of the way, however, because a tapestry is a static, complete thing, whereas a personality is constantly in the process of development. But it may serve to make the point that counseling is basically a *perceptual* task. It is not possible to learn to say the right thing at the right time without learning to listen and watch and understand.

BASIC SKILL—COMMUNICATION

The main skill a counselor must develop is that of communicating his understanding of what the client is trying to express. It is usually not very difficult to respond to the content or factual details of a client's statement. It is the feelings that are hard to put into words. Yet it is the clarification of his feelings about the topic under discussion that is likely to be of the greatest value to the client.

There is no easy way of mastering such communication. Beginning counselors are always looking for techniques and general rules about what to say and what not to say. The more we study the counseling process, the more it appears that such rules or prescriptions for good counseling are not going to be possible. Good counselors show considerable variation in the kind of verbal responses they make. They differ from one another to some extent, in their characteristic style, from client to client, and from one discussion unit to another within an interview. They do not handle a sequence in which the facts about an occupation are being discussed in the same way that they handle a sequence in which family relationships are being examined.

We can, however, see what some of the difficulties are and look at some of the practices experienced counselors have found to be profitless. One of the difficulties is that in even a short uninterrupted sequence of "client talk" a complex mixture of facts and feelings is represented. When the person pauses, the counselor must make a quick decision about which of these facts and feelings to respond to. If the counselor can think of a brief comment that puts together several of the attitudes that have been expressed, he will have done the best thing possible. However, even if he cannot do this, whatever he says to communicate an understanding of *some* attitude will advance the interview. It seems not to make too much difference which he responds to. The immediate direction the interview takes may be affected, but it is quite certain that any significant feelings by-passed now will show up later.

In making this instantaneous decision about what to respond to, one other general principle is useful. Whenever the client's remarks have involved two or more persons, try to respond in terms of *his* side of the relationship rather than that of someone else. For example, if Hugh Rich has been talking about his difficulties with an unreasonable officer during his army years, the counselor has a choice between a remark that will lead to more information about the officer's attitudes and motives, such as "He must have been a very unpleasant person," or a remark that will lead to a better understanding of the way Hugh reacts, such as "You seem to dislike people of that sort intensely." The second alternative is to be preferred because it is closer to the major purpose of the interview, the development of understanding about what kind of person Hugh himself is.

Still another difficulty has to do with the specific words the counselor uses. The one thing he wishes not to do is to arouse defensive attitudes. Certain ways of putting things are more likely than others to affect people adversely. Words like *coward, stupid,* or *effeminate* should probably never be used unless the client has used that very word himself. It is as feasible to say, "You can't quite bring yourself to attempt it," as "You haven't the courage to try." Either is an expression of a painful emotional attitude, but the second is much more likely than the first to arouse defensiveness. Much the same rules apply here as in ordinary tactful conversation. This does not mean that reality should be watered down or glossed over. Counseling differs from most conversation in that problem areas and unpleasant facts are faced, not ignored or side-tracked. They need not, however, be presented brutally.

It is not always possible to avoid words that arouse defensiveness, since individuals have their unique sore spots. One young man, for instance, flared up when a counselor used the word *emotional* in reflecting a feeling he was expressing. "I'm not emotional," he fairly shouted. "Whatever else I am, I've always been completely rational. Nobody can accuse me of being an emotional person."

When a counselor unwittingly uses a word that touches off such a reaction the only thing he can do is to accept and understand the attitude his remark has stimulated. To apologize or to defend himself would be equally useless. He might, for example, say something like this, "You pride yourself on being a calm, rational person," and go on from there. No harm is done by bursts of anger like this if they do not occur too often. It is when the client feels it necessary to defend himself continually that the groundwork of a good relationship cannot be built.

It might be well at this point to consider briefly the source of the counselor's understanding. How is it that he can comprehend vague and subtle emotions, often very haltingly expressed, emotions rooted in the backgrounds and personal relationships of very different individuals? There seems to be only one answer, unless we are willing to accept explanations which are not naturalistic. The understanding must come from his own experience. Different as their lives are on the surface, the struggles, anxieties, and aspirations of the persons he is interviewing resemble his own enough for him to experience them vicariously. The hazard for the inexperienced counselor is that the empathy he feels will stimulate an urge to talk about himself. He can hardly escape impulses to show clients how well he understands them by citing incidents from his own life.

In general, such impulses should be inhibited, although it may well be true that some counselors have succeeded in helping some people by such methods. It is inadvisable to talk about oneself because it tends to confuse the client about the structure of the situation, blurring one of the main distinctions between counseling and conversation, the fact that in counseling the spotlight is focused on one participant, not on both. More important still, it is inadvisable because it may very easily have an effect exactly the opposite of the one intended. Because his grasp of the client's meaning is incomplete and because his own experience is not comparable with the other person's in all particulars, the

recounting of it may give the impression of a *failure* to comprehend. The client's reaction may be, "He thinks he has me classified. He doesn't realize that mine is no simple decision such as his
was. How little he understands!" Therefore it is wiser on the
whole not to succumb to the temptation to talk about oneself.

Similarly, it is not good practice to bring the cases of previous
counselees into an interview, even if their problems appear to
be similar to the client's. In all probability they are not similar
enough that someone else's solution can be accepted by this individual. And again there is a risk of stirring up unfavorable attitudes. The client may say to himself, "I wonder if he talks about
everybody to everybody else. I don't know whether I want to tell
him any more if he is going to pass on the whole story to the
next person who comes in." Whether such an interpretation of
what the counselor has done is fair or sound is not the point. If
there is a considerable possibility that it will be taken this way,
the practice should be avoided.

DEALING WITH SILENT INTERVALS

One problem that often puzzles inexperienced counselors—
and experienced ones, too, for that matter—is what to do about
periods of silence. Suppose the client sits for a minute or even
longer without saying anything. The seconds drag on like hours.
What should the counselor do? The answer again depends more
upon perception of the structure of the situation than upon knowledge of correct techniques. Silence can mean many things. If it
follows a sequence in which a person has been expressing himself
freely, it may simply mean that he has reached the end of one
line of thought and is deciding what to bring up next. In such
cases, some act or word indicating that the counselor accepts the
silence and is not embarrassed by it is all that is called for. An
understanding smile may be enough. If the client shows doubt
about his adequacy a remark like "It's all right to take some time
to think if you wish" may clear it up.

Another sort of silence occurs when a client is there under
duress, as it were, and is motivated by conscious or unconscious
negativism. Under such circumstances it would be useless for the
counselor to attempt to pry information out of him through direct
questioning. If the nature of the referral makes it probable that

this silence means resistance, a remark which will show recognition and acceptance of the attitude is in order, perhaps something like "I suppose you don't relish the idea of coming here very much."

In many cases the silence is not explained by circumstances and the counselor is at a loss to know what it means. Unless one knows the background of events leading up to counseling, it is hard to differentiate between hostility and shyness. In such instances an attempt at general conversation about non-threatening topics, even the weather if necessary, may at least produce some clues as to what the attitude is.

Occasionally the client's failure to say anything is a consequence of the mental set he has about the counseling procedure. He expects that the counselor will ask him questions and on the basis of his answers will analyze him and tell him what to do. He may show that this is his conception by asking, "Well, what do you want to know about me?" It is well in such cases to say something that will start the person off in the right direction and let him discover for himself how counseling works. One might say, "Just tell me some of the things that come to your mind about yourself—the sort of person you are, what has happened to you, what your plans are, the people who have been important to you." Suggestions as to things he might bring up can be formulated in terms diverse enough and general enough that he will respond on the basis of his own associations.

One of the rewards of continuing counseling experience is the realization that what one says need not be fluent or elegantly phrased in order to be effective. A counselor who really accepts a client and understands him even partially need not be too concerned about saying "the right thing." Somehow his meaning will get across.

It may help to make clear what a counselor does during an interview if we think of it as similar to the mental activity of a trained musician listening to new music. To grasp the essential structure is his first task. This means listening for *themes*. Once he senses what some main themes are, he can follow them through all their ramifications as the musical work progresses. As in all analogies, there are hazards in this one. The themes that will be developed are not stated explicitly in a client's "opening bars," and a counselor may have to tolerate long periods of confusion before he senses any structure at all. What he must be willing to do, however, is the same in both kinds of situation—listen, think, respond. It is the hardest kind of work, but worth the effort.

Research Summary

WHAT ASPECTS OF THE INTERVIEW ARE MOST IMPORTANT?

The evidence that the kinds of interview procedures we have been recommending produce favorable results is scattered and, it must be admitted, far from conclusive. But it is encouraging that there are increasing numbers of studies of the interviewing process itself and that some of the things that make for successful outcomes are becoming clear. One of the earliest of these studies was reported by Campbell (1945). Thirty classification interviews with naval recruits were recorded. Twenty of the subjects were then re-interviewed by the psychologically oriented members of the project staff, using a procedure much freer, more accepting, more encouraging than the Navy men who had done the original interviewing had used. Letters were sent to schools the men had attended in order to check up on errors and misinformation in the interview data. Such errors turned out to be twice as frequent in the original interviews as in those by the project staff. No significance tests are reported and the total number is of course small.

Seeman (1949) obtained reactions to preliminary interviews from 20 clients of each of six counselors. The majority were expecting to take tests and be given vocational information. There were significant differences in the favorableness of the response to different counselors, but they were not related in techniques used. Counselor *responsiveness* seemed to be the quality that produced the favorable reactions.

Cowen and Combs (1950) report a follow-up study of 32 clients treated by non-directive therapy. The average time elapsed since the conclusion of the treatment was twenty months. The finding most significant for the problems we are considering here is that there were pronounced individual differences in responses to various aspects of the procedure. In some cases the sex of the counselor was important, in others not. Some resented note-taking. Some interpreted not being urged to return as rejection. Some responded unfavorably to the attempt made to "structure" the situation for them. Emphasis is also placed on the counselor as a person rather than on technique. Results obtained by student counselors were not so good as those of experienced workers, and "warmth" seemed to be very important.

A study by Reid and Snyder (1947) suggests that the ability to recognize and name correctly the feeling expressed in a counseling sequence probably is not an indispensable ingredient, since experienced counselors cannot do this reliably. The task given the subjects, a clinical psychologist and fourteen graduate students specializing in this area, was to name in fifteen seconds the feeling involved in each of 144 client statements. The over-all agreement was rather low. About 50 per cent of the subjects agreed on as many as 50 per cent of the feelings. Good counselors showed significantly more agreement than those not so good, but even among them there were individual differences in the frequency with which certain kinds of feelings were named. That is, one tended to prefer "Lack of Confidence" and "Self-defense," another "Insecurity."

The ways in which various aspects of interview technique are related to one another and to outcomes have been studied in a co-ordinated research program at Ohio State University and reported by Robinson (1950, Chap. 6). Most of these have also been reported in separate papers (Carnes and Robinson, 1948, Davis and Robinson, 1949, Elton, 1950, and Tindall and Robinson, 1947). It is difficult to summarize general trends indicated by these studies. The number of categories becomes very large when one works with four types of interview—study skills, scholastic questions, therapy, and vocational problems—a number of counselors, several kinds of counselor technique, and several types of client response, simultaneously. However, a few conclusions can be drawn with some assurance. Carnes and Robinson (1948) show that while the amount of talking done by the client is related to favorable outcomes in some kinds of interview units, in general it is only a minor criterion of counseling effectiveness and may well be a symptom rather than a cause of what is happening. Davis and Robinson (1947) show that counselors use secondary techniques for reducing resistance more in units showing low rapport than units where it is high and more in units showing stronger "leading" by the counselor than in others. Again it is not clear which is cause and which is effect. Elton (1950) shows that "responsibility-taking" by the client is correlated with favorable ratings for both "insight" and "working relationship." The technique they call "urging" accompanies the lowest ratings on "client responsibility." A much more detailed report of all the studies in this series is available in Robinson's book (1950).

Another kind of attempt to find out which characteristics of the counselor affect student clients favorably and which unfavorably was that of Pohlman and Robinson (1960). Their 109 subjects were members of college classes who were asked to respond to a list of kinds of counselor behavior using a five-point scale running from extreme dislike to extreme liking. The behaviors most consistently rated as highly annoying were those indicating a lack of respect for the client—items like "aloof," "insincere," "in a hurry," "interrupting," "yawning." Unusual mannerisms and physical handicaps were only mildly disliked. The results suggested that the counselor's attitudes are more important than his specific behavior patterns.

In a different kind of research investigation, Polansky and Kounin (1956) interviewed 150 clients who had just experienced the counseling interviews normally provided by various agencies in Wayne University and Detroit. They identified two main types of interview situation, overlapping to some extent, the *problem-centered* and the *relationship-centered*. The effects were somewhat different. The more relationship-centered the interviews were, the more willing clients were to see the interviewer again. The more problem-centered they were, the more willing clients were to follow the counselor's advice.

The fact that there are many kinds of difference between counselors and between interviews carried on by the same counselor is becoming apparent from a number of studies. Seeman (1948a) has shown that there are significant and consistent individual differences in the frequencies with which experienced counselors in preliminary interviews use different kinds of responses such as questions, responses to content, reflection of feeling, interpretations, suggestions, and information. However, in the study cited above, these differences turned out not to be related to favorableness of client reaction, whereas responsiveness was.

DIFFERENCES IN COUNSELOR STYLE

Berdie (1958) has summarized a program of research carried on by the staff at the Student Counseling Bureau of the University of Minnesota. During the first phase of this research, in the years 1940 and 1941, evidence was obtained that counselors differed significantly in the frequency with which they used six different interview procedures. During the second phase from 1948 to 1952, using a more elaborate series of categories differentiated both according to purpose and according to technique, they again showed that the four counselors they were comparing had distinctly different styles of counseling and that these styles could be reliably rated from typescripts or recordings.

A somewhat similar group of studies has classified units of counselor interview behavior according to the *roles* counselors play—listening, reflecting, tutoring, informing. Working with typescripts or recordings of interviews carried on by counselors at five different universities, Danskin (1955, 1957a; Danskin and Robinson, 1954) found that the frequencies for the different roles differed from place to place and from client to client as well as from counselor to counselor within any one agency. The type of problem under consideration in a particular discussion unit was related to the kind of role the counselor played. A similar study by Hoffman (1959) showed the same kinds of differences and established that each counselor plays a number of different roles at different times. Of the 20 counselors whose interviews were analyzed, 17 used more than 9 of the 15 subroles on the list.

DIFFERENCES RELATED TO
TOPIC OF DISCUSSION

Using typescripts of 40 initial interviews from five different universities, S. E. Davis (1958) worked out a reliable system of rating four client characteristics and showed that at interview transition points the behavior of the counselor, classified in terms

of the Robinson categories, was related to these client characteristics.

What these studies seem to add up to is that experienced
counselors, whatever their theoretical viewpoint, do adapt their
mode of response to the particular features of any individual
interview. Several studies have suggested that the principal distinction between discussion units that underlies differences in
counselor response is the distinction between "cognitive" and
"affective" expressions on the part of the client. A co-ordinated
research program at the University of Missouri, the results of
which have been summarized in a paper by Callis and others
(1957), points to this kind of distinction. Analyzing 17 cases
representing six counselors, Dipboye (1954) also found that different types of response were used for cognitive and affective
discussion units, although two of the counselors showed less of
this variation than did the other four. Working with typescripts
of 37 interviews with 20 high school senior boys, Weeks (1957)
found the same variation in counselor style for units differing in
"level of affect."

COUNSELOR DIFFERENCES AND
COUNSELING OUTCOMES

To what extent are the variations in counselor style related to
counseling outcomes? The Missouri group mentioned above has
been interested in this problem, and two of the doctoral dissertations in the series, those by Proff and by Chappell, were attempts
to develop ways of measuring movement during counseling. The
one study in the series that focused specifically on client satisfaction as a criterion, that of McGowan, indicated that this outcome was not related to counselor style, but rather to whether the
counselor was an experienced person or a novice. Weeks (1957)
also showed that client ratings of counselors were not related to
particular styles of response.

VOLUNTARY VERSUS REFERRED CASES

The desirability of voluntary consultation rather than required referrals has been brought out in two reports, neither very
conclusive. Habbe (1939) compared 50 cases coming to a psychi-

atric clinic in response to a well-planned newspaper story with 100 regular clients referred by community agencies. The self-referred were slightly superior in intelligence and schooling, and counselors felt they had a better attitude to begin with. Kirk and Headley (1950) analyzed 110 cases who discontinued counseling before completion at the University of California Center in 1947. The interview material was not complete enough to identify the reasons for the failure to return, but the percentage of referred cases was unusually high in this group (44 per cent as compared with 28 per cent in the completed group). Williamson and Bordin (1941c) in the study cited in the previous chapter also found voluntary clients to be of a higher ability level than referred clients.

Evaluation

Research of the kinds summarized here has been making less and less justifiable an emphasis on any one kind of orthodox interview procedure. It seems clear that each counselor develops his own style and that he varies it as circumstances demand. Warmth and responsiveness are important and increasing skill comes with experience. Counselors seem to be making a distinction between cases and between parts of the same case on the basis of whether affective or cognitive communication predominates. Comparisons of referred with voluntary cases remind us that the attitude a client brings to a situation as well as the counselor's own attitude must be considered. Individual differences of all sorts are apparent. A procedure that works well with one counselee may antagonize others.

Such research findings are compatible with the emphasis of this chapter—on perceptions rather than on responses, on understanding rather than on techniques.

CHAPTER THREE

The Initial Interview

SPECIAL IMPORTANCE OF INITIAL INTERVIEWS

The first interview is in many ways the hardest. Within the framework of the general principles that apply to all counseling interviews, let us consider how they can be applied to the situations one faces when he first meets new clients. As we do this, let us keep in mind that in a sizable proportion of cases, one interview is all there is. In the common situation in which high school counselors work, it is not possible for them to see more than a few of the students assigned to them more than once during a semester. In counseling agencies serving the general public it is not unusual at all to have a person come in to talk over a particular problem with someone with no thought of initiating a series of interviews. A single 30-minute interview can be counseling in the truest sense of the word. In other cases, where one or more subsequent interviews are scheduled later, it is the first one that sets the pattern for the total interaction. So for any case, short or long, it is important that the initial interview be productive.

HOW TO GET STARTED

Of the two underlying attitudes we have stressed, acceptance is more fundamental at the beginning than understanding and must somehow be communicated first. This is because the people with whom we are dealing are likely to have mixed feelings about being understood. They must be sure that understanding can in no way constitute a threat before they can welcome it. Many of us are afraid that someone will "see through us," uncovering our hidden weaknesses. We have put up strong defenses against this. Much of what we say, many of the things we do, are designed to hide rather than to reveal our underlying motives and traits. For this reason if it happens that the counselor shows by some penetrating remark that he has seen through a new client's defenses, the person may very well retreat in panic from the whole situation. It is only when he has become certain of a thorough-going unshakeable acceptance that he can run the risk of trying to make his real feelings understood. All of this does not mean, of course, that a client is clear about his own attitudes and is deliberately trying to keep the counselor from finding them out. It is against his *own* understanding as well as another's that he has fortified himself and it is *self*-acceptance as well as the con-sciousness of acceptance by someone else that makes it possible for him to let down the bars.

The first things that are to be done in making acceptance evident to the counselee can be thought of simply as hospitality. How near the fundamental attitude is to true hospitality becomes beautifully clear in the verse from Laotzu (Bynner, 1944):

If the sign of life is in your face
He who responds to it
Will feel secure and fit
As when, in a friendly place,
Sure of hearty care
A traveler gladly waits
Though it may not taste like food
And he may not see the fare
Or hear a sound of plates
How endless it is and how good.

There are many specific things a counselor can do to express this warm hospitality. He will arrange for personal introductions as much as possible. If a receptionist or secretary is the first person a client sees, it is important that she greet him in a friendly way and if possible present him by name to the counselor. He will be careful to be on time for all his appointments so that no client will need to wait. Too often, waiting generates a feeling that nobody cares about one's problems. An office that is not too bare, chairs that are not too hard, freedom from interruptions either by personal call or by telephone—all these things help to create the right atmosphere. There are many others. Sometimes so small a thing as indicating a place to dry a wet coat or adjusting a shade which is letting in too much sun is a way of showing consideration for another's comfort.

Just what should be done varies from one interview to another. Experienced interviewers usually recommend to novices that they carry on some sort of general conversation during the early part of the interview until the counselee begins to feel at ease in this new situation. The skill involved here is that of picking up clues to topics of conversation likely to interest the person. If the counselor has seen him at a game, an art exhibit, or a concert, to mention that fact may be a good beginning. Something the person is carrying with him—a book, a package of phonograph records, or a tennis racket—may be a good point from which to start. Mutual friends or a part of the country they both know may furnish material for conversation. In using any of these clues, one must, however, be alert to the possibility that it is a disagreeable rather than a pleasant topic. The girl may have gone to the art exhibit not because she has any interest in art but because all of her housemates were out on dates and she was too miserably lonely to stay home. The book a boy happens to be carrying may turn out to be the text for a course he is failing but cannot bring himself to study. The mention of a mutual friend or a member of the client's family may constitute a very touchy subject if the client feels that he is being compared with this person to his own disadvantage. When something like this happens at the beginning of an interview the counselor, realizing that he has unwittingly irritated a sore spot, will ordinarily do as he would in any tactful conversation—shift smoothly to some other topic.

But even this is no invariable rule. Counseling is not conversation, and it is not essential that it be maintained or even begun on a pleasant level. Occasionally someone will come in so obviously disturbed about something in particular that to start out with a calm, reassuring conversation is neither possible nor desirable. In such instances just the simple question, "What is it that you would like to talk to me about?" is all that is needed after the person has been seated and made physically comfortable. Similarly, in situations like the one mentioned in the preceding paragraph, when a touchy subject is uncovered through a chance remark, often the best thing to do, once this has happened, is to recognize the feeling that has been shown and allow the client to enlarge upon it if he wishes. Take for example the following sequence:

COUNSELOR: Good morning, Mr. Murdock. Are you any relation to Arthur Murdock who graduated here last year?

CLIENT: Yes, worse luck. He's my brother. Everybody I run into seems to know him and asks me if I'm going to make a big name for myself the way he did.

(The counselor notes at this point two kinds of negative feeling that he has touched off by his ill-advised question. One is Joe's doubt as to whether he is going to be able to live up to his brother's reputation. The other is a trace of hostility toward the counselor for raising the same uncomfortable question that everybody else raises. In view of the client's evident willingness to talk about it, it seems that this is as good a point of departure as any for getting into the real problems. There is no reason why acceptance now of these doubts and negative feelings cannot help to demonstrate genuine acceptance of Joe Murdock as a person. So he proceeds accordingly.)

COUNSELOR: I suppose it's a little annoying always to be greeted as Arthur's brother rather than as a person in your own right.

CLIENT: Well, I do get tired of it. All my life that's been the way it was. When I started kindergarten the teacher still remembered what a cute, smart little boy Arthur had been. I got into high school just the year after he graduated and the same thing happened. He'd been salutatorian, captain of the debate team, and I don't know what all. If I could do all the things he can I wouldn't mind. But I'm the dumb one in our family, I guess. . . .

Thus this particular interview is started on its main course, having skipped almost entirely the putting-the-client-at-ease, making-him-feel-accepted stage. Whether to go ahead in this fashion or to retreat into conversation about superficial, non-painful topics for a while longer must depend on the counselor's judgment of the client's probable response. In this instance, if his answer to the question about his brother had shown a less definite feeling it would probably have been better not to let things take this course. Had Joe simply said, "Yes, he's my brother," with indications of some discomfort, the counselor might have followed with "After a person has been around for as many years as I have he gets familiar with some of the names connected with the college. You're a freshman this year?" thus opening the way for a more general conversation. In general it is better not to begin an interview by asking a question about a brother or other relative, since it leads away from the feeling we wish the counselee to get—that he is accepted for his own sake.

What this example is intended to illustrate is that even after something has been said which jeopardizes the relationship upon which progress depends, the skillful counselor can make use of what has occurred and set the relationship right again. To do this requires a kind of alertness and sensitivity that are called for in few other types of human activity. Counseling is hard work. It also requires a large amount of what Theodor Reik in his fine book on psychoanalysis, *Listening with the Third Ear* (1949), describes as "moral courage." One must be prepared to face whatever turns up without flinching, no matter how unexpected or unwelcome it is. If some such matter, a hostile impulse or an unreasonable fear, happens to show itself in the first five minutes of the first interview, that is the time it must be faced. Usually things will not work out this way. The really significant attitudes are more likely to appear after the client has developed some confidence that he is liked and accepted than at the beginning. The business of making acceptance clear to the person may take two minutes or five hours, but it is an essential feature of counseling.

We have said that understanding means *perceiving* the client's psychological world as clearly as possible. This perceptual skill is a matter of registering and responding to a great many kinds of stimulation as they are presented in the interview situation. It requires a high degree of both alertness and sensitivity. Perhaps it is most similar to the keenness of observation we admired so much in the Indians and woodsmen we read about as children. Instead of responding as they did to faint footprints, broken twigs, and almost imperceptible distant sounds, the counselor picks up slight changes of color, tensing of muscles, hesitation in speech, change of vocal pitch, or undue emphasis on certain words. He keeps in mind at the same time the words the client is speaking, the *fact* that he is there and saying these things, the *associations* between ideas that the sequences of interview topics reveal, and all the complex, *motivational* processes that his previous experience has taught him underlie verbal expression.

CLIENT EXPECTATIONS AND THE COUNSELING RELATIONSHIP

Although there are no systematic procedures to follow, there are certain guiding principles that show us what to look for. We know in the first place that one's personality is organized around relationships with others and attitudes about oneself. There is one personal relationship directly open to observation—namely, the client's relationship to the counselor himself. The self-attitudes that are most accessible are the ways he sees his role in the counseling situation. Thus to sense the structure of this present situation is to get hold of something to which many other things can gradually be related.

Counselors have had much to say about "the counseling relationship," and psychoanalysts have had still more to say about "the transference." What has not been stressed enough in all these discussions of "*the* counseling relationship" or "*the* transference" is the fact that *each* relationship has its own individual characteristics; each is unique. It is on these unique characteristics of this particular relationship that the counselor should focus his attention at the beginning.

In doing this, the first questions he asks himself are "What are this person's expectations from counseling?" "What does he think is going to happen?" "What does he hope to get out of it?" Even before the first interview begins we can sometimes get a clue as to some components of a client's attitude if we know how the referral has been made. If Miss Lane has come voluntarily, on the recommendation of a friend who has been counseled, she will be prepared to be treated as her friend was. If her friend took tests, she will expect to take some. If her friend liked Mr. Brady she will probably expect to like him too, and no lengthy process of "ice-breaking" may be necessary. Completely different is the situation of John Grew, whom the high school principal has sent to Mr. Hughes, the counselor, because of repeated truancies. Mr. Hughes can expect John to regard him as one of the authorities with whom he wages a continuous guerilla warfare. He realizes that there is probably nothing he can say about a counselor's intentions which will change that attitude at the beginning. The boy is likely to be wary, defensive, and non-communicative, and it is only by accepting him that way that the counselor has a chance of developing a healthier relationship.

Or consider still a third sort of referral leading to an unsatisfactory structuring of the counseling situation. Mike Madison, a college sophomore, has felt increasingly moody and morose following a disastrous love affair. His faculty adviser, noticing these changes, inquires about his health. Mike tells him about his terrific nightmares which sometimes cause him to cry out in his sleep. The adviser is frightened by the possibility of some serious psychiatric condition and shows this alarm in the way in which he recommends to Mike that he make an appointment at the Counseling Center. Under such circumstances Mike is likely to approach the first interview with considerable apprehension. Is there something seriously wrong with him, and will the psychologist recognize it immediately?

We could go on and on indefinitely, multiplying examples of the diverse and highly individual expectations that different clients bring to counseling. It is usually worth the counselor's while to find out, if he can, what the circumstances of the referral were, and thus "get set" for some of the attitudes he may encounter. Then by careful attention to what is said and how it is said, he can begin to perceive the pattern of the psychological structure existing at the very outset of the first interview.

Although it is possible for counseling to proceed regardless of these initial attitudes, it goes more smoothly and expeditiously if referrals are made in an optimum way. The administrator who is responsible for the organization of a program can help here by making other personnel people such as teachers, advisers, and receptionists acquainted with the features characterizing a good referral. It is advisable that it be personal if possible, so that the warm friendliness we have stressed earlier can be in it from the very start. If it is possible to introduce the client to the counselor, that is the best way. When this is not feasible, a telephone call may be used to bridge the gap. It is always a good plan to give the prospective counselee clear information about where to go and when, so that he will be spared unnecessary doubt and uncertainty. Counseling should be recommended to him in such a way as not to commit the counselor ahead of time to any one plan of action. For instance, it is much better to say to a student who has been shifting uncertainly from one major to another, "Did you know that over in Emerald Hall we have a counseling service to help students decide what they want to do?" than to say, "I suggest that you go over to Emerald Hall and take some vocational aptitude tests." Another important consideration is that there should be no threat, actual or implied, attached to the recommendation. When the Dean of Men says to a student, "I tell you what. Either you make an appointment at the Counseling Center or you'll have to drop out of school next semester," he creates by these words an initial relationship which is very difficult to handle constructively. Finally, it is better to let the client himself decide when he wishes to come than to arrange it for him and assign him a time. With busy schedules, there are limits, of course, to the amount of self-determination possible.

Besides these factors related to the circumstances of referral there is another whole set of factors affecting the structure of the initial relationship—the client's general attitudes toward broad categories of people. These are extremely varied, as human beings classify their fellow men in all sorts of ways. It is harder for the counselor to anticipate these, but if he can it facilitates understanding. Sometimes an item entered in the person's record gives him a clue as to what to be prepared for. One young man applying for vocational counseling, for example, answered a question on a preliminary information blank, "What sort of activity do you enjoy most?" with the reply, "Talking to an intelligent woman." The woman counselor scheduled to interview him assumed that he would come to his first appointment with pleasant expectations and that rapport would be no problem. Ordinarily, however, one simply does not know before meeting a client just what these attitudes are likely to be. One must look for them during the interview itself. There are some areas, however, in which complications arise often enough that it is worthwhile to consider them especially.

The first of these has to do with the individual's attitudes toward the sexes. Because this classification is the most universal and obvious one the child meets, it is almost inevitable that he should develop some general conceptions of what men are like and what women are like. Research studies have given evidence for this sort of categorization as far down as the nursery school age. Obviously, since a counselor must be either a man or a woman, some of the client's feelings about the sex as a whole may color the counseling relationship. Often apparently irrational signs of hostility or dependency can be accounted for in this way.

A concrete example will illustrate the way these attitudes work. Bob Regis, a college freshman who has been subject to acute attacks of anxiety, makes an appointment with Mrs. Martin, on a friend's recommendation. At the time of his first visit he sidles into the office and takes a chair in the farthest corner of the room. He sits there on the edge of the chair looking acutely uncomfortable, as though he were about to take flight at any moment. Mrs. Martin does what she can to put him at ease by adopting a relaxed attitude herself and conversing for a few moments about general school happenings. During the latter part of the hour he outlines his symptoms, talking about them rather flatly and objectively as though they were not really part of him. There is still no evidence of a good working relationship when the hour is over, but he does make an appointment to return the next week. On this occasion his behavior is quite different. He goes directly to a chair beside Mrs. Martin's desk. The first thing he says is, "I thought I'd better tell you why it was so hard for me to talk to you last week; I've always hated women. I suppose it's because of the sort of person my mother was . . . ," and he branches off into an account of the tangled emotional relationships in his family. In this case there was nothing Mrs. Martin could have done at the time of the first interview that would have released this confidence. There was no way she could know for sure what it was that was blocking him. The only course possible for her was the one she followed, to accept him as he was without impatience and wait for the attitude that would clarify the structure of the relationship to become apparent.

Cases such as this raise the general questions as to the advisability of having counselor and counselee of opposite sex. Most high schools and many colleges arrange for men to take care of the boys and women the girls. There is no evidence, however, that this is the best practice or the one making for best rapport in all cases. If a boy has had a stern, unloving father and a sweet, indulgent mother, he will probably feel more at ease with a woman than with a man. Furthermore, these questions are too complex to be thought through on the basis of rapport alone.

Counseling is a *learning* process, a situation in which emotional attitudes are *modified*. Once he overcame the initial obstacle, it seems quite likely that Bob Regis could learn what he needed to know more effectively through his contact with Mrs. Martin than through knowing a male counselor. On the other hand, it might be better for the boy with the severe father to find out through counseling that all men are not like this. Thus he might learn more from dealing with a man even if he felt less comfortable about the situation in the beginning. We simply do not know enough about these things to decide wisely. Probably the best procedure, in view of this ignorance, is to let the client decide, if counselors of both sexes are available.

One thing is fairly certain. For the counselor to be aware of broad sex attitudes and accept them naturally whether they are favorable or unfavorable advances the counseling process. It is not a matter that can be approached by direct questions, however, and we must be careful not to jump to conclusions or make interpretations that go beyond what the client has said. Such comments as "What do you think about women?" or "You don't trust men very much, do you?" are most likely to put him on guard than to elicit his true feelings.

Some other broad attitude categories that may influence the initial stages of counseling are those centering around age, around parents, and around teachers. Young people, especially teenagers, often have what seem to their elders quite fantastic ideas of the ways in which age groups differ. If one would understand how a girl sees the counseling situation at the beginning, it is sometimes necessary to understand what her age stereotypes are. It is almost inevitable that attitudes carried over from parent-child relationships should weave themselves into the complex fabric of the counseling relationship. Similarly, since so much of this work is done in a school setting, it is natural that many boys and girls at first identify counselors with teachers and principals.

Since the number of combinations of even these few factors we have been able to single out is large, it is not strange that there can be no one standard relationship that we attempt to set up for all comers. Mr. Hendricks, a forty-year-old college counselor, must realize that he is a very different figure to the different individuals he sees during the course of a day. To seventeen-year-old Elsie Bliss he appears to be a middle-aged man something like her father, a decent sort on the whole, but probably given to sudden bursts of anger if one acts loud or silly. To Mr. Jensen, a forty-five-year-old veteran trying to make a new start after losing the small business he owned before the war, he looks like a young upstart who has probably been more successful than he deserves and who is likely to be contemptuous of a man who at forty-five is a failure. To Miss Blair, a thirty-year-old schoolteacher who has returned to college because she is tired of sixth graders and wishes she could find something else to do, he is an interesting-looking man whom she would very much like to know better. She wonders whether or not he is married and decides that she mustn't be too open with him and tell him everything she has been thinking about because, after all, she would like to make a good impression.

If the counselor is a psychologist, or the organization for which he works is connected with a psychology department, attitudes are still further complicated by feelings clients have about this profession. In some cases their beliefs are based largely on psychiatric movies they have seen. In others, a smattering of Freud has given them some facility in talking about catharsis, the super-ego, and castration complexes. Some come directly from courses that have given them more realistic ideas of the benefits to be derived from counseling. Whatever bits of facts or fancy the person is carrying with him will be woven into the fabric of the initial relationship.

COUNSELOR ATTITUDES AND THE COUNSELING RELATIONSHIP

So far we have been talking about the counseling relationship as though it depended on the attitudes of the client alone. We must not lose sight of the fact that it has another side. The counselor's own feelings are bound up in it too. We have said earlier that he should be an accepting person who finds it easy to be interested in diverse kinds of individuals and to wish them well. This, however, is not a blanket attitude that covers all with equal warmth. Inevitably he will like some clients better than others and will feel more kinship with some than with others. Inevitably also, since he is a sensitive human being, he will react on an immediate unconscious level to subtle indications of hos-

tility in a person he is interviewing. These things will be true no matter how well-integrated a person he is and even if he has set his own personality in order through some thorough-going psychotherapy before beginning his work.

In general, these attitudes of the counselor will not prevent a good relationship from developing if he can recognize and accept them in himself as naturally as he recognizes the attitudes clients are showing. The two are threads of different colors woven into the complex pattern of the relationship. Blindness for one of the colors distorts the pattern. He need not demand of himself that he like all kinds of people equally well or understand them all with equal facility. He is no superman. To insist that he is is simply to shut his eyes to a part of the reality he faces.

The one counselor attitude that militates strongly against a favorable outcome is active dislike. Occasionally anyone in this kind of work, no matter how high his principles or how broad his sympathies, will encounter someone for whom he feels nothing but repugnance. When this happens it is best that he work out some arrangement that will terminate his connection with the case after the first interview. This may mean introducing the prospective client to another counselor at the same agency whose attitudes are thought to be more favorable toward persons of this sort. It may mean referring him to a different type of organization, perhaps for medical or psychiatric help. It may even mean abandoning any attempt to help him and explaining to him that there is nothing your service can do. Even this is preferable to continuing a relationship not built on a solid foundation. Fortunately such a situation occurs but rarely. Fortunately also, we do not all dislike intensely the same kinds of people, so that one counselor can help where another cannot.

It is well that no one make such a dislike judgment in too much of a hurry, however. There is a curious perceptual shift that sometimes takes place during an interview with an individual who initially makes an unfavorable impression. It is as sudden and definite as what happens when the well-known staircase figure flops over. It seems to come, as Rogers (1951, p. 32) has pointed out, when the counselor succeeds in adopting the internal rather than the external frame of reference with regard to the person. For example, a woman counselor finds herself becoming intensely irritated with a young man who is explaining what high standards he has always had, how much emphasis his family put on cleanliness, punctuality, and good manners, and how hard a task he faces "trying to train his lower-class wife in these desirable habits." "What an opinionated prig he is!" she thinks to herself. "How does his wife ever endure it?"

But as she says nothing and listens to the rest of what he has to say about his childhood and his parents, suddenly his whole aspect changes for her. Here is a pathetic boy making a desperate effort to be perfect and to do everything right because his mother and father expect it of him. He has never managed to satisfy them, but he cannot stop trying. Their standards are part of him. He is still struggling to keep everything under control and thus head off some vague but very threatening disaster he has been led to expect. All at once she feels part of that struggle for she too has experienced it. The dislike and annoyance have vanished without a trace.

If we ever come to know more about how to make this shift take place, we shall have discovered something that will carry us far beyond the confines of counseling into broader areas of human relations. For the present all we can be sure of is that we are most likely to achieve the experience if we concentrate all our efforts on trying to see the client's life from his own viewpoint.

We have discussed in considerable detail the questions that the counselor carries with him, somewhere in the back of his mind, during the first interview. The phrase, "in the back of his mind," prescientific as it sounds, was chosen advisedly. The "front of his mind" is completely occupied with listening and observing, trying to put himself in the other person's place. Judgments about the client's expectations from counseling, his attitudes toward people of the counselor's sex, age, and position, and recognition of one's own feelings toward this particular person constitute the "ground" against which the "figure" shaped by the client's problems will be made manifest. It is the high degree of awareness which we have been recommending that most distinctively sets the counseling interview apart from general conversation.

By this time many readers may be asking whether it is really necessary that *all* counselors think in this way. How about the man in a vocational guidance office whose work is confined to matching young people and jobs? How about the high school

adviser whose interviews are concerned almost entirely with helping students to choose courses wisely?

The answer is that to be aware of all the nuances of feeling is as valuable in these situations as in those we label psychotherapy. Vocational and educational counseling will be far more effective when this is realized. Such awareness does not lead us to over-complicate essentially simple situations. When a student who seems to be doing well in all he undertakes states that his only difficulty is choosing between medicine and engineering, there is no reason to insist on involved unconscious motivations. The kind of sensitivity we have been describing is as well adapted to the perception of a simple design as a complex one, if a simple design is what is there. But it is becoming increasingly clear that an individual's unique personal attitudes are as much a part of his vocational and educational choices as they are of his friendships and love affairs. Thus we cannot assume that *all* educational and vocational problems are simple. The boy mentioned above who is hesitating between medicine and engineering *may* simply lack information about the demands and rewards of each, but his un-certainty *may* represent something as intangible as deep-seated doubts about his own masculinity, doubts which are impelling him toward engineering as a way of proving himself a man. Far-fetched as this may sound, vocational conflicts often involve just such emotional undercurrents. The counselor whose eyes are closed to them loses his opportunity to help the person. The ad-vantages of the approach we have been advocating is that it enables the skillful worker to face problems realistically at all levels of complexity. We cannot on any superficial basis classify the problems into those which require skillful handling and those which do not.

THE GOALS OF THE INITIAL INTERVIEW

Before the initial interview ends the counselor hopes to have achieved three things. First and most important, the foundation for a relationship between counselor and client will have been laid down. In the previous section we have considered some of the factors entering into these relationships, the raw material, so to speak, out of which they are built. Let us look now at the qualities they must have in order to be fruitful.

As has been indicated, they must be warm and friendly. It is characteristic of beginning counselors that they phrase this task in somewhat this way: "I must make him like me." As one gets more experience, he is more likely to turn the sentence around and say instead: "I must like him." A counselor knows better than a client does how to begin to like a stranger. The process of finding out what the other person wants, what he prides himself on, what he is really concerned about, is likely to produce this warm feeling as a by-product. And if the counselor really feels it, a client will usually return it.

Besides this liking there are other qualities the counseling relationship needs. There must be respect and confidence in it. A client must be able to rely on the counselor's competence as well as on his goodwill. There should be something in the counselor's manner that will cause the client to say to himself, "Here is someone I can trust."

There is one quality that the counselor's attitude should *not* express. This is pity. No matter how pathetic the client or how unfortunate his circumstances, pity will not help him. It is a response to his weakness rather than his strength. All of us have to struggle against self-pity if we expect to achieve maturity and accomplish the tasks we have set for ourselves. The kind of sympathy that is pity for our misfortunes handicaps us in this struggle.

In cases where a client expresses a great deal of self-pity we can apply our principle that acceptance does not mean approval or agreement. Certainly he should be left free to express this feeling, but the counselor need not contribute to it. If he can maintain his neutrality without showing any annoyance or disapproval, such feelings will eventually give way to something else.

To build a sound working relationship is the first objective of an initial interview. The second is to begin to open up all of the psychological realities in the client's situation. This emphasis on *opening up* is what makes counseling different from most ordinary conversations. When a friend or acquaintance says something that suggests anxiety or self-doubt our immediate impulse is to stand off the troublesome emotion by a bit of reassurance, a witty remark, or a change of subject. Counseling acquires that we do just the opposite—that we say something to help the person penetrate more deeply into the feeling he is trying to express or look at it more closely. When a student speaks of his anxiety about

passing an important examination, a good counselor does not say, "Of course you'll pass it. Remember how well you've done before," but perhaps, "So much is at stake for you this time—and there is no way to be sure of coming through successfully." When a woman of 38 says, "I've never done anything well in my whole life. I've quit jobs, failed my family, let my friends down," a good counselor does not say, "But your record shows you have done many things successfully," but rather, "Up to this point your life seems to you to be a failure." We try always to think of something to say that will show we understand the meaning the client has been expressing and will encourage him to open this door a little wider.

How much of this "opening up" should be done depends, of course, on circumstances. There are some dangers if we facilitate the release of more emotion than the client is prepared to handle or than we are able to help him handle. We shall consider later the matter of referral—what to do if therapy rather than counseling is called for. But generally speaking, we shall not go wrong if we *follow* the client's train of thought and feeling rather than probe deliberately for hidden meanings. And every client does need this scrutiny of his own psychological landscape if he is to make good decisions and manage his own life well.

The third special objective of the initial interview is to "structure" the situation for the client—to give him some idea of how counseling can help him and to make plans for further work. We hope that when he leaves at the end of this first hour any misconceptions he may have started with will have been cleared up and that he will be sure just what he is supposed to do next. Standard techniques for explaining the counseling process to clients have been generally unsatisfactory. A sentence or two to answer a particular client's question about the process is of more value than a lecture, however short, on the whole procedure.

Too often such attempts to explain leave a client feeling that we do not really know what we are doing. Sometimes, I think, we tend to be too apologetic about our tests, too doubtful about our own procedures. The counseling interview itself is not the place for criticizing or defending. Our aim here is to select the best tools that we have for doing the particular job this individual needs to have done. We are here to help people make better ues of their potentialities. We *do* know how to do this. If the client senses that we do he will revise his ideas of counseling as he sees what happens. Our real job is to *make something happen.*

We should, however, make it clear what is to be done by and for this particular individual. A few minutes before the end of the scheduled time the counselor should begin to think about what needs to be settled before he and the client part company. Then the two of them can go over these arrangements together, thus clearing away any confusion or ambiguity about what comes next.

In the simpler situations where the client has requested or seems to need only some information about specific educational or vocational requirements, he can be put in touch with the sources of such information and invited to return if he has other questions. If, for one reason or another, the counselor has decided to place the case in someone else's hands, the shift can be explained and the necessary introductions and appointments made. If tests have been requested or seem to be advisable, a little time can be devoted to discussing them and deciding which ones are to be used. (This will be discussed in some detail in a later chapter.) If personal problems suggest the need for psychotherapy the possibility of further interviews can be pointed out and the next one definitely scheduled.

The important qualities during this last phase are co-operativeness, clarity, and warmth. Counselor and client decide *together* on what is next to be done. This is true even if, as often happens, it is the counselor who makes the suggestions. There is a difference between explaining what the available resources are and telling an individual what he must or should do. Implicit in the whole procedure is the counselee's freedom to accept or reject any proposed course of action. If, after it has been explained that tests can be taken which will answer many of a person's questions about himself, a client says that he does not wish to take any, that should settle the matter. He should not be urged or coerced. If, on the other hand, an anxious dependent individual, whose problems seem to have their roots in much deeper soil than the vocational indecision he complains of, chooses to take vocational tests even after the counselor has outlined for him the alternative procedures of psychotherapy, his wishes should be respected.

It is extremely important too that the closing moments be pervaded by a warm friendliness rather than a laissez-faire neutrality. It can easily happen that in his attempt to be scrupulously careful to leave the choices in the client's hands, the counselor unwittingly makes the person feel rejected or unimportant. The freedom he is given may be interpreted as indifference or as pessimism about his prospects. That such misunderstandings actually occur in a fair number of cases most counselors find out in the course of their own experience. Phrasing, manner, facial expression, and tone of voice should all express the feeling that there will be real satisfaction in seeing more of the client. Little indications make a difference. It is better to say positively, "I'll look forward to seeing you then, next Thursday at two," than to say with a questioning tone, "You'll be back next week at the same time?"

We have been thinking about three objectives the counselor has in mind for the initial interview: (1) getting a sound counseling relationship started, (2) opening up the psychological realms of feeling and attitude within the person, and (3) clarifying the structure of the helping process. To me the order in which these have been stated corresponds to their importance. In individual cases one should always sacrifice number three for number two, and either of them for number one. If, for example, an hour ends while a woman is still pouring out her bitter resentment toward the husband who is in the process of divorcing her, one would never cut her off to discuss vocational tests. She has come in because she wishes to get a job and go to work. Tests will eventually be helpful in deciding what kind of job to try for. But right now the resentment is so strong that it must be dealt with before she can take the next step. It would be best simply to say to her, "The hour is up now, but I'll be glad to have you come in again Thursday at this time if you wish." In this case no structuring or making of plans occurs, but a good relationship and a willingness on the part of the client to explore her own feelings have been achieved.

Or, to take another example, 17-year-old Nancy who has been expelled from high school for truancy and defiance spends all of the first counseling hour telling the counselor what a fine person she is and how the world misunderstands her. Guilt about her behavior, anxiety about the soundness of her personality, apprehension about the future, lie just under the surface. But the counselor makes no effort to touch them or to get her started in some constructive direction. Sore as she is from much buffeting around by the rough winds of experience, she must know the healing that comes from being sure of a friend whom she can trust before she can take these next steps. In this case both the planning and the opening up are sacrificed to enable the relationship itself to be built on a sound basis.

The initial interview is the hardest part of our task—the part that demands from us the most intensive concentration. Each person constitutes for us a new adventure in understanding. Each is destined to broaden our own lives in directions as yet uncharted. Each initial interview renews our appreciation of the challenge and the fascination of the counseling task.

CHAPTER FOUR

Diagnostic Activity in the Initial Stage of Counseling

DIFFERENT POINTS OF VIEW ABOUT DIAGNOSIS

So far as the ways of conducting the first interview are concerned, counselors representing various viewpoints would not be likely to disagree too seriously. It is with regard to what comes next that one of the most basic differences arises. Once rapport has been established and the client has had an opportunity to explain the nature of his problem, what then? (This introductory stage may, of course, take several interviews rather than one, or it may be completed in fifteen minutes, but the issue is the same.) Until the rise of the non-directive movement it was assumed without much question that an important, if not the most important, part of the counselor's skill lay in making a diagnosis on the basis of which treatment for the individual could be intelligently planned. Rogers and his co-workers have very directly challenged this assumption. Because of the controversy on this point many an average counselor in a high school or college situation finds himself confused and puzzled as to what he ought to do.

To add to the confusion different meanings have become attached to the term *diagnosis* so that persons who argue over it are not always using it in the same way. In its simplest, most obvious sense it is a concept carried over into psychology from the field of medicine. The first step in medical treatment is to label correctly the disease from which the individual is suffering.

It seems reasonable to follow this example and give psychological treatment only after the condition causing the difficulty has been identified. In psychiatry, which of course is a branch of medicine, this has been standard procedure. Counseling is similar enough in its method and aims so that it has naturally attempted to do the same thing.

A closer scrutiny of this concept of diagnosis, which at first glance seems so obviously sound, shows us that it actually has little to contribute to psychological counseling. The principal difficulty is that in the situations with which we deal there is nothing analogous to a separate disease entity like tuberculosis, ulcers, or scarlet fever. Psychiatrists have pointed out that their categories—schizophrenia, manic-depressive psychosis, paranoia, and the others—are not like these either, since they are based on observations of symptoms that appear to be correlated, rather than on an understanding of causal factors. If one can object to psychiatric terms, he can object even more strongly to the use of labels for conditions within the normal range. They do not even come in reliable clusters. If we use "vocational indecision," for example, as a diagnostic label, it is difficult to see that any useful purpose has been served. There is an unlimited number of different combinations of attitudes and circumstances out of which vocational indecision can arise, and no standard treatment for the state of mind is known. Classifications of this type may be of some value in facilitating record-keeping and the writing of administrative reports. There their usefulness ends.

If we shift over to the concept of counseling recommended in this book, seeing its major goal as the facilitation of individual development through choices rather than the general improvement of personality, the use of diagnostic labels becomes even more meaningless. It is conceivable that a whole new set of categories focusing on kinds of choices, obstacles to choice, and developmental levels in choice-making may eventually be worked out, and such categories might serve a useful purpose in organizing the counselor's thinking about a client. But the presently available systems of psychiatric labels and others derived from them or modeled after them do not contribute much to the thinking clients and counselors do about life decisions.

There is another use of the term *diagnosis* in books and papers on counseling which makes considerably better sense.

Writers such as Williamson and Darley have thought of diagnosis as the comprehensive picture that the counselor develops of his client, his strengths and weaknesses, his interests and aptitudes, his past experiences and hopes for the future. This sort of diagnosis becomes a crucial step in vocational and educational planning. When a counselor had succeeded in fitting into a coherent pattern all the information about a person that is available to him from many sources, including records, tests, and interviews, he is in a position to make a prediction as to what is likely to occur if the person decides in each of several different ways. If the prognosis in one of these directions is decidedly unfavorable he can interpose some treatment which will make it less likely that the client will make that choice. For a number of leaders in the counseling field, this is the essential task—this making of diagnoses leading to prognoses which in turn lead to wise decisions. They would not, of course, discount the importance of tact and skill in communicating information to the client, but they would place the emphasis on the thinking done before the decision interview begins.

Many smoothly functioning school counseling organizations and many training programs for student counselors have been built with diagnosis as a central concept. The whole Veterans Administration vocational advisement program after World War II embodied this philosophy more than any other. It has the virtue of bringing clarity and order into a very complex field. Furthermore, few would quarrel with the idea that it is good for a psychologist or educator to learn to fit many diverse items of information about an individual into some understandable pattern. Many workers feel that the ability to do this is one of their most indispensable skills.

OBJECTIONS TO DIAGNOSIS AS A CENTRAL CONCEPT

There are, however, some rather serious objections to organizing counseling around diagnosis, even when it is of this thorough, skillful variety. For one thing, the textbook outline is far more clear-cut and uncomplicated than the procedure itself is. The trouble is that we do not really succeed in separating "diagnosis" from "treatment" and postponing treatment or decisions until all the information is in. This means that in some cases what we do in our attempt to make a diagnosis may turn out to be the wrong kind of treatment. The act of taking tests and filling out questionnaires influences clients' attitudes in certain directions rather than others. A dependent or evasive individual may be less ready to face the real sources of his difficulties when he comes for his second interview than he was at the time of his first. The eight hours he has spent taking tests have reinforced his tendency to look to someone or something outside himself for decisions. Whether we like it or not, everything from the first moment of the first interview on is actually part of treatment. We cannot really isolate the diagnostic aspects from the rest.

A more serious objection to placing diagnosis at the center of counseling and organizing everything else around it is that we are accumulating more and more evidence that clinical predictions, no matter how experienced and skillful the psychologists who make them, are not accurate enough to warrant their use as a basis for important life decisions. Several studies now testify to the fact that impersonal statistical predictions using a regression equation based on a few variables are more likely to be correct than are the best intuitive judgments based on all the information available.[1] We simply cannot trust our prognoses. Moreover, we know very well that the statistical predictions are inadequate bases for crucial decisions. Seldom does a multiple correlation between a criterion and the optimally weighted combination of predictors run higher than .60 or .70. Such a relationship between college success and test scores, for example, is very useful in setting selection standards if the institution doing the selecting does not mind rejecting a considerable number of students who would have done satisfactory work. But if one's concern is with the individual rather than the group, as the counselor's primarily is, this is not good enough. How is one to know whether the course of this specific person's life is likely to follow the main trend indicated by the correlation coefficient or to constitute one of the marked exceptions which its magnitude leaves room for? It is at this point that we have always fallen back on our clinical judgment, and it is precisely this kind of judgment that has been

[1] P. E. Meehl, *Clinical versus statistical prediction.* Minneapolis: University of Minnesota Press, 1954.

called in question by the research studies to which we have referred.

There is still another objection to placing diagnosis and prognosis at the heart of the counseling process. It is the one which has been most stressed by the proponents of non-directive techniques. In order to make a searching diagnosis and evaluate prognoses in various directions, the counselor must adapt an objective, third-person, attitude. That is, he must see the problem from an external frame of reference. This is quite a different approach from the one he takes during an interview, when he attempts to get the "feel" of the client's experience. It would not seem that the conflict between the two attitudes is necessarily irreconcilable, since a large part of the diagnostic thinking goes on *between*, rather than during interviews. It is while the counselor is thinking over all the circumstances that have been recounted to him and trying to fit test scores and background information into a pattern that he must be objective and matter-of-fact. He can still "listen with the third ear" while the client is talking to him. A person is not confined to a single frame of reference but may shift from one to the other, if he wishes, at different stages of the counseling process. To Rogers and other non-directive workers, however, the necessity for such shifts is a handicap to be avoided if possible. On this point little actual evidence is available so far, but it is worth consideration because of its relationship to the whole philosophy of counseling.

DIAGNOSIS AS COMPREHENSIVE PICTURE OR WORKING IMAGE

Nevertheless, in spite of these criticisms, this attempt on the part of the counselor to see the whole picture, whether we call it diagnosis or not, and whether it results in prognosis or not, is an important activity of the counselor. To some extent, it forms a part of every human relations activity. Madison Avenue has given us a term for such comprehensive pictures—the *image* an individual projects. From the moment he first encounters a client, a counselor begins to form what may be called a "working image" of the person. What he finds out through interviews, tests, observations, and background sources serves to modify this image, filling in details, making it more complex and accurate. By means of it he is able to organize large amounts of information in an organic, personal way, and understand in a manner so direct as to appear almost intuitive what alternative courses of action are really possible for the client. There is probably a good deal of variation from one counselor to another in the complexity and accuracy of the working images they form, variation which as yet has been studied very little in its relationship to the processes and outcomes of counseling.

VARIETIES OF DECISIONS: WHETHER TO CONTINUE THE RELATIONSHIP

We can avoid much of the controversy over the diagnosis issue if we abandon the term itself and turn our attention to some specific questions which are more likely to be answerable. At what stage in a case is it necessary for the counselor to make a judgment? What kind of judgment is required? What factors need to be considered in making it?

We have noted one such choice-point typically occurring at the end of the first interview, although there is certainly nothing fixed about the time. This stage in the proceedings may be reached either sooner or considerably later, but the question that the counselor cannot dodge if he works for an agency to which many kinds of people go for help is "Shall I continue with this case? Is this person likely to be benefited by counseling?" In large, specialized services, an intake interviewer may make this judgment. Unless a highly skilled individual is available for this special task it is probably better that the counselor do it himself.

The simplest type of case for which one decides to give no further service can be classified under the heading, "No apparent need for counseling at this time." A high school counselor may schedule routine interviews with all the boys and girls for whom he is responsible. Only a fraction of them may need to come in again for any purpose during a school term. To identify that fraction and make sure that these individuals know that further services are available is an important part of the counselor's task, whether we call it diagnosis or not. A college counselor will also encounter in the course of a year's work a fair number of well-adjusted people whose plans are already satisfactorily worked out and who, in spite of minor difficulties, are handling their lives as well as they could be expected to. Often such a person will have come in out of curiosity or because of an enthusiastic recommendation by a friend or roommate. Since the counselor realizes that he may have missed something and that it is quite possible for an individual's circumstances to change, he does not close one of these cases with an air of finality. Rather he will end the first hour in a manner that leaves the channel open but makes no definite arrangement for more interviews. He might say, for example, "I'm glad you came in. You know where I am now. If anything comes up that you want to talk over I hope you'll make another appointment."

At the opposite extreme, counselors encounter with some frequency prospective clients who are so seriously disturbed that they are outside the range of people the counselor is equipped to help. Sometimes psychotic manifestations such as delusions, hallucinations, or bizarre schizophrenic thinking become apparent during the initial interview. The textbook disposition of such cases is simple. They are to be referred to a psychiatrist without delay. In practice this is often more easily said than done. There are large areas of the United States where psychiatrists are scarcer than the proverbial hen's teeth. Even in places where they are available the expense of psychiatric treatment puts it out of the question for many people. Furthermore, the client may be horrified at the idea of such treatment since to seek it would involve an admission that something is seriously wrong. Because of these difficulties no one solution is always open to the counselor. Sometimes exploration of all the circumstances brings out the fact that the client is eligible for treatment at some free clinic such as the Veterans Administration Mental Hygiene Clinic. Sometimes voluntary commitment to a mental hospital can be arranged. It goes without saying that discussions of such plans should be carried on in an atmosphere free from alarm and as friendly and kind as that characterizing the rest of counseling activity. One should of course never give the impression, "Your case is too serious for us to handle," but rather, "Your problems are of a different sort from those we are set up to help people with, but perhaps we can work out an arrangement for you to see someone else who can help you."

The counselor should realize, however, that even if he cannot send the person for psychiatric treatment it is not advisable for him to work with a psychotic case himself, unless he is a member of a psychiatric team, as counseling psychologists are in increasing numbers of mental hospitals and rehabilitation agencies. To disturb whatever precarious organization a psychotic or near-psychotic individual has been maintaining is unwise unless he is in a controlled environment where the consequences of disturbance cannot possibly be harmful to himself or others. It is often hard, especially for a young counselor with high ideals, to close the door in the face of a person with serious problems. It is necessary to realize, however, that good intentions do not guarantee good results and that there are some people we cannot help.

A still more difficult decision is forced upon the counselor when he knows that the client's condition is extremely serious and that commitment to a mental hospital is the only satisfactory course. In taking the necessary legal steps to bring this about, the counselor will have to break confidences and thus reinforce the client's feeling that he is surrounded by enemies and can trust no one. Again there is no single procedure that suits all cases. If the person can be persuaded to commit himself, it is the best solution. If members of his family seem likely to make the necessary arrangements, it is best to leave it to them. If the person's symptoms involve suffering for himself but no actual danger, it may be advisable to leave matters as they are, at least for a time. In some few urgent cases, it may be necessary for the counselor to take the initiative in commitment proceedings.

Such psychiatric problems constitute only a very small fraction of the average counselor's work. A considerably larger fraction is made up of persons who might be described as neurotic, although this may not have been established through actual psychiatric diagnosis. The standard prescription in such cases is to refer them for psychiatric help. But in practice, this decision is even more complicated than in the case of psychotics. In the first place, there is no clearly identifiable line between neurosis and normality. No red light flashes to warn us that neurosis is present. Secondly, counselors differ greatly in their backgrounds of training and experience, so that cases that would be outside the field of competence of one might be suitable for another. Thirdly, what can be done for a neurotic individual whose case is likely to be more time-consuming than the average must always depend to some extent on the agency's total counseling load.

Perhaps the best basis for a sound decision as to whether or not to continue work with a person showing psychiatric difficulties is the nature of the service to be rendered rather than the seriousness of the symptoms. The distinction between counseling and psychotherapy proposed in the first chapter can help with this distinction. A long-drawn-out search for the origins of intrapsychic conflicts is not counseling. However, a patient with psychiatric symptoms can often be helped to explore his resources, decide on some actions he can take on his own behalf, and carry out these plans. Since such reorientation often results in an improvement in his total condition, it could be considered a kind of therapy, but it is a process different from that usually designated by the term. We shall have more to say about this kind of treatment in Chapter 11. The point here is that if the first interview or any information the counselor has access to at the beginning suggests that this distinctive counseling experience is likely to help the client, he may try to provide it, centering his and the client's attention on strengths and promising possibilities rather than on disabling symptoms or overwhelming anxieties. Obviously this is not an easy diagnostic decision to make. Consultation with psychiatrists and psychologists is of great value. Fortunately such consultation is usually easier to arrange than is a psychiatric referral for the client.

The decision not to continue contacts with a definitely neurotic client is easier to make if psychiatric help for the person is available. But here as with the psychotics it is important to realize that there are situations in which an effort to help an individual, no matter how well-intentioned it is, may leave him in worse condition than it found him. A neurotic pattern of adjustment is, after all, a form of solution to the person's problems. To unsettle this solution is hardly an ethical procedure unless there is a fair probability that he will be able to work out a better one.

In communities where facilities for psychiatric referral are in existence, the results of diagnostic tests such as the Minnesota Multiphasic Personality Inventory, the Rorschach, and the Thematic Apperception Test will sometimes help the counselor to decide on whether or not to refer the client to the other agency.

In such cases, the reason for asking him to take the tests can be presented clearly and without alarm at the close of the first interview. For example one might say, "The University, as you may know, has a Mental Hygiene Clinic that is set up to help students with certain kinds of problem, just as we are organized to help them with others. I'm a little doubtful at this point whether you would get along better with them or with us. If you can spare the time to come in and take a couple of tests, it will help us to decide." He can be told that if the recommendation is that he see the psychiatrist at the Clinic, the test results will be sent to that agency. Then the first appointment with the Clinic can be arranged from the counselor's office so that the client need not suffer a moment's uncertainty about the next step.

In places where psychiatric referral facilities are not available, the use of tests to help with the diagnosis of a neurotic or psychotic condition suspected to be serious is ordinarily ruled out by the nature of the situation and the basic ethical axiom that we must not leave the client in worse condition than we find him. To appreciate this fact, a counselor has only to put himself in the client's place for a moment. If a person who already has some doubt as to his normality or sanity is requested to take a test like the MMPI, the experience is likely to reinforce those doubts. Whatever the counselor does afterward will be almost certain to increase the anxiety. This heightening of the anxiety may not be a handicap if the condition turns out to be one which the counselor decides that he himself can treat. But if it appears to be a variety of maladjustment more serious than he wants to deal with himself there may be unfortunate after-effects whether or not any report on the test results is given. The client might conclude that things were far worse with him than he had thought if diagnostic tests indicated that he was beyond the reach of counseling.

It is only by constantly putting himself in the other person's place that the counselor can make distinctions like this one as to when diagnostic tests are feasible and when they are not. Adopting this point of view will also enable him to phrase his explanations of why further appointments are not recommended in such a way that they will not frighten a client or give him an impression that his case is hopeless. It is quite possible to combine honesty and realism with kindness and consideration. To one person, for example, he may say, "What people with problems like yours usually need most is a chance to talk things over at considerable length with a psychiatrist. It often takes several months of interviews several times a week to bring about a change. We don't have the facilities for that sort of service here, but in a year or two, when you are out of college and earning your living, you can probably arrange it. Meanwhile if you go on as you are it is not likely that things will get any worse, and you have shown that you can accomplish things in spite of the handicap." To another he may need to explain: "I know how hard it must make things for you to have to struggle against this fear of crowds all the time. But a fear like that is tied up with the rest of one's personality in such a complicated way that it usually isn't possible to get rid of it without spending a great deal of time untangling the whole skein. So for the time being perhaps the only thing to do is put up with it. If it ever gets enough worse to warrant the expense and trouble, you will want to consult a good psychiatrist who is experienced in helping people with such problems."

It is especially difficult to turn down these cases of serious maladjustment when they have been referred by a faculty member or personnel officer of the school of which the counseling service is a part. The counselor can hardly help feeling that the person who made the referral will say, "What good is a special service of that sort if it can't help the very students who need it most?" Thus he is put on the defensive or perhaps feels a little guilty about the whole thing. The main thing to keep in mind is that another person's expectations cannot constitute an adequate basis for a counselor's decision. In many cases it may be possible for him to explain to the colleague who sent the student to him the reason for the termination of counseling. Such explanations can lead to better referrals and sounder public relations in general.

Besides the cases which the counselor decides not to continue because they are too serious or not serious enough, there is a third category of one-interview cases. These are the ones in which some treatment other than counseling seems indicated, at least to start with. One example is the person whose symptoms point in the direction of organic disease requiring medical care. Another is the student whose low grades seem to be accounted for by a severe reading disability. Still another is the college freshman with a percentile rank of three on the college aptitude test who is considering giving up college and getting a job because his grades are so low. The boy with the reading handicap can be put in touch with some agency giving intensive remedial training; the low-aptitude freshman can be confirmed and encouraged in his decision to go to work. An adolescent who is at sword's point with his homeroom teacher and is petitioning for a change may simply be allowed to transfer to another group where the outlook for him is more promising. The girl with too heavy a load of course work for her ability can be permitted to drop one subject.

In all these instances, the counselor is not really recommending some non-counseling treatment. All he is doing is to concur in the individual's own proposal that he try something else first. There is a subtle but probably important difference between the two things. In order to have grounds for recommending something as a solution to the problem presented, he would need to know much more about the individual than he can possibly know at the end of one interview and even then, as we have seen, his judgment might be wrong. Furthermore, for him to make a recommendation to the authorities for a change of homeroom or living quarters is to give the relationship with the client a structure that will not be favorable for later counseling in case that turns out to be necessary. He must not get himself typed as "the person who tells you what to do" or "the person who gets you out of trouble" if he wishes to create a situation in which it is clear that the client makes his own decisions and accepts the responsibility for his own mistakes.

He can, however, accept the person's decision to try some other way of coping with his deficiencies and still leave the way open for counseling if this does not work. It often turns out this way. Languid, apathetic, obese Sharon Logan may indeed have a thyroid deficiency which medical treatment can help, but it does not rule out the possibility of psychological complications. After her basal metabolic rate has been brought up to normal she may still be unable to meet academic or social competition, still held back by crushing feelings of inferiority. Whether she then returns for the counseling she needs will depend partly on what was said at the close of the one interview she had with the counselor. The student with the reading handicap may still be unable to concentrate on his essential science courses even after tests indicate that his speed and comprehension are within the normal range. The high school boy may soon find himself as much at odds with teacher and classmates in the homeroom to which he has transferred as he was in the one from which he escaped. Thus it is well in these cases where no arrangements are made for more than one interview that the counselor show by his words and expression that he will welcome the client back if need arises.

As has been mentioned earlier, this sorting-out process, the act of separating those who are immediately to be given further service from those who are not, is a more important feature of the work of some counselors than of others. In a college with a number of specialized personnel departments the functions of which are well-known to the students, most of the sorting out may be accomplished by the students themselves. Those who wish help with vocational and educational decisions will come to the Counseling Center. Those with serious emotional problems will consult the Psychiatric Clinic. Those who need remedial work will apply to the appropriate agencies. This system, however, never works with one hundred per cent accuracy, and in the more general situation where probably the majority of counselors work, the necessity for some differentiation between the students they are equipped to help and those they are not is an inescapable responsibility. The heavier the load, the more urgent the need for this sorting out.

VARIETIES OF DECISIONS: WHAT KIND OF TREATMENT?

Once a counselor has decided that he will continue a counseling relationship with a client, other decisions become necessary. He must ask himself the question: What does this counselee seem to need most? Is it *information, clarification, support,* or any combination of these things?

The form that the *information* question is likely to take at this early stage of the counseling process is: Shall I arrange for this client to take any psychological tests in order to find out more about what sort of person he is?

Controversy over the use of tests in counseling has existed for a long time, but out of it has come a considerable measure of agreement on the general value of test information in helping with vocational and educational decisions. (See Chapter 6.) In the beginning of the vocational guidance movement, guidance consisted mainly in disseminating information about jobs so that young people would have a more adequate basis for choosing from among them. With the rapid development of psychological tests after World War I the importance of analyzing individuals as well as jobs began to be stressed. During the twenties and thirties many workers argued vehemently against testing on the grounds that the reliability and validity of these techniques were very inadequate. The reply that test users could and did make to this charge was that *other* bases for vocational decisions were even less valid and reliable. They argued that by combining test results *with* the other sources of information the errors likely to arise from either technique could be avoided. Gradually enough data accumulated in follow-up studies to furnish dependable evidence that this was true—that sounder vocational decisions could in fact be made with tests than without them.

With the rise of the non-directive movement in the forties another sort of objection became prominent. This was that the use of tests had the effect of giving the counseling relationship the wrong structure, that it encouraged the client to look to someone else for the answers to his questions instead of working out answers for himself. Since the counselor is the person who chooses tests and interprets what scores mean, the client sees his own role as that of taking advice from an expert rather than as that of endeavoring to think maturely about his own life. Discussions of this issue have led to the trying out of new ways of incorporating testing in the counseling process without authoritative structuring. As evidence that these methods are feasible has accumulated, this objection also has lost much of its weight. There seems now to be no reason why the values coming from both test information and a client-centered attitude cannot be combined in the facilitation of vocational and educational decisions.

There is no incompatibility in the two approaches if we think of testing in terms of information for the use of the *client* rather than diagnosis by the *counselor*. In deciding whether or not the opportunity to take tests should be presented to a client the basic question is: Does he really need more information about himself? In discussing the conduct of the first interview, we stressed the acceptance and understanding on the part of the counselor which help to make it possible for the counselee to accept and understand himself. It is important to realize that the contribution tests make is to the *understanding*, not to the *acceptance* aspect of the process. Intelligently chosen and interpreted, they can show the person what some of his important characteristics are, but they can do nothing to help him come to terms with what he finds in himself. Thus if his problem lies primarily in unhappy self-attitudes, the exploration of these should probably take precedence over the accumulation of more facts which it is unlikely he will be able to accept when he gets them.

In specific cases, how is the counselor to know whether or not the person can profit by taking tests? In the first place, he asks himself how much information about the client is already available? In most high schools there are testing programs for all students, at least in the areas of intelligence and achievement, and a considerable amount of information about each person can be obtained simply by going to his cumulative record. A college student or adult client may have had some previous vocational testing and counseling. He may be able to report in some detail on the test results but still be as undecided as he ever was. This is an indication that it is not really test information that he requires and that further testing might only prolong the period in which he tries to fasten the responsibility for a decision on something outside himself. In still other instances so much information from non-test sources may exist that testing seems irrelevant. A high school boy who has spent the last five summers in his uncle's garage, has demolished and rebuilt a Ford of his own, and spends all his spare time working with engines does not need mechanical aptitude or interest tests. In the choice of a field of specialization there may, of course, be other questions to which tests might help him find answers. It may, for example, be important to ascertain whether he is good enough at mathematics to consider mechanical engineering rather than auto mechanics as an occupation.

Another obvious but often-neglected point to be considered in deciding whether to test or not is the question of whether there *are* any tests which will tell this particular individual the things he wants to know. We do not have an assortment of psychological tests covering all the important human traits even in the limited sphere of vocational adjustment. There are any number of doubts that young people bring to counseling which cannot be resolved by means of tests. What are my chances for success as a real estate salesman? Do I have enough art talent for a career in industrial design? Am I better suited to mechanical or electrical engineering? If I become a junior high school teacher, will I be able to handle the discipline? Have I the right kind of personality for social work? Are my aptitudes more like those of barbers or bakers? These are all legitimate informational questions. If there were clear-cut, objective measures of the traits involved, decisions could be made with less difficulty and the counselor's task would be much easier than it is now. But we do *not* have such tools and it is only honest to say so when clients raise the issues. They should know that decisions on such matters have to be based on other kinds of data—success in related courses, tryouts in similar jobs, and general attitudes toward the kinds of task involved.

To what extent should the client's own request govern the decision about tests? At first glance it might appear that in any thoroughly client-centered program this should be the deciding factor. However, the situation is not quite so simple as this. More important than the literal meaning of the words, "I'd like to take some aptitude tests," is the feeling that lies back of them and the wish that prompted the person to speak them. It has already been emphasized repeatedly that it is these attitudes upon which attention is focused in the interview. Therefore it is the counselor's duty to accept this statement in the same way in which he accepts everything else the client says, responding to it in such a way as to encourage the clarification of the motivation behind it. If the interview begins in this way, the appropriate response is not, "All right. We'll make an appointment for you to come in for testing tomorrow," but rather, "O.K. You might tell me a little more about yourself and what you would like to find out." Notice too that it is better to say it this way than to ask directly, "What do you want to take tests for?" since such a question is likely to arouse defensiveness.

The situation is somewhat different at the end of an interview in which *both* lack of information and difficulties in accepting what the person does know of himself have become apparent. If he decides at this point that he would like to find out what tests can tell him before doing anything else, his decision should be respected, provided, of course, that there are tests that will tell him what he wants to know. It is not necessary that lack of information be the whole problem. If it constitutes any part of the difficulty, tests may be useful. Those cases in which doubts about real abilities and interests are tied up in some complex way with conflicting self-attitudes actually constitute a large part of a counselor's work. There is no reason why we should either leave the person in doubt about his strengths and weaknesses in order to focus on the personal conflicts or ignore the attitudes and try to force a decision on the basis of objective evidence alone.

The counselor's function here is primarily clarification. He should try to make it possible for the client to *choose* what he wishes to do next rather than simply to wander into the course that he happened to see first. He may explain it in some such way as this: "A person who is trying to come to important decisions often finds that it helps to talk over all his feelings about it in the way we have been talking during this past hour. It also helps, when a person isn't sure just what his greatest strengths and weaknesses are, to take some tests that show how he stands in comparison with other people. We can make arrangements for you to do either one of these things next. If you would like to come back for another talk next week, we'll make an appointment for it now. If you think you'd better get some new information about yourself first we can decide right now what tests you want to take and when it will be convenient for you to come in for them." The warmth and friendliness in the counselor's tone and manner will make it plain that the help and support the client came to find are there whichever course he decides upon.

Not infrequently it happens that a client who asks first for tests is in reality seeking something quite different. If they concentrate on his meaning rather than his words this will become clear to both participants as the interview proceeds. The first request will then become irrelevant. One young man, obviously deeply troubled, came to the college counseling office asking to be given a Rorschach test. As the interview went on and he came to trust the counselor more, he explained that for years he had been tortured by doubt as to whether he was basically heterosexual or homosexual in his outlook. He had hoped that a Rorschach would give him a clear answer so that he could stop struggling with the problem and with all the other problems of personal relationships that arose from it. When it was explained to him that there was no test which would furnish him with such a clear unequivocal verdict, but that counseling could perhaps help him find a way out, he was more than willing to come back for more interviews rather than to be given what he had at first asked for.

Another student, a brilliant girl majoring in languages, asked to take some tests because she was "curious about them." She went on to tell how she had taken dozens of IQ tests during her childhood years and that she still volunteered whenever possible to act as a subject for psychology students struggling to meet their course requirements in testing practice. As her ideas developed in the favorable atmosphere of the counseling room, she found herself putting into words something she had never really faced before. She admitted that she had been troubled for as far back as she could remember by a haunting sense of inferiority. High test scores and outstanding academic successes served to hold it in check but did not dispel it. There was always somewhere in the back of her mind a feeling she knew to be absurd but could not get rid of—a conviction that she was not really the brilliant person people gave her credit for being and that someday she would be unmasked. Out of this state of mind came both the compulsion to keep taking tests and the motivation to keep studying. Each time some new person would tell her how well she had done it would reassure her for a little while, but each time the old feeling would eventually return in full force. By the end of the first interview she had realized that what she wanted was not just to go through the old reassurance-discouragement cycle once more but to come to grips with the inferiority attitude itself. It was not necessary for the counselor to do anything about the request for testing which she had made in the beginning.

We have considered the decision of whether or not to test at some length because it is one that frequently faces a counselor. This does not mean, however, that information about psychological characteristics of the client is the only variety of information to be brought into the counseling situation. At the time these early decisions are being made, a high school or college student may undertake to explore some occupational possibilities using printed materials in the library. A woman contemplating a divorce may get the legal information she must have if she is to clarify her alternatives. A physically handicapped person seeking rehabilitation may arrange for a thorough physical examination. All sorts of information enter into the counseling process before final decisions are made.

It has been suggested earlier that in cases where the initial interview indicates that the client is confused or undecided even though his information about himself and his situation appears to be adequate, the most sensible decision is to offer him the opportunity for further interviews to help him clarify his attitudes and ideas. This does not mean therapy, although the techniques used overlap to some extent with those psychotherapists use. If we keep in mind the definition of counseling set forth in Chapter 1—to facilitate an individual's development through his own choices—we can strike the right note in explaining to the client what we have in mind. As indicated earlier, it is often advisable to let the client choose whether or not he wishes to return for a "talking over" session to help him decide what to do. When we phrase the offer in this way we weaken any belief he may have that all of his problems are going to be solved for him or that he is to be transformed through some magical sort of psychoanalysis.

It sometimes becomes clear during the first stage of a counseling relationship that the best thing that can be done for a client at this time is to offer him a measure of *support* in his efforts to cope with the circumstances of his own life. This happens in some of the psychiatric cases we have considered in some detail. During the difficult period while Henry is on a waiting list for treatment in a Child Guidance Clinic it may give him strength and courage if his high school counselor sees him for only ten minutes a week, not to discuss emotional problems or psychiatric symptoms but just to keep him in touch with someone who likes him and is interested in him. Bill Bergson may have made all of his plans for college and career when he comes to see the counselor. But he needs the support that comes from having someone he respects corroborate his thinking and agree that his decision is sound. Even when interview time is minimal and verbal expression is limited, the counseling relationship can contribute in an important way to an individual's development.

VARIETIES OF DECISION:
IS CONSULTATION NECESSARY?

Besides these decisions as to whether to continue a case and what kind of help the person needs most, the counselor will often have to decide at this early stage whether or not to seek some kind of consultation with regard to it. It is in accord with generally accepted ethical principles for him to talk the case over with other professional persons on the staff of the agency in which he works. In many agencies it is customary to hold staff meetings at which group decisions can be made with regard to a case one counselor is handling. Such consultation constitutes a real resource for a counselor, even if he is a person with considable experience, and it is wise for him to arrange for it if he has any doubts about his own decisions.

As indicated at the beginning of this chapter, *diagnosis* is an ambiguous word. We have tried to separate out a part of its overall meaning, the part related to the decision-making activity of the counselor in early stages of the counseling process, and clarify this one aspect. Other aspects, especially the synthesizing activity that comes later, will be discussed in later chapters. Counseling theory and practice has reached a stage of maturity that makes it unnecessary for us to argue about whether or not diagnosis is necessary but instead to concentrate our attention on what counselors actually do. Further progress lies in this direction.

Research Summary

DIAGNOSTIC CATEGORIES FOR COUNSELING

One kind of counseling research has consisted of specific attempts to develop diagnostic categories that can be reliably judged. Pepinsky (1948) showed that counselors agree fairly well in their classifications of cases under the following headings: Lack of Assurance, Lack of Information, Lack of Skill, Dependence, Cultural Self-Conflict, Interpersonal Self-Conflict, and Intrapersonal Self-Conflict. Choice-Anxiety was also included, but there were only two cases in the series analyzed that fell under this heading. In a similar study Sloan and Pierce-Jones (1958) found fairly good agreement between counselors on all categories except *Dependence* and *Choice-Conflict* (similar to Pepinsky's Choice-Anxiety). When the groups high on each category were compared with student norms for the Minnesota Multiphasic Personality Inventory, a number of significant differences appeared. Diagnostic categories could be ranked according to the severity of the personality deviation they represented. For males this order was: (*a*) Lack of Information; (*b*) Lack of Assurance and Lack of Skill; and (*c*) Self-Conflict I and Self-Conflict II. (Studies cited at the end of the research summary following Chapter 1 also suggest that in the minds of both counselors and clients there may be a sharp distinction between the self-conflict categories and the others.)

These diagnostic categories correspond much more closely to the decisions counselors must make with regard to the disposition of cases than the standard psychiatric classifications do. However, there is some evidence that the formulation of *goals* for counseling is not so reliable a process as the identification of problems. Poole (1957) asked counselors in training, persons from public school and high school settings enrolled for summer practicum courses, to make judgments before and after each interview with a high school client as to his problems and the counseling goals. Other graduate students in the counselor training program were then asked to read through the interview typescripts and make the same kinds of judgments about problems and goals. There was significant agreement between readers and counselors on problems but not on goals or on counselee achievement of goals. These results might lead us to question how necessary the formulation of goals is for the counseling process. The judgment about what the problem is would be related to a number of other decisions such as those we have discussed in the text.

The efforts to design a set of diagnostic categories specifically for counseling have not as yet led to more effective work in the practical counseling situation, but they are useful tools for the research worker who may wish to differentiate the processes that occur in different types of case.

THE DIAGNOSTIC PROCESS

A different sort of research effort has been directed toward finding out the mental processes of a person engaging in diagnostic activity. Koester (1954) asked ten counselors to think aloud while making diagnoses of three cases. Three judges analyzed the resulting protocols to determine the frequency of the following types of responses: (1) indeterminate response, (2) response as an interpretation of datum, (3) response as a comparison and evaluation of data, (4) response as a hypothesis based on synthesis of data, (5) response as an evaluation of an interpretation or hypothesis, (6) response indicating need for additional data. There were differences between counselors in the frequency with which they used the various categories, but eight of the ten were consistent in their use of them from case to case. Category 4, Formulating Hypotheses, was used most frequently, and Category 1, Indeterminate Responses, least frequently.

C. A. Parker (1958) used these same categories to classify the verbalized thoughts of ten counselors about a client while they (a) read materials in a case folder, (b) predicted his behavior in the next interview, and (c) listened to three recorded interviews. There was significant consistency in frequencies shown from one counselor to another. Contrary to expectation, there was no increase in the diversity and richness of the predictions as more information became available and not much relationship between this diversity and richness and the validity of the predictions (agreement with what the client actually did in the next interview). The concept of the diagnostic process as a hierarchical one—interpretation, synthesis, forming and evaluating hypotheses—was not supported.

The idea that a counselor constructs what we have called a *working image* of the client with whom he is dealing is supported by a study McArthur (1954) has described. As part of the Study of Adult Development at Harvard, distinguished visitors were invited in as discussants at a case conference. Each was asked to organize a large amount of material about a subject (up to graduation from college) and then predict the person's behavior during the next ten years. These clinicians handled the task by developing a sort of construct of the person—"He seems to be the sort of person who. . . ." It was from such constructs rather than from separate facts or theoretical formulations that good predictions came. Judges using different theoretical systems made equally valid predictions. Pepinsky (1955) has described this kind of mental process as that of a theorist who constructs a *model* of the other person.

Evaluation

The reliable classification of counseling cases into diagnostic categories has been shown to be feasible, but there is no evidence that such classification makes for more effective counseling. Study of the mental processes counselors use while studying case materials suggests that they do more than categorize. Their thinking is not so much an orderly problem-solving procedure, as it is a construction of a working image of the person being studied.

CHAPTER FIVE

The Use of
Background Information
and Case Records
in Counseling

NATURE OF FILED INFORMATION

One of the first things a counselor does when preparing for an interview with a client is to go to the files of the agency in which he is working, seeking whatever information is available about the person. If he is a school counselor, the student's cumulative record is likely to tell him a good deal about abilities, school achievements, interests, home background, special difficulties encountered at previous developmental stages, attitudes toward various aspects of the school program, and characteristic kinds of behavior. If he is a counselor in a rehabilitation agency, his client's file may contain information about his disability, work experience, and previous contacts with social agencies, as well as facts about his age, education, residence, and marital status. If he is a counselor in a psychiatric hospital, material about the course of the patient's illness, reports of psychological tests given for diagnostic purposes, and some account of the treatment he has undergone will probably be contained in his file.

OBJECTIONS TO THE USE OF CASE RECORDS

At the outset we must recognize that much be said against case records as an adjunct to counseling. There is no doubt that they can be used in ways that prevent rather than facilitate good counseling. We shall examine these objections and difficulties first, so that in thinking about how to use records skillfully we can keep in mind the pitfalls to be avoided.

The most serious way in which they may interfere with the kind of process described in the previous chapter is by encouraging categorizations and snap judgments. Because they are made up of bits of factual information it is easy for the person reading them to adopt the external frame of reference. It is then natural for him to classify the "case" according to his own psychological theories. For example, Mr. Gordon notes an IQ of 85 in the first section of a boy's file and says to himself, "That's it. Of course that explains the trouble George has been having. These low-IQ boys are always difficult to handle in regular classes." Because this diagnosis strikes him as so plausible it keeps him from noting in later sections of the record some evidences of a considerably higher degree of mental ability and blinds him during the interview to signs of the client's anxiety over his appearance and social inadequacies.

As she goes over another record, Mrs. Barnes is impressed by the fact that Lucille's sister, eighteen months her junior, is in the same school grade. "No wonder Lucille is sulky and unhappy," she thinks. "She is obviously jealous of this sister who is brighter than she is. We'll have to see what we can do about getting them into different rooms." Because her mind is made up ahead of time she fails to grasp the complexity of the situation Lucille tries to describe in the interview, the mixture of love, resentment, and admiration she feels for her sister, her relationship with an older brother now at college, and her dreams of becoming a concert violinist. Later she wonders why the treatment she recommends, placing the two girls in separate homerooms, fails to help Lucille. She does not realize that it had no relevance to the whole pattern of the girl's attitude toward school and toward life.

These are extreme examples because they represent the making of a diagnosis from a single item of information. But even when many facts are brought together, it is still possible to fall into similar errors. Miss Larson, Dean of Girls at Lakeside High School, examines very conscientiously the material on Rose Borini, a ninth-grade girl whom she has been asked to see because of repeated truancies and apparent lack of interest in school. The picture that emerges in her mind is something like this: "Rose is a fifteen-year-old Italian girl from a laborer's family, the oldest of six children. Her intelligence, according to several tests, is within the average range, and until last year she has done satisfactory work in school, getting above-average grades in art and music. Previous teachers describe her as a pretty child, neatly though rather shabbily dressed. Entries from anecdotal records show that in the seventh grade, boys were beginning to take an interest in her and she in them. No health problems are mentioned, and there is no record of any sort of delinquency." What Miss Larson makes of this is that Rose is probably a girl who has matured young and become more interested in dates and possibly in marriage than in academic work. She sees her role during any interviews they may have as one of convincing the girl that school has something to offer her, since the compulsory education law requires that she stay in school at least a year longer. She is also prepared to arrange any changes in schedule necessary to create more interest on Rose's part. To have this case clearly outlined in this way is a handicap only if it prevents the counselor from recognizing that there are other features much more important in the whole picture than the ones the written data have shown her. If she begins too soon to try to impress Rose with the value of school she may never find out that Mrs. Borini is an alcoholic whose condition has become increasingly serious as the years have passed, that Rose has gradually been taking upon herself more and more of the housework and care of the younger children, and that she is torn by the conflict aroused by her boy friend's insistence that she marry him and stop trying to carry the burden of the family. Such emotional material lies just under the surface and usually never gets into the cumulative record. Premature diagnoses, however comprehensive and reasonable they may appear, must be avoided if counseling is to encourage the expression of real feelings.

A particular objection that is often raised to cumulative record systems in school arises from the possibility that damaging information from one period of an individual's life will be used against him at some later date. Many boys, for example, are involved at one time or another in minor delinquencies. To have down in black and white that eleven-year-old Charles stole twenty dollars from his teacher's desk may make it more difficult

for him at the age of eighteen to get a job for which he is qualified, even if his reputation for honesty during the seven-year
interval is unblemished. Janet, a bright, capable high school
senior, shows in her record that during her sophomore year she
was sullen and unpopular and made low grades in everything.
If this information is used to disqualify her for the editorship of
the school newspaper, it will prevent her undertaking what might
have been the most valuable experience of her school career. Such
situations are particularly unfortunate because the student himself usually has no idea of what his record contains and thus is
puzzled and resentful at being passed over for a post he had every
reason to expect to get.

Still another objection to systems of case records in both
schools and social agencies is that the labor of filling in forms
and keeping files up to date is likely to become burdensome and
to constitute a waste of counselor time that might better be spent
in direct service to clients. Complaints about "paper work" are
very common among counselors. Because of the confidential
nature of the data that must be processed, what is essentially a
minor clerical task must often be done by professional persons
who chafe against the necessity of doing it. They come to see
records as a source of frustration rather than as a valuable counseling tool.

Having admitted that there are such difficulties inherent in
the maintenance and utilization of case records, we can see that it
is not necessary to give up the practice of keeping them in order
to meet these objections. Knowing them is the first step toward
overcoming them. The answer to the criticism that records encourage premature diagnoses is to select and train better counselors
who will not stumble into this trap. As for the possibility that
facts in the record may prove damaging to the individual, there
are various ways of preventing this from happening. Some schools
make a practice of going through the records at the end of each
year and removing anecdotal reports of this kind. Control over
the accessibility of the files so that placement officers are never
allowed to see the records themselves is another method. Here
again more psychological understanding on the part of *all* school
personnel—teachers, counselors, and placement officers—will go
far to prevent the misuse of information. The objection to the
labor involved in maintaining usable records can be met by

keeping all standard forms as simple as possible and providing enough professional secretarial service to do most of the paper work.

THE VALUES OF CASE RECORDS

If such precautions are taken, a case folder can be a most useful counseling tool. It can be read in such a way that it enables the essential processes of acceptance and understanding to function smoothly from the beginning of the first interview. The counselor can use it to help him "get set" for some of the things he may encounter and realize enough of the individual's peculiar problems and circumstances to adopt his frame of reference from the beginning. It is quite true, as was said above, that the problem he is prepared for may turn out not to be the real problem, and the facts that stood out most clearly in the record may prove to be the least significant, but the *attitude* his intelligent and sympathetic reading has engendered is the attitude out of which good counseling comes. Without previous information, for example, the counselor might well have reacted to Jerry Cranston, a noisy, belligerent trouble-maker, in the same way that all his teachers do. Knowing that the boy has recently moved to the city to live with his grandmother after a much-publicized divorce case makes it possible to look *through* his behavior, as it were, and try to sense the attitudes behind it. It should be emphasized again, since confusion is likely to settle around this point, that this does not mean classifying Jerry in any predetermined category, child-of-divorced-parents. There should be no diagnosis, no plans for treatment, no abstract generalizations. The facts from the record simply serve the purpose of creating a friendly, accepting attitude toward the boy out of which will eventually grow a genuine understanding of just what this and the rest of his experiences have meant to him.

A counselor with the developmental viewpoint advocated in this book is especially likely to find information in the case folder helpful. The working image he tries to formulate is a four-dimensional picture, as it were; it has a *time* dimension. As he tries to interpret facts that have been recorded at different stages of the client's life, he asks himself: What are the directions of development here? What changes have been occurring? What lines of development are still open?

One practical value of cumulative records is that they make it unnecessary to spend precious interview time in the collection of factual information. The whole interview hour is left free for the exploration of the psychological realities, the fears and hopes, the likes and dislikes. Some would say that it is only these things that have any effect on the person's life anyway and that factual details such as age and IQ, economic status and work experience, can be ignored, but most counselors would agree that these facts do have to be considered when decisions are in the making. If we are to have them it is certainly more economical to keep them in a permanent file that grows with the person than to ask for them again and again.

HOW TO STUDY A CASE RECORD

If a case history is to serve this purpose in preparing a counselor for his first interview with a new client, it must be studied in an appropriate manner. One cannot read it like a book, starting with the first line and working through systematically to the end. It is necessary rather to bring together items from different sections and try to link up those that belong together. One should have in mind, as he starts, a rough outline of areas to be covered, such as family circumstances, abilities and achievements, interests, relationships to other people, and special difficulties. Then, depending upon how materials are arranged in the record, he turns to different parts of it to fill in the gaps. Under family circumstances he notes first the address where the person lives and pictures to himself the part of the city it represents. He tries to imagine how it would feel to live in the sort of tenement, cottage, or mansion that prevails in that area. He notices the father's occupation if the client is a student, his own if he is an adult. What standards, aspirations, and expectations for one's children tend to go with this occupational status? What are the characteristic attitudes of people in these circumstances toward school? In connection with this question he turns to another section where test scores are recorded. Are the individual's mental abilities and school achievements in line with the expectations of families like his? Is it possible that he feels himself to be a disappointment to them? Or does he perhaps feel himself superior to the surroundings in which he is growing up? How happy is the home? Here there are likely to be no entries unless conflict has been severe enough to lead to a divorce or to an investigation by some social agency. What about the person's relationship to other children in the family? Are his brothers and sisters older or younger, and how much? Are there older children or relatives of whom the family are particularly proud?

The counselor considers now in more detail the evidence with regard to the client's abilities and his understanding of them and reaction to them. He looks for scores on standardized tests, noting especially any developmental trends they show. Over a period of years a sequence of IQ's running 120, 110, 94, 91, 85 suggests something quite different from the sequence 95, 102, 98, 105, 100, although the average in both cases is exactly the same. The fluctuation in the second case is about what would be expected in view of the standard error of intelligence tests, but in the first case there appears to be a steady decline in comparative intellectual status. He tries to think of possible explanations for this drop and wonders about its effects on the person's total adjustment pattern. Test scores in reading and other school subjects are similarly scrutinized. There may also be some aptitude test scores in the file which can be used as an indicator of special assets and liabilities.

The counselor never considers test scores by themselves. In connection with them he thinks about school grades and occupational history, again looking for developmental trends in over-all average and in particular fields. Has there been any consistency and continuity about jobs? Have they been such as to leave any residue of skill? How about extracurricular activities? Is there evidence for athletic, musical, or executive experience?

There may be no clues as to the person's attitude toward his own abilities, since this is the sort of thing that is more likely to show up in what he says than in facts and figures, but if there are any such indications they will help the counselor with his initial understanding. For instance, Bob's record may contain an anecdotal report of an instance when the boy refused to take a committee chairmanship. Does this mean that he lacks confidence in his ability to carry a task through? In Henrietta's case, the fact that a girl with an IQ in the 90's has made a consistent A and B record right up through high school suggests that she may be overestimating her own mental capacity and heading for trouble when she gets into college. Needless to say, such hypotheses must be kept extremely flexible so that they can be modified during the interview if necessary. Bob's refusal may have meant nothing more than a lack of interest in the particular work the committee was appointed to do. Henrietta may be much brighter than the IQ indicates, or she may be bitterly aware of her mediocre intelligence and achieving the high grades through an extreme effort to make up for it. To have thought about these attitudes, however, is to be sensitized to whatever feelings do turn out to be present.

Still another kind of information the counselor will try to synthesize from the record has to do with the individual's interests. What have his enthusiasms been, in and out of school? Have some of them persisted over a period of years? In general, does he seem to be the sort of person who attacks any new activity eagerly but soon loses interest, or is he a person who always finishes what he starts? Tentative answers to these questions also may come from several different parts of the record— tests, school grades, extracurricular activities, work experiences, and anecdotal reports. Again the preliminary formulations must be tentative—a way of getting ready for whatever attitudes are expressed in the interview rather than of deciding ahead of time what those attitudes are.

The file may contain some indirect information about the client's relationship to other people. Developmental trends are again important. Is there anecdotal evidence from which periods of comparative popularity and unpopularity can be charted? Are there possible complications produced by physical deviations from the norm, such as smallness, fatness, or a bad case of acne? Does he get along well with girls? How many of the activities he has engaged in are things involving both sexes? Here too, as the counselor puts together these bits of information he tries to imagine how it would feel to be a person in these circumstances, with these physical characteristics and these kinds of social experience.

Problems and difficulties an individual has had are likely to be stated quite explicitly. Perhaps there has been a persistent reading handicap only to a limited extent overcome. Perhaps he has been repeatedly reported by his teachers for infringements of rules. If there has been a chronic illness or a physical handi-

cap, a foreign language background, a speech defect, or a traumatic childhood experience, it is obviously valuable for the
counselor to know of it ahead of time.

In reading for the kind of general orientation we have been
discussing, the counselor pays particular attention to discrepancies
and conflicts. Why did this boy do so well in arithmetic and so
poorly in geometry? How does it happen that his teachers all
complain that he is lazy, whereas the proprietor of the grocery
store where he works after school describes him as the best
worker he has had on the job? If he is interested in public speaking, as he said he was in a questionnaire filled out in his homeroom, why did he refuse to take part in a school declamatory
contest? With an IQ of 132, why isn't he making better grades?
Why does he state "lawyer" as the occupation he would like to
enter and then not sign up for a college preparatory course? Innumerable questions of this sort can arise as one scrutinizes student files. Sometimes tentative answers are to be found in other
sections of the available information. More often the questions
become part of the mental background with which the counselor
approaches the initial interview, the background which will make
it possible to understand clearly the pattern of the client's experience.

Studied in this manner, a good case record can facilitate both
acceptance and understanding. It will often help with the initial
ice-breaking stage by suggesting topics in which the client is
likely to be interested. It may furnish warnings as to areas to
be avoided at the beginning. Often when he has finished his
preliminary study the counselor can make a tentative plan for
begining the interview. It would not, of course, be advisable for
him to plan the whole thing, as that might prevent his following
where the client leads.

OBTAINING CASE INFORMATION

The problems involved in setting up and organizing a system
of records are outside the scope of this book. A school counselor
who is called upon to carry out this personnel task will find a good
discussion and many examples of forms that have been used in
Traxler (1956). It is better to limit the scope of the undertaking
and include only the most helpful kinds of background material

than to let the task of recording and filing become burdensome. It is preferable that items kept in this way be factual, objective, and non-judgmental rather than opinions of members of the school staff about students. It is obviously better, for example, to state simply, "John was kept after school for copying from Peter's algebra paper," than to say, "John is showing dishonest tendencies." The first allows anyone who really wishes to understand John to try to piece out a coherent picture of his motivation from this and other items of information. The second tends to create an unfavorable attitude in a new teacher or counselor before he even sees the boy. Similarly it is better for a teacher to write, "When the children choose up sides for a game, Gladys is always last to be chosen," than to say, "Gladys is the most unpopular child in the room." It is again a matter of internal versus external frames of reference. Items descriptive of an individual should be phrased so that they facilitate the seeing of the experience from the individual's own viewpoint.

In counseling programs for college students and adults, where very often the transfer of records from previous situations is not feasible, a substitute technique is the use of some sort of information blank to be filled in by the counselee himself.[1] Such blanks are designed to include some of the same types of information as school cumulative records, and they have the advantage that facts must of necessity be presented from the student's point of view. What he puts down is what he is presumably willing to talk about in his own experience. Thus counselor and client have a common meeting ground. This method is obviously impractical for poorly educated clients.

One other technique that has been used in some counseling programs for somewhat the same purpose might be briefly mentioned. This is the autobiography. It may be written as an English assignment or a homeroom activity and thus not require extra time from anyone on the staff. Whether such papers are dry, stilted statements of fact unwillingly made or vivid expressions of significant experience will depend on how the assignment is made and on the morale of the class and the school as a whole. As a preliminary or adjunct to counseling the autobiography has the advantage pointed out in the preceding paragraph—it tells

---

[1] See Appendix A for an example.

something about his life experiences from the counselee's own point of view and consists of things which he is presumably able to recognize and willing to talk about. Thus it may assist the counselor to handle the beginning stages of the interview smoothly. If Genevieve, for example, devotes considerable space to an account of her happy childhood years in a little town in Iowa, this may be the best topic with which to begin a conversation with her. It may easily and naturally lead on to a discussion of her main difficulty, about which she did *not* write in her autobiography, her loneliness and failure to make friends in the city where she is now living.

If autobiographies are required as a class assignment and are to be used in counseling, the purpose should be made clear to the students. They should know just who is to see their papers and whether or not they are to be filed in their permanent records. Only thus can the confidence on which counseling rests be insured and maintained.

RECORDS OF THE COUNSELING PROCESS

We turn now to the topic of records that should be kept of the counseling process itself. One point on which counselors of all schools of thought agree is that fairly detailed notes should be kept so that the course of the previous interview can be reviewed before each new contact. Counseling is a process rather than a single event, and the only way one can sense the direction of movement is by knowing where one was at different times. Theoretically, perhaps, it might be possible for a counselor with a prodigious memory to keep the details of all his cases in mind without resorting to written records. Practically this does not work. The process of forgetting details and confusing one person's problems with another's sets in so soon after an interview that the individualized understanding we have been stressing is seriously impaired if notes have not been made.

The most complete and meaningful method is to make a tape recording of each interview and play it back to oneself before the next. More and more college counseling services are making this a standard part of the procedure for some of their cases. The sense of counseling as a process of growth and change is more easily obtained from these recordings than from any written account of what an interview contained, since such things as inflection, tone of voice, hesitation, and pauses all carry significance. Counselors in training find it valuable though often disconcerting to be able to observe the relationships between their own remarks and the client's reactions.

Some are likely to object that clients will be constricted in their expression if they know that a recording is being made. As a matter of fact this does not seem to happen. It would appear that freedom of expression depends so much more on a feeling of confidence in the counselor than it does on mechanical features of the situation that ordinarily, after the first few moments, a counselee pays no attention to the recording equipment. In some cases it even seems to make for a more constructive attitude on his part, since he feels that he is really being taken seriously and given the finest kind of professional attention. We are assuming, naturally, that there is no secret about the matter. He is told as the interview begins that it is customary to make a recording which can be played back between sessions for study. If he objects, it is of course not made. Just as in the matter of autobiographies and written records, since counseling success depends so largely on maintaining attitudes free from suspicion and distrust, it is never advisable to make secret recordings. There would always be the possibility that the person might discover what had been done and feel that the counselor had taken an unfair advantage of him.

Of course, we can never be sure that a recorded interview is exactly the same in its sequence and structure as it would have been had the recording not been made. It may well be that it is not. A counseling relationship is an extremely sensitive complex psychological entity. It seems likely that anything which is added or subtracted changes it to some extent. But, for practical purposes, this is a relatively unimportant issue. As has been repeatedly stated, there is no one standard counseling relationship. Each is unique, and the process of growth can occur in different settings. Recording the interviews may modify the situation, but it need not make it less favorable. The important fact has by now been substantiated by a large amount of evidence, the fact that successful counseling can take place through recorded interviews. The question as to the strict comparability of recorded and nonrecorded situations is an interesting research problem but is not crucial in clinical work.

Unfortunately, even if mechanical equipment for recording all interviews were available, which it usually is not, time schedules ordinarily make it impossible to handle records entirely in this manner. To do so means that for each interview there must be allowed at least twice as much time as it actually takes, since the replaying takes as long as the original conference. Thus economy of time usually dictates the use of written notes which can be made and read through rapidly. The making of such notes is an important counselor skill.

Whether or not they are taken during the interview itself seems not to make much difference. Some counselors prefer to do it that way so that they can be sure of recording accurately in the proper sequence the topics that come under consideration. Others feel that to write while a client is talking interferes with the attention they wish to give to his words and expression. They prefer to jot down what has occurred as soon as the interview is over. Whichever practice is followed, there should be no secret about this affair. If the question comes up at all, the client should be told that the counselor keeps notes to help him remember what they have talked about.

What can be said about the nature of these interview notes? Naturally they cannot be standardized, since each counselor imposes upon them his own style. If we keep in mind their purpose, we can see what their essential qualities must be. Their function is to enable the counselor to remember the interview over a fairly short period of time. Since he can trust his memory to supply the details once the necessary cues are given, what he needs most in the notes are these reminders that will touch off the memory process. The main topics that have been discussed should certainly be listed in the order in which they came up. Often it is important to include the nature of the transition from one to another. If something the counselor said produced the shift or was the occasion for a pronounced emotional response, then his remark as well as the client's reaction should be noted. Usually it is more essential to get down what the client talked about than what the counselor said. If any tentative decision or plan for action was made at the end of the hour, it should of course be in the record. Counselors working under the sort of pressure for time that exists in so many agencies will have to learn to streamline the records, to use abbreviations as much as possible, and to sacrifice elegance of style to completeness of content.

It is much better, in the notes as in the interview itself, to avoid judgments, interpretations, and technical phraseology. Thus one would say, "Jim talked at length about his fondness for his mother," rather than, "Jim shows evidence of an unresolved Oedipus complex." It is better to say, "Frances is concerned because the periods when she feels 'on top of the world' are always followed by periods of gloom," than to say, "Frances shows manic-depressive tendencies." "Horace told about his difficulty with the chemistry and geology courses required of premedical students" is to be preferred to "The problem seems to be one of wrong vocational choice." If we are to maintain an internal frame of reference with regard to the person, to understand rather than to categorize, these differences in phrasing are not superficial or insignificant.

There is another reason also for keeping the interview notes free from judgments and interpretations. It is good practice to keep them open to the client's inspection if he wishes to see them. Not infrequently a question will arise about what was taken up during some previous conference, and the simplest way of answering is to turn to the notes taken on that occasion. The fact that he is allowed to see the record seems to give a client that confidence and freedom from suspicion that we have been emphasizing as the most favorable attitude for counseling. Client and counselor are seen as partners working from the same data.

PROFESSIONAL USE OF SCHOOL
CUMULATIVE RECORDS

In a school system that maintains a cumulative record file, a distinction must be made between these interview-by-interview case notes and the cumulative record itself. Case notes are for the use of the counselor—and at times of the client. They do not go into the file to be carried on down through the years. At the termination of counseling service to an individual, whether that service consists of one interview or twenty, the counselor will write a brief report for the record. It will include a statement of the nature of the problem, the nature of the treatment, and what was accomplished. If standardized tests were given as a part of vocational counseling, either the scores themselves will be stated or information will be given as to where they may be found. Samples of these brief summaries as well as of the more detailed case notes are given in Appendix B.

In discussing school counseling records we cannot escape questions about who shall be given access to them. Theoretically the answer is simple and straightforward. When school administrators set up a cumulative record system, they do it with the aim of helping all the people who must deal with a student to understand him better and thus individualize their treatment of him. This means primarily teachers, since they make up the largest proportion of a school staff and have more contact with students than anyone else. Ideally then, it should be easy for teachers to make use of these records. They should be filed in the classrooms themselves in the lower grades where one teacher has the same class all day and in some convenient central location in the junior and senior high school so that all teachers can find them without red tape or delay.

But there is a danger here, as realistic school administrators and counselors are quick to point out when the subject comes up for discussion. Under such circumstances it can easily happen that confidential information about students and their families becomes the subject of lunch-table gossip. Instead of helping to create attitudes of acceptance and understanding, talking about the facts in this way serves to generate unfavorable attitudes and to rationalize teaching failures.

"Of course Jack Koshevsky can't learn anything. His IQ is only 90, and look at the kind of family he comes from!"

"He isn't doing anything in my class either."

"I don't know why they keep boys like that in school. Let him get out and get some kind of laboring job. That's all he'll ever be good for . . . ."

The conversation goes on, relegating one child after another to the class of hopeless cases. It is quite true that if this is the use she is going to make of the information, it would be much better for Mrs. Sears not to know that Jack's IQ is low and that his family is of the "lower-lower" variety. But the remedy for this sort of difficulty would seem to lie in re-education of teachers rather than in secrecy about facts. The use of personal information as a basis for gossip and rationalization is highly unprofessional conduct. In a school where it is common the student will not find the help and encouragement he needs whether or not his record is kept secret. So if a counselor is required to work in a setting where malice and hostility flourish, his first job is to attempt to build up a personnel point of view in the school. What this means is a subject to be discussed in greater detail later. At this point it will suffice to say that denying teachers access to student records is a temporary expedient at best. In a school characterized by good morale and high professional ethics it will not be necessary.

PROBLEMS WITH REGARD TO CONFIDENTIALITY

The foregoing rule applies to the basic cumulative records but not, of course, to the counselor's own interview notes. It is generally understood that these are to be considered confidential. A student will ordinarily assume that this is the case without anything being said. If he asks about it, he can be assured that this is so. Occasionally special problems and conflicts arise in the carrying out of this policy. It is to these we now turn.

The first of these arises from the fact that in most places a counselor does not have the same legal status as a person in one of the older professions concerned with human relations—medicine, law, or the ministry. If it should happen that a client reveals information about an action which makes him subject to legal prosecution and it becomes known that the counselor has such information, he can be forced to testify or be considered in contempt of court. This is a very rare occurrence. Only once in the author's twenty years of counseling practice have the police asked for a report on a case. In this instance the client, a kleptomaniac, was quite willing that she should testify, since information about the motivation behind his symptoms could only lead to better rather than worse treatment for him. However, rare as it is, the possibility of such a development is something every counselor should have thought through. There is no one right policy. One thing that can be done is to make clear to the client at the time he begins to bring up a matter of this kind just what the counselor's position is. He may then decide to keep silent about actions in which officers of the law might be interested. Whether or not he decides to go on, the counseling relationship will be modified to some extent by what has happened, but it will still have the clarity and honesty on which good outcomes depend. Under no circumstances must a client feel that he has been let down or betrayed.

The necessity for taking such special steps usually does not apply to incidents in the person's past life. It is a fairly common thing for a college student to tell of past delinquencies, thefts, vandalism, or sexual misconduct. These can be accepted in the same way as anything else he talks about, since the lapse of time makes it unlikely that they will ever get him into trouble.

There is another sort of conflict which bothers school counselors more than these rare cases when court action is involved. It arises from the situation in which one learns of some condition which calls for disciplinary action. Suppose he finds out that there is a little coterie of homosexuals in one of the dormitories or that cheating is rife in a certain class. Is it his duty to inform the proper authorities of these facts so that matters can be set right? If a poll were taken of counselor opinion there would undoubtedly be considerable disagreement.

My own answer would be "No." The risk that the counseling service could come to be regarded as an espionage agency is one which is too great to be taken, as it would rule out effective work from that time on. There are other channels through which knowledge of bad conditions can reach the authorities, and it is better that these channels be used. The counselee himself may decide to report the facts to the responsible officials. Another reason for the counselor to take no action himself is his realization that he is always working in the realm of attitudes and beliefs, not facts. What a client sees as homosexuality in his dormitory associates may only be a projection of his own desires. His belief that everyone else is cheating may be a rationalization of his own failure rather than an objective picture of what really occurs. As has been said before, the counselor is not in a position to sort out fact from fancy, and it is not important that he do so. It can only lead to confusion and complication if he drops this orientation.

In still another conflict situation the counselor sees in what a client has told him some reason to believe that a talk with some third person might improve a relationship that is giving the client a great deal of trouble. Is it advisable for him to go to this parent, sister, teacher, or friend of his counselee and tell him—in strictest confidence, of course—what is giving rise to the difficulty? Will this create a more favorable emotional climate for the individual outside the interview situation itself? Again there would probably be some sincere disagreement among counselors as to the best policy. And again my own answer would be "No," at least if the client is an adolescent or adult. The point made in the preceding paragraph is just as relevant here. From what the person has said we know only what his psychological reality is. We do not get objective facts. Furthermore, even if such a conference with friend or relative is handled in the most tactful manner, the implied criticism of the way another person is dealing with a problem individual can easily lead to resentment and defensiveness. If it does, the emotional climate will be made worse, not better. Another reason for avoiding this treatment of a problem is that it makes for ambiguity about the counseling relationship. A situation has first been created in which the client will see the counselor as a person who gives him support and understanding while he grapples with his own decisions. If now he learns that the other has been taking an active part in his affairs, he is confused and no longer knows what his own role is in the situation. Finally, and perhaps most important of all, a problem in personal relationships that is discussed early in the course of the counseling process often turns out to be not the real problem at all. To accept a boy's complaints about his mother's domination as the basis for his difficulties before the whole complex structure of interlocking attitudes is made manifest may mean forfeiting whatever opportunity there may have been to change this structure. By the time it has been completely clarified, the boy himself may have handled the things that need to be changed without any necessity for the counselor's intervention.

In this as in many other areas, however, no absolutely hard-and-fast rule can be laid down. It is standard practice in children's clinics to interview parents, teachers, or any other individuals who are important in the child's life. There is no critical age below which parents should be called in, above which they should not. The considerations we have discussed constitute guides for the counselor, not directives. A useful rule is "When in doubt, wait."

One thing that can be done in the cases of counselees who

have reached the age of responsibility is to consult them before conferring with others and get their permission before releasing records. If Henry's abilities, interests, and desires all point toward a career in science and he is deterred only by his knowledge that his father is depending on him to take over the family business, the counselor might well ask, "Would you like me to talk things over with your father?" If Henry welcomes the suggestion, as he probably will, an interview can be arranged at the father's convenience, perhaps a three-way conference at which Henry is present. This has the advantage of keeping the situation clear for all participants. The counselor will not argue with the father but simply make him acquainted with the facts about Henry's aptitudes of which he is not aware. If a parent comes to see the counselor on his own initiative, he can be allowed to talk over his attitudes and uncertainties with regard to his son or daughter but not given any confidential information. Afterward the client can be informed that his father has been in and the situation shifted to something more like the one previously discussed. Mutual confidence and understanding is the goal.

In high school situations where counselors are helping students make long-range plans for college and career, it is often advisable to bring parents into the picture from the beginning. The counseling in such cases is as much with the parents as with the students themselves, since they must necessarily be involved in the carrying out of any plans that are made. These situations obviously constitute no violation of confidence. Their structure is clear to all participants from the beginning.

The foregoing discussion may well have given the reader an impression that the handling of confidential information is an individual matter, varying from case to case. To some extent it is. Certain general principles, however, apply to all the cases. First, the counselor should constantly remind himself that his province is attitude and feeling rather than objective fact and that the counseling process works mainly through attitude changes rather than through modification of surroundings. Second, the client's faith in the counselor's integrity must be maintained. Third, the responsibility for decisions and action is in the client's hands and the structure of the situation should show clearly at all times that this is so. Within this framework of guiding generalizations there is considerable allowance for individual variation.

Since this chapter on the relationships between records of various kinds and the counselor's work has touched on a number of diverse types of records, it is well that we summarize at the end the ideas that are most important. First, the counselor uses records that have been kept by others to help him sense how life looks and feels to his counselee and thus to start the first interview smoothly and productively. Second, he keeps fairly detailed notes on each interview for his own use, and at the conclusion of his counseling service to the individual writes a brief summary for the permanent record. Third, school cumulative records should be available to all who deal with the student with proper safeguards to prevent misuse of the information they contain. Fourth, the counselor's personal files of confidential information should be open to no one else, and in all but a few exceptional cases the counselor should avoid making even oral reports on what they contain.

CHAPTER SIX

The Use of
Tests in Educational
and Vocational Counseling:
General Considerations

THE PURPOSES TESTS SERVE

As indicated in the first chapter, counseling is concerned with the making of choices—with the individual's search for an answer to the question "What shall I do?" When these choices involve decisions about education and career, an important part of the information about himself the client needs often comes from an analysis of his performance on standardized tests. Thus every counselor working in this area needs to be thoroughly grounded in the basic principles of mental measurement and thoroughly familiar with a number of the more commonly used tests.

To present all of the information about all of the tests a counselor will use is obviously far too ambitious an undertaking to be included in a book on counseling. Special courses on tests and measurements are an essential part of counselor training. But even with such specialized knowledge about measurement principles and particular tests, one may run into difficulties when he tries to apply it in the day-to-day situations he encounters in his consulting room. It is to this liaison between the theoretical and the practical that the present chapter is devoted.

In general, what the information about himself a client obtains from tests can do is to help him clarify the alternatives toward which his thinking about choices should be directed. It is well for the counselor to recognize at the outset that this may not be all that the person expects from a testing program. He may be trying to use it as a substitute for his own thinking about life decisions rather than as an aid to such thinking. There is a widespread belief among students and in the public at large that vocational aptitude tests will "tell you what you should do." If disappointment is to be avoided later, it is important that the counselor try to restructure this attitude during the interview when tests are selected. This can best be done by focusing attention on the kinds of questions tests will be helpful in answering rather than by explaining in detail why they will not accomplish what the client wants them to.

The information about an individual represented by test scores is especially useful in *ruling out* areas it will not be very profitable to consider. Generally speaking, low scores are more predictive than high ones. It is commonly found, for example, that scatter plots representing correlations between scholastic aptitude tests and school criteria usually show a larger number of exceptions to the general trend in the lower right-hand quadrant than in the upper left (as scores are usually tabulated, with the lowest at the left and at the bottom). This means that a bright student is more likely to achieve less than was predicted for him than a dull student is to achieve more. In a way, this is what common sense would predict. There are innumerable reasons why a person with the ability to grasp the most complex subject matter may fail to do the work required for even a minimum passing grade; there are fewer ways in which exceptions in the other direction can occur. Similar trends have been found for a variety of tests. A college student with exceptional motivation impelling him toward a career in science may decide to go ahead even though he ranks in the bottom tenth of his class on a mathematics test, and he may be able to overcome his deficiency and carry out his plans. But ordinarily a score of this kind can be used as a guidepost to indicate that the road will be rough in the mathematical direction and that the remaining alternatives are more promising.

SPECIFIC QUESTIONS TESTS HELP TO ANSWER

There are certain specific kinds of questions tests help to answer. One of the most common of these is, How high an educational level is this person likely to be able to reach? A well-selected test of what we commonly call general intelligence but what is more accurately labeled scholastic aptitude is one of the best bases for such inferences. With almost universal secondary education, the average IQ level for high school students is about 100, and a comprehensive, diversified high school program will have something to offer students of any level of ability so long as it is within the normal range. But colleges are more selective, and the decision as to whether to plan for college or not is one each high school student must make. College students in turn often need to consider the feasibility of graduate work. Embree (1948) and Wrenn (1949) have analyzed the scores made as entering freshmen by people successfully completing various amounts of college work. The average IQ (equated to 1937 Stanford-Binet) for students entering college is 118, for those completing bachelors' degrees 123, for those taking advanced degrees 126, and for the Ph.D.'s, 141. There is of course a range of values in each of these distributions and naturally half of the individuals in each group are below the mean. These data are obtained from only two institutions, but at least at the graduate levels their requirements are probably similar to those of other established institutions. Knowing these facts is helpful for a counselee who is attempting to decide for or against a career that will require graduate training at a time long before he is actually ready to enter graduate school. The doubts of a student who has nearly completed his undergraduate work can be resolved by less circuitous means; the counselor may use either the Miller Analogies or the Graduate Record Examination along with his scholastic record.

The judgment as to whether a high school student will be able to succeed in college or a freshman complete his work for a degree is complicated by wide differences from college to college and from course to course within the same institution. There have been several studies showing how marked these differences can be (Embree, 1948). Their specific findings are not of much use to a counselor because the whole question is very much a local matter. The worker in the high school needs most to know the level of ability which is necessary for successful functioning in each of the colleges in his vicinity or in those colleges which he is most apt to deal with. The college worker needs to know the requirements for different courses and majors within his own school. Some information of this sort is sure to filter in to him as he works in one location for a period of time. To get more precise quantitative evidence requires the setting up of a research study. Usually this is well worth the effort involved.

Another specific question that must often be considered when life plans are being formulated is: How good is the client's educational background for the specialized training program he is considering? Are there gaps in it anywhere? Such questions are best answered by scores on achievement tests. They are available in all the major subject-matter areas at all levels from the primary grades to the graduate school and constitute a major resource in educational counseling.

Another specific question is, Does the person have to a sufficient degree a special aptitude required for some kind of work he may wish to consider? It is this question more than any of the others we have considered that may be tied in with the clients misconceptions about what tests can tell him. For some reason, aptitude tests were oversold to the public. There are no so-called vocational aptitude tests that have consistently given high correlations with occupational criteria. In fact the correlations Ghiselli (1955) has brought together from many sources are not high enough or consistent enough that we can feel at all confident of any prediction based on them.

There are indications, however, that even though they do not predict degrees of success *within* an occupation they do measure characteristics that differentiate *between* occupations. There is evidently an automatic sorting-out process that occurs as people attempt to find their places in the world of work. A boy with too little mechanical aptitude for the job with the telephone company he tried first quits or is fired and turns to something else. The girl whose clerical aptitude is inadequate does not last long at the office where she is too slow to keep up. Thus in the fields where good norms for special occupational groups are available, low test scores can be legitimately used for ruling out areas, as explained in our previous discussion. They can make it unnecessary for the person to fail at a task in order to find out that he is not suited to it. Employment service counselors using the General Aptitude Test Battery do not usually attempt to predict *how* successful a prospective worker will be on a job. They base their interpretations of test performance on whether the person is below or above cutting scores that have been set for each group of occupations separately on the tests of aptitudes required in this particular field.

The other major question tests enable us to answer is, What kinds of people does this client resemble in his interests? The form in which this question is stated is important. Misconceptions are prevalent here also. Interest tests cannot tell us *how much* interest a client will have in any particular field of work or study. They will not tell us how successful he will be, or even how well satisfied he will be. An *A* score on the Strong Vocational Interest Blank or a profile on the Kuder Preference Record similar in shape and elevation to that of a particular group of workers or students shows us that the person tested *fits into* the group in question—that his outlook and orientation is in many ways like theirs. This is an important thing to know. Here too information from the test may substitute for painful experience. But it is only one aspect of the complex thinking upon which good vocational decisions must be based.

COUNSELING USES OF TESTS DISTINGUISHED FROM OTHER USES

The most important principle about the use of tests in counseling—and a useful guideline in deciding which tests to keep on hand in any particular agency and which tests to select for any particular client—is that the information to be obtained is *for the use of the client himself*. It is this more than anything else that differentiates the counseling uses of tests from their uses in many clinical and industrial situations. Psychologists who have had thorough training and a great deal of experience in the use of projective personality tests for the diagnostic evaluation of psychiatric patients or employment tests for the selection of various kinds of personnel in a large department store do not thereby become qualified to make decisions about counseling tests. A test is useful for counseling purposes only if there is a considerable amount of evidence as to just what characteristic it is measuring and if the counselor can state in clear, unambiguous terms what the significance of an individual's score is in relation to various life decisions.

PRINCIPAL TYPES OF COUNSELING TESTS

The types of tests that should be available to furnish partial answers to the questions listed above are tests of intelligence, academic achievement, various vocational aptitudes, and interests. There should be enough specific tests of each of these main types that one at an appropriate *level* for each client can be selected, within the range that the agency serves. For example, a college counseling center uses mainly intelligence tests of a difficulty level suitable for entering freshmen, consisting largely of verbal and quantitative rather than performance items. But if some of the clients are college seniors considering graduate study, a more difficult and specialized test of mental ability, such as the Miller Analogies Test or the Terman Concept Mastery Test, should be available to help such persons with their decisions. And for non-college clients and college students who have not measured up to the intellectual requirements of the situation, a less specialized test that will indicate how the person compared with the general population in a broader kind of mental ability is needed. An individual test such as the WAIS often contributes to the evaluation such a client must make of himself.

PERSONALITY TESTS—SPECIAL CONSIDERATIONS

The use of personality tests in educational and vocational counseling is a subject on which there is at present no general agreement among counseling authorities. There is a need for this kind of information in connection with two kinds of question that commonly arise in counseling situations. The first is: Does this client need something more than information and a chance to clarify his thinking about his future through discussions with the counselor? In other words, is he suffering from personality handicaps of one kind or another that should receive some direct attention in the course of the counseling process? The other kind of personality question is: Does this client have a suitable pattern of personality characteristics for the occupation or training he is considering?

Both of these are legitimate and very important questions. The doubt about whether or not personality tests should be used is a matter of whether or not any existing instruments for measuring personality really answer them. So far as the second question is concerned, the matter of the suitability of the client's personality traits for any given occupation, it is quite clear that we do *not* have research data that enable us to answer it, except insofar as vocational interest tests constitute an answer. Attempts to relate sales aptitude to scores indicating extroversion or dominance, or to identify the measured personality attributes of teachers, social workers, or physicians, for example, have failed again and again. Because if a client takes a personality test he will be inclined to try to use the scores in these ways which research indicates are unsound, he is perhaps better off without information that might well lead him astray.

The other purpose, to identify counseling needs beyond the facilitation of vocational and educational choices, is more feasible. The general level of adjustment or emotional stability can be assessed by any one of a number of paper-and-pencil inventories or more complex projective methods. Many of these instruments are designed to show also the kind of faulty adjustment or the area of life in which difficulties arise. There is considerable ambiguity in the interpretation of these tests, because of response sets of various kinds that have been shown to influence scores. Some persons automatically give the socially desirable response to each question and thus come out with a "good" score even though their general adjustment is precarious. Some tend to agree with all statements, positive or negative. Some tend to choose extreme responses such as "strongly agree," others moderate responses such as "agree." But even with all of these obstacles to accepting any score at its face value, a psychologist familiar with the idiosyncracies of a particular test, such as the MMPI, can learn much about a person from analyzing his test performance.

If personality tests are to be used, their place in the whole structure of the counseling situation should be made clear to the client. If the counselor wishes to use a personality test mainly to enable him to understand a client better and does not intend to give him any report on his own scores, he should explain this in the interview in which tests are selected. If he does give the client a report on personality scores, he should phrase it in simple, non-psychiatric terms. If a college student, for example, scores more than two standard deviations above the mean on the Hs, D, and Pt scales of the MMPI, it is obvious that it would not be advisable to tell him that he showed to an unusual degree personality characteristics found in hypochrondiacs, depressives, and obsessive-compulsive neurotics. But it would be quite possible to say, "The test shows that you are more likely than the average person to be concerned about symptoms of possible illness, to feel discouraged and depressed at times, and to get ideas and impulses that you can't shake off," and then use this statement as a starting point for further discussion.

Fortunately, there are now several tests that lend themselves to this kind of use in counseling better than the ones developed especially for psychiatric situations do. The Edwards Personal Preference Scale, the California Psychological Inventory, and the Minnesota Counseling Inventory are all made up of items that fall within the range of experience of normal persons, and are scored for non-psychiatric sounding traits such as Need Achievement, Socialization, or Family Relationships. They are being increasingly used in high school and college situations as a means of encouraging thinking and discussion about the individual's personality as he participates in counseling interviews. The evidence that they really serve this purpose more effectively than does a procedure of simply creating an interview climate where the client feels free to discuss anything he sees as important has not yet been presented. But such tests constitute an extra resource that is available to counselors who wish to use them.

VALIDITY CONCEPTS IN COUNSELING

In choosing particular tests from among published tests that are available and in interpreting the scores his clients make on them, the counselor uses the concepts fundamental to test theory —with special emphasis on the nature of the counseling situation. The most important of these concepts for him is *validity*. He must have a clear idea of what it is that the test measures. This means that he must be familiar with the evidence, consisting of correlations with criteria and with other tests, and differentiations between means and distributions of various separate groups. The more of such relevant data there is available, the more illuminating the results of the test will be as he uses it to evaluate the characteristics of individuals.

This leads to a generalization of considerable importance. For counseling purposes old tests are better than new ones. The rule holds only within limits, of course, and exceptions constantly arise, but it is still essentially sound. A test can never be pronounced valid on the basis of a single research study, or even two or three. It is only after it has been tried out in many situations and its relationship to many criteria ascertained that we are in a position to say much about what a score means. For this reason tests like the Minnesota Clerical or the Minnesota Paper Form Board are far more meaningful to the counselor than newer tests of clerical and mechanical aptitudes, even though these may have some advantages in convenience or attractiveness of appearance. It is only recently that the amount of knowledge based on experience with the Kuder Preference Record has given it even approximately the value of the Strong Vocational Interest Blank for situations in which either one could be used. What makes scores on any test meaningful is the total background of information on what such scores have been shown to predict. The test must *have* this background; the counselor must *know* it.

Since 1954 when the American Psychological Association published technical recommendations for published tests, it has been customary to consider four different kinds of validity evidence. *Content* validity rests on evidence that the items constitute a satisfactory sample of some universe of content that is generally agreed upon. *Concurrent* validity rests on correlations between test scores and criterion measures obtained at the same time from the same subjects. *Predictive* validity rests on correlations or regression equations showing the extent to which test scores predict criterion measures obtained at a later time. *Construct* validity rests on correlations between test scores and other measures that are in accordance with theoretical reasoning about the trait in question, even though no one of these measures is a direct indicator of the characteristic.

The first three of these kinds of validity evidence are of particular importance to counselors. In achievement tests, it is the content validity that matters. One needs to know that a student who receives a high score on an American history test, for example, actually has command of the full range of subject matter in this area that his test score would suggest. For aptitude tests of all sorts, including academic aptitude, it is predictive validity evidence that is required. We need to know what the person is going to be able to do in the future. However, for a new test, concurrent validity evidence linking it to an established test about which we know a great deal more may serve a useful purpose.

On the other hand, if the evidence for the validity of a test is solely of the *construct* variety, the test should not be used for counseling purposes. The fact that some evidence based on reasoning generated from psychoanalytic theory suggests that a certain test measures "ego strength," for example, is of no use to us unless we know what various levels of this measured trait have been shown to mean in the lives of persons who have taken the test. There are a great many tests that can legitimately be used for research purposes that have no place in counseling.

The most common source of confusion is the battery of aptitude tests based on factor analysis. A considerable number of such published tests is now available. What we must remember is that *factors* are only *constructs.* When we rearrange the correlations between tests in such a way as to suggest what ability or personality trait it is that several of them have in common, we can define a new trait and give it a name, such as Spatial Ability or Thinking Introversion. Special tests can then be devised for measuring such traits directly. But until a great deal more research has been done, we still know nothing about the meaning of such traits in the world outside the testing room. The factor batteries have many advantages in convenience and economy of time over other sets of tests. They are of great potential importance in counseling as well as in many other areas of human affairs. Some day we may be able to measure in a few hours all of a person's basic abilities, abilities upon which the structure of his special skills must be built. When we know which abilities or which combination of them is important in specific occupational and educational fields, much of the doubt and uncertainty can be taken out of vocational decisions. What the counselor now must keep in mind, however, is that it is precisely this knowledge that we do not as yet have for most of these published tests. Such information is being accumulated, but it will be a long time before there is enough of it to constitute a groundwork for sound interpretation. Face validity can be as misleading here as elsewhere. A few studies, for instance, show that scores on the "Number" factor are less closely related to mathematics than to English grades. Workers in applied fields of psychology may not know the factor analysis methods well enough to realize that names are assigned to factors on a purely subjective basis. The research worker must use his own judgment about what tests with high loadings have in common, and this judgment, like any other, may be wrong. Factor batteries that are to be used in counseling situations must meet the same standards with regard to predictive validity that other types of tests are expected to meet. Factorial validity is not sufficient.

COUNSELING USES OF TEST NORMS

The second most important consideration in test construction and interpretation for the counselor is the matter of norms. All workers who use tests must of course learn to pay attention to the nature of the group on which the derived scores are based if they are to know what any single score means. This becomes difficult for the counselor because he must often use several separately standardized tests at the same time and attempt to make intra-individual comparisons between scores rather than comparisons between one person and another. Differences in norm groups can make a psychogram very deceptive. A decided peak may not indicate at all that the ability it stands for is the individual's highest. It may show how he compares with a general population group, whereas the other scores show how he compares with college students. Counselors attempt to allow for these discrepancies by using "clinical judgment," but it seems probable that too great a strain is often put on this rather elusive faculty. Thus unsound or doubtful interpretations pass unchecked since this is another fine point that we cannot expect clients who know nothing of test construction to be aware of.

Fortunately this is an area in which even a very modest research program can pay big dividends in increased clarity of interpretation. It is quite possible in a large institution to develop local norms on all the most commonly used intelligence and achievement tests and on some of the special aptitude tests so that an individual's scores on all of them can be referred to the same baseline. In smaller institutions where there are not enough cases for respectable norm groups it is at least possible to get comparative data showing where the group as a whole stands as compared with the norm groups on which scores in some counseling tests are based. Having this knowledge leads to more intelligent decisions about academic problems at least. If it is known that the average score for freshmen at College X is a half standard deviation above the high school mean on one scholastic aptitude test and a half standard deviation below the college mean on another, the significance of a particular score on either of these tests in this particular institution is easier to determine. For statistical reasons which we assume are familiar to all readers it is advisable that such adjustments be made in standard scores rather than in percentiles. One might almost lay down a general rule that the counselor should do his *thinking* about the clients' test results in standard-score terms even though he may have to use percentile norms as a starting point if they are all that are available. The ability to think of one sort of distribution in terms of the other is one of the skills that should grow out of work in statistics and measurement courses.

Consideration of the norm problems brings us by another route to the same conclusion stated earlier—that well-established tests are more valuable counseling tools than new ones. A test that has been in use for a number of years has usually accumulated a variety of sets of norms. From those that are furnished, the counselor can choose the ones most relevant to an individual's characteristics and questions. On the Minnesota Clerical Test, for example, the possibility of finding out how a person compares with employed clerical workers as well as with men or women in general adds a great deal to the information obtained from a score. One caution, however, is in order. Because a test maker furnishes norms based on several types of populations, it does not follow that his test is *valid*. The two problems in test construction are completely separate. To give norms based on a group of machine-shop operators does not constitute evidence for the validity of a mechanical aptitude test. To present norms for Negro children on an intelligence test does not prove that the test gives an adequate measure of Negro intelligence. The counselor must constantly evaluate tests on the basis of *both* validity information and suitability of the norms for his purposes. In any conflict, validity is the more important consideration.

RELIABILITY CONCEPTS IN COUNSELING

The third basic concept is reliability. Because of the many meanings and connotations of the word *reliable*, most clients and many counselors tend to attach too general a significance to it. When a counselee asks, "How reliable is this test?" he usually means, "How good is it? How much confidence can we place in it?" His question should be answered in terms of the meaning he attaches to the word.

But in the counselor's own thinking, "reliability" should refer to only a single characteristic of tests, namely their freedom from chance errors affecting scores. Because no test is entirely free from the effects of chance determiners, we must learn to think of a score as a *zone* rather than a single point. The score tells us approximately where in a distribution an individual belongs. Because of the scarcity of satisfactory tests for some purposes and the necessity for making validity the primary consideration governing the choice of tests, counselors are often forced to make use of tests that are less reliable than they would wish. Many of the vocational aptitude tests in common use have reliability coefficients of .85 or lower based on the kind of group within which discriminations are to be made.

The standard error of measurement is likely to be more useful to the counselor than the reliability coefficient, since it is expressed as points of actual score. Thus it represents the zone of inaccuracy that surrounds any particular score. For example, if a counselor is considering a score of 48 points made by a client on a test whose standard error is 3 points, he can say to himself, "It is quite likely that this client's true score lies somewhere between 45 and 51, and practically certain that it lies between 39 and 57." He then has only to translate these reference points into percentiles or standard scores to decide how specific he can be in reporting to this person how good this particular test performance is. If a score of 45 corresponds to a percentile of 38 and a score of 51 to a percentile of 60, it is obviously going to be impossible to tell the person whether he is below or above average in this ability.

It is possible to use tests that are less reliable than one would wish to be used in counseling if one keeps in mind the principle that the less reliable the test the less specific can be our designation of ability level.[1] For tests with reliabilities of .90 or above, we can use terms like *very high, high, above average, below average, low,* and *very low* to defferentiate levels of performance. For tests with reliabilities of about .6 we should use fewer categories, perhaps, only *above average, about average,* and *below average.*

The interaction between imperfect reliability and the use of percentile norms in interpreting and reporting test results has not always been thoroughly understood by counselors. Because of the shape of the percentile distribution and the way it is derived from the distribution of raw scores, differences between one percentile and another throughout the middle range represent considerably less difference in raw score than do differences in percentile at either the high or the low end of the distribution. But reliability and unreliability are concepts applying to the raw scores. This means that any given standard error of measurement affects percentiles of average magnitude far more than it affects low or high ones. On many tests of moderate reliability, standard errors corresponding to twenty or thirty percentile points in the middle of the scale may occur. It is the counselor's responsibility to see that clients do not come to erroneous conclusions about their own ability patterns because they do not take this inaccuracy of percentile scores near the middle of the distribution into consideration.

If we see counseling as a partnership between counselor and client, there is no way in which we can avoid taking the kind of responsibilities we have been outlining here with regard to the choice and interpretation of tests. With very few exceptions the clients who come to us know nothing of the special field of mental testing. It is quite possible for them to hold completely erroneous notions as to what tests can do and to misunderstand what their own scores mean. If we use tests at all we must try to see that this does not happen. And we must do this not by delivering lectures on test principles but by using a few well-chosen phrases that indicate simply and precisely what a test is designed to do and what a specific score means. It is not an easy task. The next chapter will be devoted to methods for accomplishing it.

[1] B. S. Bloom. "Test reliability for what?" *J. Educ. Psychol.*, 1942, 33, 517-526.

Research Summary

EVIDENCE THAT TESTS CONTRIBUTE
TO COUNSELING SUCCESS

One of the most valuable series of reports in the counseling literature establishes beyond the possibility of any reasonable doubt that vocational guidance which makes use of tests in the objective analysis of the individual produces better results than guidance which uses the interview alone. The authors are a number of British psychologists who made careful studies of their procedures during the 1920's and 30's (Earle, 1931; Allen, 1932; Gaw and others, 1926; Hunt, 1943; Hunt and Smith, 1944, 1945; Jennings and Stott, 1936; Macrae, 1932, 1939; Myers, 1932; Oakley, 1937; Rodger, 1937; Smith, 1951; Stott, 1943). The two largest of these studies involved respectively more than 600 clients of the National Institute of Industrial Psychology, and more than 1600 school-leavers in Birmingham. Similar data on smaller numbers were obtained in Cambridge, Fife, and Glasgow. Since both methods and results were comparable in all of these, we shall summarize only the final reports on the largest and most conclusive, Rodger (1937) and Hunt and Smith (1944). The NIIP clients with whom Rodger was concerned were secondary school students aged fifteen to eighteen, predominantly boys, followed up at least two years after counseling was completed. They were divided into two groups according to whether they were still at school or at work and were classified as to whether what they had done was suitable or unsuitable (consistent or not with the counselor's recommendations) and as to whether they were successful, unsuccessful, or doubtful. Results were more striking for the workers than for the students, although the direction of the differences was the same for both groups. Those who had gone into fields recommended as suitable showed a much higher proportion of successful adjustment than those who had not. Of the "worker" group, 89 per cent of those in "suitable" occupations were successful as compared with only 43 per cent of those in "unsuitable" occupations.

In the Birmingham project summarized by Hunt and Smith, subjects were children leaving school at fourteen to go to work. Half of them were given counseling based on test information; the other half had only the regular vocational planning interview which was standard procedure for school-leavers. Some 1600 of them were followed up after a two-year interval and some 600 after a four-year interval. Besides comparing experimental subjects with controls these investigators followed the procedure set up in the NIIP studies and compared those in "accordance" posts with those in "non-accordance" posts. (An "accordance" post is one that is in line with recommendations made by the counselor on the basis of tests or in the absence of tests on the basis of other case data.) A variety of criteria of occupational adjustment were worked out. Results on all criteria and in both the two-year and the four-year groups were consistent. The tested subjects made better adjustment than the controls. *Within* the tested group those who took "accordance" posts were doing better than those who took "non-accordance" posts, but this was not true within the control group. Evidently recommendations made by the counselors who worked without benefit of tests did *not* result in superior placements. Another interesting difference was that subjects in the experimental group who began with non-accordance posts were likely to shift in the direction of accordance posts as time passed, whereas in the control group what shifts there were tended to be *away* from the jobs recommended by the counselor. Thus we have clear-cut evidence that in spite of their many limitations, vocational tests do add to the effectiveness of vocational counseling.

A supplementary study by Macrae (1937) reports that when the same psychological techniques were used to select boys for work parties in Borstals (reformatories), allocations resulted which were successful in 70 per cent of the cases as compared with 45 per cent when the selection was based on housemasters' recommendations. Another early study from a Spanish vocational guidance agency (Cardenal and Granada, 1933) also gives similar results, showing that the success of these methods is not confined to English-speaking countries.

EVIDENCE WITH REGARD TO
WHAT VOCATIONAL TESTS PREDICT

It has been somewhat disconcerting to psychologists that vocational aptitude tests, not given in connection with counseling, seem to correlate to only a very slight extent with measures of occupational success in the fields they are designed to predict. The widely discussed study by E. L. Thorndike and associates, *Prediction of Vocational Success* (1934), indicated that the only prediction that could be made was the highest grade that would be reached in school. Intelligence tests, educational achievement tests, and school marks all predicted this criterion fairly well. None of the correlations between scores on vocational tests taken at the age of fourteen and occupational criteria four to eight years later were high enough to be of any practical value, although they were somewhat higher for clerical than for mechanical work, and in clerical work somewhat higher at the 20-22 age level than at the 18-20 level.

A more recent study by Latham (1951), better designed in many ways, points in exactly the same direction. The subjects here were 1600 high school seniors who in 1947 took a battery of 27 aptitude tests. The follow-up was by questionnaire a year after graduation. (The author explains in some detail the steps that were taken to secure maximum returns, but fails to give the figures as to what the percentage replying finally was.) A system for weighting aptitude test scores was devised to give a quantitative index of *job suitability* for each job chosen or undertaken by an individual. This would seem to represent a quantification of the sort of counselor judgments we have been discussing, which could be used in a situation where no counseling occurred. The criteria used here were employer ratings of success on the job and worker satisfaction as expressed in the questionnaire. The most striking finding is that the correlations of both success and satisfaction with job suitability indices is practically zero. There seems to be no evidence whatever that individuals going into work which a counselor would have considered suitable on the basis of test scores get along better than those who go into unsuitable work.

Another study with similar implications is the large-scale investigation by R. L. Thorndike and Hagen (1959) reported in the book *10,000 Careers.* About 17,000 men who had been given the comprehensive Air Force battery of tests during a five-month period during 1943 were sent questionnaires in 1955 and 1956 to obtain career information. Over 10,000 of the subjects replied. The tests were classified into five groups: (1) general intellectual; (2) numerical fluency; (3) perceptual-spatial; (4) mechanical experience; and (5) psychomotor. Jobs were grouped into 124 categories, and seven kinds of criterion information were used as a basis for success ratings. The results showed almost no correlations between test and criterion scores. The different kinds of jobs were, however, clearly differentiated in terms of mean scores on the kinds of tests, so that patterns of scores characteristic of each job family could be delineated. Ghiselli's summary (1955) of validity information available on vocational aptitude tests also indicates that correlations between tests and criteria are typically low and vary widely from study to study.

It seems unlikely that we are going to be able to predict degree of success very accurately by means of tests. However, the well-documented finding that there are *patterns of abilities* characteristic of different occupations should not be ignored. Evidence for this was produced by the series of studies carried on under the auspices of the Minnesota Employment Stabilization Research Institute and reported by Dvorak (1935). Similar evidence is presented in the Thorndike and Hagen (1959) study mentioned above. Berdie (1955) made a follow-up study of 1500 students ten years after they had been given a battery of aptitude, achievement, interest, and personality tests when they entered college. Curricular groups were clearly differentiated by their patterns of scores, although the correlations of test scores with grades in the courses chosen were low. Interest measures gave the best differentiations, achievement tests the next best, and aptitude tests the least. Strong's (1955) follow-up studies furnish clear-cut evidence for the differentiation of kinds of occupations followed over long periods of time on the basis of interest scores.

The fact that groups of persons in different occupations are significantly differentiated on test scores made years earlier is intelligible in terms of choice or decision concepts. During the period when workers are exploring the possibilities and becoming established, there is probably a strong tendency for persons who lack some characteristic aptitude or interest to quit (or be fired from) the job to which they are unsuited. Thus through decisions made by them or about them, they would tend to gravitate toward kinds of work for which they possessed at least the minimum essentials.

Such an explanation is in keeping with the fact noted in the text—that low scores are more unambiguous in their meaning for the individual than high ones are. Fisher (1949) has brought together a considerable number of validity studies in diverse areas all showing this trend. It is possible to predict failure from an unsatisfactory test score with significantly greater accuracy than to predict success from a high score.

APTITUDE BATTERIES BASED
ON FACTOR ANALYSIS

During 1956 and 1957 the *Personnel and Guidance Journal* carried a series of articles dealing with published tests of this sort. In each case, the test author presented the distinctive features of the aptitude battery, including all statistical information he considered relevant. Donald E. Super then commented on the strengths and weaknesses of each battery and the purposes for which it could legitimately be used. The papers have been collected in a single reprint volume (APGA, 1957). Test batteries included are the *Differential Aptitude Tests*, the *General Aptitude Test Battery*, the *Guilford-Zimmerman Aptitude Survey*, the *Holzinger-Crowder Uni-Factor Tests*, the *Factored Aptitude Series*, the *Segel-Raskin Multiple Aptitude Tests*, the *Flanagan Aptitude Classification Tests*, and the *SRA Primary Mental Ability Tests*. Super's analyses indicate that the predictive validity of all of these batteries is less clear than one would wish, although some of them have accumulated enough information to be used intelligently in counseling situations by persons who know this informational background.

PERSONALITY TESTS IN COUNSELING

There have been more studies of the MMPI than of any other single personality test. Jensen (1958) found that low-ability, non-achieving college students obtained significantly more deviant scores than did the other ability and achievement groups with which they were compared. Swan (1957) found a few significant differences between couples showing different degrees of marital adjustment on the Marital Adjustment Scale. Kleinmuntz (1960) attempted to differentiate three curricular groups, business, engineering, and education, on the basis of MMPI records. The groups did not differ on the clinical scales, but special keys developed by means of item analysis differentiated between them with a fair degree of accuracy (65 per cent correct classifications). In only one of the curricular groups, however, was cross-validation of the keys carried out, and for this education key the proportion of correct classifications dropped from 74 per cent to 62 per cent. A special 43 item MMPI key constructed by Kleinmuntz on the basis of item analysis, designed to differentiate between students who were maladjusted enough to seek help from a college Mental Hygiene Clinic and non-clinic students, produced better results. Even on cross-validation, the adjusted could be distinguished from the maladjusted with very few misclassifications.

A considerable amount of work on counseling uses of the MMPI has been carried on by L. E. Drake and E. R. Oetting. In one reported study (Drake and Oetting, 1957), they showed that a profile with peaks on the *Sc* or *Ma* scales is predictive of underachievement in college students unless accompanied by a *Mf*, in which case normal achievement can be expected. They have developed a codebook for counselors (Drake and Oetting, 1959) showing what kinds of personality characteristics are associated with different MMPI profiles.

In summarizing the implications of the MMPI research for counselors, one can say that scores on the clinical scales themselves may contribute a little but not much to one's assessment of a client's adjustment status or achievement potential. The prospects are brighter that profile analysis and special scales for specific purposes, based on item analysis, will be more valuable. But much more research will be necessary before these tools are available for general use.

Some investigators have concerned themselves with tests developed specifically for persons within the normal range rather than for psychiatric patients. Since such tests are newer, there are not many studies as yet of the way they function in the counseling setting. Goodstein, Crites, Heilbrun, and Rempel (1960) have shown that counseling clients differ significantly from nonclients in both the elevation and the shape of the profiles obtained on the California Psychological Inventory. Clients who received personal adjustment counseling differed significantly in the expected direction from clients who received vocational-educational counseling. Merrill and Murphy (1959) used the Edwards Personal Preference Schedule in differentiating between groups of achievers and non-achievers, both groups consisting of low-ability freshmen for whom predictions of college success would be low. They found significant differences on several of the EPPS scales. Among low-ability students, the ambitious, deferent, conforming persistent individuals are better risks than those whose measured need structure is of some other variety. Berdie and Layton (1960) have summarized some validity research on the Minnesota Counseling Inventory showing the relationship of some of its scores to delinquency and to dropping out of college. In this paper they also report additional evidence with regard to stability of scores over intervals up to a year, sex differences, and differences between high school and college students. These three non-psychiatric personality tests show promise of usefulness in the screening of students who need counseling and the identification of characteristics unfavorable for academic achievement.

The question not clearly answered in any of the research on personality tests is, Does the test contribute more to the thinking of counselor and client than alternative methods of getting at the same characteristics do? Until this has been demonstrated, some counselors will continue to use the information from records and from counseling interviews themselves in preference to tests with considerable ambiguity surrounding individual scores.

MISCELLANEOUS WORK ON TESTING

The standards of reliability, validity, norms, and other matters, standards that tests should meet in order to be considered acceptable, are discussed in the monograph published by the American Psychological Association (1954). The distinction between types of validity evidence discussed in this text can be found in this monograph.

Silvania (1956) has tabulated the returns from a survey of tests used in counseling centers approved by the American Personnel and Guidance Association and compared present practice with that indicated by two previous surveys in the 1940's. The four top ranks in the most recent study are as follows: (1) Kuder; (2) Wechsler-Bellevue; (3) ACE; and (4) Strong.

The story of Project TALENT, a large-scale testing program carried on in the spring of 1960 to obtain an inventory of aptitudes, achievement, interest, personality characteristics, and background material on a 450,000-person representative sample of high school students is told in a brief report (University of Pittsburgh, 1959). This study is potentially of the greatest significance to counselors, since follow-ups of the subjects at intervals from one to twenty years after high school graduation are contemplated.

With the increasing emphasis on counseling services for psychiatric patients, some new tests have been developed particularly for such clients. Walter and Jones (1956) and Stotsky and Weinberg (1956) have demonstrated that a sentence completion test can be scored in such a way that it helps to predict success of patients in work situations. Stotsky (1956b) reports that some specially constructed aptitude tests are also useful for this purpose.

Evaluation

Tests are a valuable counseling tool, but a counselor needs to have an extensive background of knowledge in order to use them intelligently. The value of intelligence, achievement, aptitude, and interest tests for certain purposes has been demonstrated, but they will not do all the things their enthusiastic adherents expect of them. Predictive validity is the all-important consideration. Tests measuring various aspects of personality and adjustment are more questionable, but research findings are now at hand to support at least their limited use for particular purposes.

CHAPTER SEVEN

The Use of Tests in Educational and Vocational Counseling: Integration with Counseling

PLANNING THE TESTING PROGRAM FOR AN INDIVIDUAL

We have been assuming that mental tests have something to contribute to counseling in cases where an individual needs dependable information about his own characteristics. In the previous chapter we were concerned with special aspects of test interpretation that are of particular importance when tests are used for this purpose. In this chapter we shall take up the problem of bringing tests into the counseling situation without changing its structure in an unfavorable way. It is evident that if tests are a part of it the counseling pattern will be different from what it would be without them, but this difference is not necessarily a disadvantage. As has been stressed before, no two counseling relationships are identical, and everything said or done makes some difference in the structure of the situation. The potential hazard that accompanies testing is in making the counselee *less clear* what counseling can do for him and *more dependent* upon the counselor for the answers to all his questions. We wish to facilitate both his understanding of himself and his acceptance of what he learns. Information must be brought in in such a way that he can incorporate it in his picture of himself instead of building up defenses against it. These general purposes give us a background against which we can examine some specific problems and procedures.

How well these purposes are achieved will depend first of all on the way in which tests are selected. It is not so many years ago that Bordin and Bixler (Brayfield, 1950, pp. 173-183) first proposed that tests should be chosen by the client rather than by the counselor. This seemed to many workers to be a fantastic idea, but as it was tried out the procedure began to seem quite natural. Its great advantage is in keeping an essential feature of the situation clear for the counselee—namely, that *he* is to make the decisions by which the course of his life will be governed. This does not mean, of course, that good counseling has not been done under the other system. The fact that the counselor makes minor decisions about tests does not obligate him to make major ones about careers. But a certain amount of confusion about roles is circumvented by arranging to have all decisions, in and out of the counseling room, in the client's hands.

Our principal difficulty in attempting to organize our procedure in this way is that the clients who are to make the choice know nothing about tests and thus may decide what to take on the basis of completely erroneous ideas. They come to counseling with all sorts of attitudes and beliefs on the subject. Some have developed an almost superstitious faith in test scores and are quite prepared to take at face value anything the results may suggest. Others, acutely skeptical and critical even before they sit down to work on a test, seem to be preparing defenses against it. Few if any of them have any notion of the elementary concepts of reliability, validity, and the meaning of relative scores.

The first method by which the counselor can get around this difficulty is to limit the list of tests which may be chosen. Not all techniques used in clinical work are suitable for counseling if we are seeking information for the client rather than suggestions and clues which a psychologist can work up into a diagnosis. The previous chapter has explained what are the essential features of tests useful for this purpose. They must be reasonably reliable so that a score will indicate with some certainty at least whether a person is superior, average, or inferior in the trait measured. They must be backed by validity evidence showing what kinds of life situations they are related to and how close the relationships are. They should have norms that enable a person to compare himself with the kinds of people with whom he will be competing if he decides to go ahead in a certain direction. Finally, they must have been in use long enough for a body of experience to have grown up around them and their special advantages and limitations to have had a chance to show up. The number which qualify according to all these standards is definitely limited. Only the charlatan will feel that he is adding to the impressiveness of the service he offers by appearing to have tests for every conceivable human characteristic.

Having pruned down the list from which choices are to be made, one must next organize the titles in some reasonable fashion in order to make it easy for the client to relate traits about which he wishes information to tests which can give it to him. In school situations one workable classification is: (1) General Scholastic Aptitude, (2) Subject-Matter Achievement, (3) Special Aptitudes and Talents, (4) Interests. Service for out-of-school adults may wish to consolidate the Scholastic Aptitude and Achievement sections and make a further breakdown of the Special Aptitude section. There is no one way of classifying tests, but ease and efficiency are promoted if they are organized around the kinds of questions clients coming to a particular agency tend to ask about themselves.

With a limited number of tests clearly grouped under a few main headings, it is often possible to include in the printed list itself a brief explanation of what each test shows. The alternative procedure is for the counselor to explain the function of each test at the time the client is considering whether or not he wishes to take it. Whether they are presented in written or in oral form, such explanations should be brief and clear, free from pedantry and technical terminology. It is better to say, for example, "This test measures your ability to see how parts fit together, an ability that is important in many kinds of mechanical work," than to put it, "This is a test of two-dimensional spatial visualization correlating with mechanical criteria to the extent of about .50."

Presenting a client with a list of tests from which he is expected to choose is only one of many possible procedures that may be used. Perhaps a more common one is for the counselor simply to suggest a few tests that seem to have some relevance to the person's questions and situation. The client is still the one who decides whether or not this kind of information is what he really wants and whether he wishes to spend his time obtaining it. The important thing is not who initiates the consideration of a test but who makes the final choice with regard to it. As long as the client carries the responsibilities for these decisions, the counseling partnership is maintained.

It is important that decisions about testing be made only after there has been a preliminary interview which creates an atmosphere in which the client's real questions and problems can emerge. The student who rushes in asking to take some vocational aptitude tests should always be invited first to sit down and talk things over. After he has had an opportunity to examine his own motives and needs and to experience acceptance and understanding from the counselor, he will be better able to select tests that will really help him with his decisions. Tests alone can never do the job.

To start always with an interview of this sort will help to head off a troublesome situation which otherwise can arise a little later. Not infrequently the first and only question an individual poses at the beginning is one which a single test will be able to answer only in a fairly ambiguous "Yes" or "No" fashion. Can I get into a certain college? Will I be accepted for a pre-medical course? Is my reading ability low? In the Veterans Administration it was a common occurrence for a man to come in with his mind all made up about what he *wished* to do. He would see tests only as a means of verifying his choice so that the VA would be willing to finance his training. In such a case if he made a low score on a single test he took for verification purposes, an extremely awkward and unpromising counseling situation would be created. The counselor would be in the position of having to inform him that his score did not warrant a recommendation that he go ahead with the plans he had made. Knowing nothing except the facts the single test had given him about the man's pattern of abilities and interests, the counselor could not very well suggest alternative possibilities. Resentment and defensiveness would inevitably follow. Had the person's outlook been broadened at the beginning this outcome could have been avoided.

This does not mean that the counselor should argue with such a client in the initial interview or urge him to take more tests. He should rather accept the plan the client is proposing in the same spirit that he accepts all his other feelings and opinions, showing friendly interest but neither approval nor disapproval. If the interview is productive the motives and needs that lie back of the choice will begin to appear. It may be that a mother or wife is pushing him toward a professional career that he himself doubts his ability to achieve. It may reflect some fixed idea held since childhood, a dream that no longer fits the conditions of adulthood but which he has not questioned. Whatever the reasons for the occupational choice, as he discusses them and finds them accepted without criticism he is very likely to extend his horizon spontaneously and think of other kinds of life plan. If he does not do this, it is quite legitimate for the counselor to ask him whether there are not some other characteristics he would like to check up on while he has this opportunity. Then if he shows some interest in the Strong test, the question can be put to him as to what keys he would especially like to have scored. Because the client-centered attitude must be consistent and dependable in order to function at all, the client's decision is of course final. If after all this he still insists that it is a career in medicine or nothing for him and that he is interested only in tests related to this one occupation, no others should be required of him. Such stubborn insistence on one thing alone is rare, however, in interviews which place the emphasis on the needs occupational choices meet rather than on the choices themselves.

At the opposite extreme from the client who wishes to take only tests related to a single choice is the one who will read over a test list and check practically everything on it. This too can lead to unsatisfactory situations. He may find that the process he has let himself in for is far more time-consuming than he expected and decide to drop the whole thing. Thus both time and test materials are wasted. The inevitable duplication in what is measured also wastes time. Furthermore, as in the case of Strong and Kuder interest measures, two tests that apparently cover much the same ground may produce discrepant results and lead to confusion because there is no research evidence that could give clues to the reason for the discrepancy. To head off these difficulties arising from overtesting, again a satisfactory interview focusing on the motives behind the questions is the first essential. It is clearly the counselor's responsibility to explain which tests duplicate each other. Few students will realize unless told, for example, that the Engineering and Physical Science Aptitude Test has subtests on science, mathematics, and mechanical comprehension, so that it is unnecessary to take time for separate tests in these areas if the composite has been chosen. Finally, it is a good idea to tell the client before he leaves how long the test program he has lined up for himself will take. If it seems overlong, he can decide right then to leave out what appears least valuable.

High school counselors will probably find most of what has been said about individual test selection inappropriate for their situation. They work mainly with the scores from standard batteries of tests administered to students in groups. This inevitably involves overtesting for some students, undertesting for others, and the use of inappropriate tests for many. But because of the number of students to be served and the fact that the testing program serves several purposes besides counseling, they must come to terms with this way of handling the testing function.

If the counselor is himself responsible for planning and carrying out the testing program, he can apply some of the principles we have been discussing in this and the previous chapter to the task as a whole. It is important that the battery used for counseling purposes be made up of tests reliable and valid enough to permit a clear-cut report to the student. It is important that they cover enough different aspects of ability and interest that the individual can assess strengths and weaknesses rather than suitability for one particular thing, such as college education. The conditions under which they are given should approximate as closely as possible those that obtain when a person is taking tests he himself has chosen, since the attitude with which one approaches the task can influence results markedly, especially on interest inventories. Co-operation must be secured from students even when the initiative must necessarily be taken by the counselor. A clear explanation as to how the results are to be used and the kind of information about themselves they can expect to get often helps to develop the necessary morale. Finally it must be recognized by everyone concerned with the program, administrators and teachers as well as counselors, that the *reporting* of test results is a matter for individual, not group discussion, except in cases where small groups, set up especially for group counseling, have been organized. To save time by giving tests in groups does not weaken a program seriously, but to attempt to make further economies by allowing students to interpret their own scores undermines it completely. It is better to do no testing at all and leave students to judge their capabilities from other kinds of evidence than to open the way for the many kinds of misconceptions and anxieties about intelligence, aptitudes, and interests that testing without counseling creates. Unfortunately many school administrators are not familiar enough with the technical aspects of mental measurement to realize this. It is usually the counselor's responsibility to make this clear.

In situations where the counselor does not plan or help to plan the school testing program he can still preserve some of the emphasis on individualization and choice as he works with each student. It is still important to discover what the client really wants to know about himself before presenting any of the test scores that are available. It is not necessary to present all of them to him in any one interview. It is better to make sure that he fully understands the significance of the facts that are considered.

Furthermore, it is advisable for the counselor to have on hand a supply of tests he can use to supplement the regular testing program in individual cases. For instance, it is obvious that a tenth-grade boy who scores at or below the fifth percentile point on all of the Iowa Tests of Educational Development is not helped much in making his own educational and vocational decisions by this information. He knows already that he is an unsatisfactory student. The test confirms it. It is clear that advanced education is ruled out for him, but he needs the kind of information about himself that will help him to distinguish between *other* alternatives and to plan the special kind of educational program that is suitable for him. An arithmetic test that will indicate how proficient he is in adding and subtracting may be indicated if he is thinking about work in a grocery store. A test of mechanical aptitude or mechanical knowledge will help him judge his probability of success (or failure) in a vocational training program of some kind. A reading test at a lower level of difficulty than the one in the standard battery will indicate what kinds of material he should be able to study and understand. Such supplementary testing does not require much of a counselor's time, and it does add to his effectiveness.

THE ORGANIZATION OF TEST
INFORMATION INTO A PATTERN

Once a battery of tests has been given and scored, the next step is to fit the results into some coherent pattern that will facilitate discussing them with the client. There is little or nothing to be gained by presenting a client with an unintelligible mass of quantitative data and expecting him to incorporate it with the rest of his experience, much of which he may have found equally unintelligible. If we are really thinking of test results as a source of information, information that can promote and deepen self-understanding, then it is of the utmost importance that the facts be organized in such a way that they can be clearly communicated. In a busy counseling agency it is easy for this task to be squeezed out by more observable kinds of activity. A person who is sitting and thinking about the material in a case folder may not appear to be doing anything. However, the thinking is necessary and it is the counselor's responsibility to arrange his schedule so as to leave time for it before every planning interview.

In analyzing how this is done, let us begin with an example of the kind of data a counselor must organize. We have made things a little easier for Mr. Larson, the counselor, than they would ordinarily be by summarizing the background information which he would probably have had to assemble from several different blanks in the student's folder. It is the organization of *test* information and its incorporation with the background data which concerns us here.

NAME: Peter Hardy AGE: 18

SCHOOL PLACEMENT: Freshman in State University

FAMILY: Peter is the youngest of three children. The father is a brick-layer; the mother before marriage was an elementary school teacher. An older sister is married, an older brother in the Navy. The family is in comfortable circumstances and is financing his college education. Peter is living in the dormitory.

SCHOOL BACKGROUND: His high school record was satisfactory but not outstanding. Grade reports show average and slightly above-average marks in most subjects. No subject stands out as a field in which he has achieved conspicuous success. He took part in a number of activities and held minor offices in several organizations but was not conspicuously good at any of these either.

WORK EXPERIENCE: Peter had a paper route throughout his high school years. For the past three summers he has worked, one year on his uncle's farm, another in a cannery, and most recently in a grocery store doing deliveries. The last was the job he liked the best.

OCCUPATIONAL PLANS: Until recently he has never thought much about what he wanted to do when he grew up. He has vaguely considered law because "it would be a good thing to have a profession," but aside from this he has no ideas.

NOTES ON FIRST INTERVIEW: Mr. Hardy came in because of vocational indecision. This is beginning to trouble him now that he has come to college, as he keeps meeting boys his age who seem to have definite plans for their lives. He wonders sometimes if he should not have come to college but started to work in a store or office instead. Particularly when, as has happened recently, he gets back an English theme with an unsatisfactory grade or a poor exam paper in history, he doubts his own ability to complete a degree course.

It is his mother who has really set her heart on his going through college, and the thought of her disappointment if he doesn't make the grade is his chief reason for trying. She has always had intellectual and social ambitions for her family, and so far they haven't lived up to them very well. The daughter at 18 married a salesman who has a good income but not even a high school diploma. The oldest boy left high school to join the Navy during the war and decided to stay in when it was over.

Peter feels that his mother has already had more than her share of disappointment and worry. His father is doing well now, but there was a period during the 1930's when no building was going on and the family was very "hard up." He can just barely remember the uneasy feeling he used to get as a small boy when people would make cracks about the WPA—how he would hope they wouldn't find out that his father had a WPA job. What he remembers better is a period in his life from about 11 to 14 when he was a member of a "gang" that went in for minor delinquencies such as breaking into empty houses and stealing vegetables and fruit from gardens. "My mother was pretty worried about my future then," he says half jokingly. He finds it hard to understand now just what appeal the whole thing had for him. At any rate the gang broke up when the older boys in it quit school and scattered, and he "turned over a new leaf" about the time he entered high school.

He had come prepared to take "aptitude tests" and was eager to take as many as possible. After some explanation of what different tests were designed to measure we settled on a list including the ACE, the Cooperative General Proficiency Battery, the Cooperative Reading Comprehension and Effectiveness of Expression, the Minnesota Paper Form Board and Clerical, and the Strong. Because of his need for a broad survey we will score the Strong on the group keys, adding Carpenter, Printer, and Farmer to get at some areas the groups do not cover. It can be scored on other occupational keys later if it seems desirable.

TEST RESULTS:

Test	Norm Group	Percentile
ACE		
L	Entering freshmen	91
Q	" "	70
Total	" "	85
Coop. Gen. Prof.		
Natural Science	" "	60
Social Science	" "	95
Mathematics	" "	75
Coop. Eff. of Exp.	" "	22
Coop. Reading		
Vocabulary	" "	91
Speed of Comprehension	" "	80
Levels of Comprehension	" "	83
Minn. Paper Form Board	Liberal Arts freshmen	60
Minn. Clerical		
Numbers	Men in general	70
Names	" " "	80
Strong		
Group I (Human Science)	Men in the occupations	B−
Group II (Technical Science)	" " " "	C+
Group V (Personnel)	" " " "	A
Group VIII (Business detail)	" " " "	B
Group IX (Business contact)	" " " "	B+
Group X (Verbal)	" " " "	C
Carpenter	" " " "	B−
Printer	" " " "	B
Farmer	" " " "	C+

As he begins to try to fit these facts into some pattern, Mr. Larson thinks back to his first interview with Peter Hardy two weeks before. He remembers him as a slight, fresh-faced boy appearing younger than his eighteen years. It would have been easy to react to him in a fatherly, protecting way because of his youthfulness and because of a disarming simplicity of manner, free from conceit or aggressiveness. He had not thought of him then as an outstandingly intelligent person. In fact he remembers thinking that Peter's difficulty might simply be that he was out of his depth in college. Mr. Larson takes another look at the ACE and the Cooperative test scores as well as at the high school record. Here is the first question around which some of the facts can be grouped. Why has the world, including Mr. Larson and even including Peter himself, so completely failed to recognize the boy's real intellectual ability? Why has he given so little evidence of it in his high school work? The one possibility that suggests itself from the test record is the below-average English score. The counselor notes in this connection that in the information blank Peter has filled out there are six misspelled words, and that his response to the question, "What problems would you like to talk over with a counselor?" is written in a childish, almost unintelligible scrawl. Inability to express himself clearly in writing could certainly operate to pull down his grades, especially in subjects where essay examinations are the rule. He remembers that it is English themes and history that Peter mentioned specifically as giving him trouble. This line of thought leads to another question, "Why did a boy with this much intelligence and reading ability fail to develop the elementary skills of written expression?" Perhaps the contrast between his laborer father and his schoolteacher mother had something to do with it. Could his wildness at an earlier age also be a symptom of such a conflict? But Mr. Larson draws himself back from further speculation along these lines. He is committed to a client-centered philosophy and feels that such a diagnosis at this stage is not only unnecessary but might actually blind him to attitudes and feelings as they are expressed in subsequent interviews. "At any rate," he says to himself, "the fact that his motives during the junior high school years were steering him in the direction of hardness and adventure might have kept him from learning much during that period in English which is commonly regarded as a 'sissy' subject."

So much for the underachievement, but Mr. Larson remembers that it was not this that Mr. Hardy saw as his principal problem. What help can the test results give in vocational decisions? He notes immediately that the high score on the social science achievement test fits in well with the *A* on Group V, the social service group on the Strong. This suggests the broad area including teaching and school administration, personnel work, and related occupations. He asks himself why this has not occurred to Peter as a possibility before. The only profession he has even vaguely considered, that of law, is one in which the Strong gives him a flat *C* if the Group X score can be taken as an indication. He turns to the Strong blank itself to see if reading-through some of the boy's specific likes and dislikes reveals anything about his motivation. The first thing that strikes him is that there are almost no "dislikes," a few "indifferents," but the vast majority of occupations and activities marked *L*. This of course would tend to produce a *C* on the verbal group and an *A* on Group V, because this is a peculiarity of these keys. He turns to Strong's book to verify the point. But just what does the fact mean in Peter's case? Are his significant scores artifacts of some response set, or can they really be taken to mean interests like those of the occupational groups? Why does he register this indiscriminate *L* response? Could this too arise from incompatibilities in the father's and mother's value systems and the boy's attempt not to repudiate either of them? If so, could the vocational indecision arise from the same source? Again it is not for Mr. Larson to answer the question and thus make a neat diagnosis but rather to present all the facts to Peter, whose own thinking about what the facts mean will be more valuable than any his counselor could do on the basis of present evidence.

Aside from this social service emphasis there is nothing in the test record particularly relevant to vocational choice. So far as special clerical and mechanical aptitudes can be evaluated from the brief tests given, it can only be said that both appear to be within the average range. Peter would not be disqualified from entering either broad field because of inadequate ability. Mr. Larson knows too much about the reliabilities of the tests to attempt to be any more precise than this on the basis of percentiles of 60, 70, and 80. No particular interests in mechanical or scientific directions are in evidence, and science and mathematics achievement scores, while satisfactory, are not outstanding enough to warrant considering specialization along those lines. Something in business, however, might be a possibility. The B+ on Group IX, the sales occupations, fits in with his enjoyment of the work in the grocery store.

Having come this far with his own analysis of the data, Mr. Larson is ready to outline the main things he has to communicate to Peter and try to decide how to *begin* the communication task. He need plan ahead no farther than that, since from then on the interview will take whatever shape Peter wishes to give it. The principal ideas in connection with which all the test results can be discussed seem to be as follows:

1. Tests show superior mental ability and indicate capacity for considerably better school achievement than has been shown so far. The only handicap is English expression which, although not impossibly low, is considerably below the college average.
2. The one general occupational area suggested by both interest and achievement scores is social service. Business contact work is suggested by the interest test and not ruled out by anything in the rest of the data. No score is low enough to disqualify him from mechanical or technical occupations either, but the interest test does not point in that direction.
3. Two questions stand out. Why is his achievement in English low? Why does he register so few dislikes on the Strong? Answers to both of these might help to understand his uncertainty.

In deciding where to begin, Mr. Larson first rules out the third topic. He realizes that Peter will come to the interview eager to get a report on the tests he has taken and that to ask him these questions at the beginning might stir up anxiety or defensiveness rather than lead to productive thinking. The choice between alternatives 1 and 2 is more difficult. To be told suddenly that one is much brighter than one has supposed is not necessarily encouraging. To assimilate such knowledge sometimes involves a radical readjustment of one's self-concept. Perhaps it would be better to bring this in more gradually. On the other hand, to begin with the vocational question, although it has the advantage of giving the boy first what he himself has asked for, may suggest too simple a solution too soon. Suppose he quickly decides that a career as a school administrator appeals to him. In this case the underlying motivation may never come to light at all and some new crisis may catch him as unprepared as did the shift from high school to college. However, all things considered, the counselor decides to begin with the second point, but to make sure that somehow before the interview ends all the facets of the test pattern come in for some consideration. He is ready now to see Peter Hardy.

This is an example of the kind of thinking involved in organizing test results for reporting to a client. It is in no sense a model or outline to be followed. The very essence of the matter is that there can be no standard technique for synthesizing these data. Each client is unique: his attitudes toward life and work, his relationship to the counselor, and the circumstances within which he must function are not like those of anyone else. This means that even if his test profile should be identical with that of a previous counselee, the way the counselor would organize his scores and report them might be different from the way he did it on the previous occasion.

Certain general recommendations as to how to approach the task can, however, be made. In the first place, it is advisable to get the background factors firmly in mind before considering the test scores. As was stressed in the chapter on records, cold objectivity is not what is wanted here. What we try to do is to comprehend the client's world as it seems to him. To have had a satisfying first interview with him and taken good notes on it are decided advantages. From this vantage point we can anticipate to some extent how the results of the testing he has undergone are going to affect him. Will he be completely dismayed at this low score on the Miller Analogies or will he turn with something like relief to some career plan not calling for graduate training? How is he going to feel about this A on the Strong CPA scale, in view of the fact that his father, whom he hates and admires and above all wants to break away from, is an accountant? Adopting the client's point of view enables us to sort out test results into those which are in keeping with his wishes and expectations and those which are out of line with them.

Another good rule is to pay particular attention to discrepancies in the case data—items that do not seem to fit together. If two tests, presumably of the same trait, give widely different scores, the reason for the difference should be analyzed. (As indicated before, if the research background of either or both is deficient, it may be impossible to make anything of such findings.) In some cases interests and abilities seem not to go together. A student may have high academic aptitudes and high scores in standardized tests and course grades in science and mathematics and yet get C's on all the science scales of the Strong. Sometimes the claimed interests differ markedly from those the interest test reveals. A girl may insist that she wants to be an artist or writer and that she finds routine work of any sort intolerable and yet turn up with A's on the Strong Office Worker and Housewife scales. Sometimes basic emotional needs may run counter to the whole ability and interest pattern as when a brilliant, talented girl hesitates to enter a profession requiring long training for fear she will jeopardize her chances for marriage and a family.

Few case records are free from any such discrepancies. As the counselor studies each he fits the conflicting evidence into some larger pattern if he can and then looks for supporting data in other parts of the record. The fact that Mr. Bartholemew's ACE scores is so much lower than his Ohio score may show that he cannot work fast. Is there a consistent tendency for his other scores to be higher on untimed than on timed tests? Mary Stanley's protest against routine work may reflect the attitudes of the circle in which she moves, a circle in which it is the accepted thing to be contemptuous of ordinary office workers. Have we any information as to who her friends are? If no such way of reconciling a conflict is apparent, the counselor simply makes a mental note that this is something he and the client will face during the interview and try to work out together.

In vocational counseling a patterning of test information that is quite generally applicable is evaluating the significance of the obtained scores in connection with each of several alternative career plans. This is especially to be recommended in cases where clients come in with definite possibilities in mind, although it is never necessary to limit oneself to the things they have mentioned, and even with a completely undecided person like Peter Hardy the method may still be applicable. As has been said earlier, many writers on counseling have used such an analysis as a basis for prognoses, or predictions as to probability of success in each occupation, and the technique was made a fundamental part of the standard procedure the Veterans Administration adopted in its postwar counseling centers. This way of handling test data works just as well if we stop short of actual clinical predictions, which the available evidence indicates we cannot carry out accurately enough to do the client any good. The first step is to think of a number of occupations we have some reason to consider. The next is to go through the case information seeking material that has something to do with the person's assets and liabilities along each of these lines. The procedure both stimulates the counselor's thinking and suggests possible openings for the subsequent interview. Within this framework the level of achievement on a number of tests can be organized intelligibly. Its main weakness is that it is *too* well-organized, too logical to apply in all situations. Where subtle emotional undertones pervade the thinking about choices, it may not be possible to incorporate them in the scheme. It is better for a counselor to keep a flexible attitude and be ready to shift to some other type of patterning if it seems more appropriate. The attempts to fit the facts into this kind of mold may even serve to show up factors which elude the classification. And even if the interview following testing has been planned in this manner, the perceptive counselor is always ready to abandon the plans if matters take an unexpected turn.

Once a person has developed a high degree of skill in analyzing test results, integrating them with background materials, and discovering patterns in terms of which they can be organized, the whole process may require no more of his time than it has taken to read the preceding explanation of it. Always, however, some cases will take longer than others, and a few will be exceptionally intricate and puzzling. It is from his reaction toward these people whose records "just don't make sense" that a person's basic attitudes toward his clients and his work can often be judged. The good counselor accepts the challenge such cases present without any hard feelings, realizing that it is people of this sort who need counseling most, since usually their lives do not make sense to them either. Instead of exclaiming in exasperation, "What do you do with a boy who shows no special talents, gets no A's or B+'s on the Strong test, and seems to be enthusiastic about nothing except making bows and arrows!" he will think of ways of encouraging the boy to formulate in words what he really wants out of life. When one's best efforts fail to produce an intelligible pattern in the test scores, one can always begin the interview with a brief explanation of what is unusual about the record and let the client go on from there.

COMMUNICATING TEST INFORMATION IN THE INTERVIEW

After the information to be given has been organized the next problem is how best to communicate it to the client. Our aim is to enable him to form a sound idea of his own assets and liabilities, the raw materials with which he must work in building his future. It is not necessary to give him exact scores or detailed technical information about tests. It is what the test results show about himself that he wishes to know.

The first aspect of the counselor's preparation for this task, the organization of the facts into a pattern that can be easily grasped and kept in mind, has already been discussed in some detail. The second is a matter of sensing what the client is really seeking from counseling. We know enough about the influence of wishes on beliefs to realize that a person's understanding of the significance of his own test record will depend to some extent on what he *needs* to think about himself. The more clearly the counselor can sense what these needs are the more likely he will be to put what he has to say in terms that can be accepted. There is no merit in stating facts unless they mean something to the person hearing them. Communication must communicate.

An example will make this clearer. Two college students have very similar test profiles. Both are below the tenth percentile in college aptitude, below average in all subject-matter fields, but above the 90th percentile on mechanical aptitude tests. Both have A's only on Group II and the skilled labor scales of the Strong. Bill Brown is in college because his father wished to give him advantages that he himself did not have. Bill's own inclinations were to get a job in a local lumber mill, marry his high school sweetheart, and settle down to the sort of small-town life he loves. He has been making poor grades about which he feels a little guilty. The whole college situation is getting more and more uncomfortable. He has come to the Counseling Center with a half-formulated hope that something will turn up to justify his getting out of these uncongenial surroundings. John Allen, on the other hand, is the only child of a widowed mother who adores him and is certain that he has a brilliant future. She has made great sacrifices to insure that he get a college education. One of John's most fundamental assumptions around which his whole life is organized is that he must not disappoint her. He must make a good record; he must graduate; he must get into a profession. If the going gets hard he must work harder. He has come to the Counseling Center to see if he can find out why he is having so much trouble making his grades and what he can do to remedy his deficiencies. A simple factual statement such as "Your best abilities seem to be in fields that haven't much to do with college work" will be accepted eagerly by Bill, rejected completely by John. Similar as the facts to be communicated are, the wise counselor will not express them in the same way in the two cases.

For one thing there is always freedom to choose what to begin with. As we have shown in the Peter Hardy example, when a number of scores on several different tests have been organized into a pattern there are likely to be several alternatives. In choosing between them the first aim should be to minimize defensive reactions. They are a handicap in any counseling situation and are particularly to be avoided here, since they will work against the acceptance and use of the information the tests bring. One good way of forestalling the development of defensive attitudes is to relate the first statement made to something the client has previously said, a question he has asked or a choice that he has made. In the example of the preceding paragraph, one knows that the statement quoted will work very well for Bill because he has indicated in the previous interview that he thinks he is better suited for something else than for college. In reporting to John the counselor might begin, "I can see from the interest test you took why you decided on a science major. Your likes and dislikes seem to be more like those of technical scientists and men working with machinery and tools than like those of any other group. But the tests also suggest some reasons why you might expect to have trouble with some of the college courses in science." This opening does more than report what the interest test showed and lead into a discussion of the boy's deficiencies. It helps to get across at the same time the counselor's acceptance of John, his respect for his capacity to understand himself, and a generally sympathetic but not protective attitude. Again it must be emphasized that if it is to be effective the counselor must really feel that way about John. Any contempt for students who score low on intelligence tests will poison the atmosphere in spite of efforts to conceal it.

Often but not always it is well to begin with interest tests rather than ability tests, since clients are less likely to feel a need to be defensive about them. Often but not always it is advisable to mention high scores before low ones for the same reason. But no general rule can be laid down about these things, human motivation being as diverse and complicated as it is. A boy who is in active protest against a dominating physician father may be more upset by being told that he himself has the interests of a doctor than by anything else the counselor might tell him. The girl who has convinced herself that her poor grades are the result of a lack of reading skill may find it difficult to accept the fact that her reading test scores are excellent, since believing this opens the way for vague anxieties as to what really *is* wrong with her.

The only essentials for making good decisions as to how to begin are perceptiveness and good will on the part of the counselor, arrangements that permit a leisurely, comfortable first interview in which underlying motivations can be expressed, and enough time for the counselor to think over the meaning of the test results before attempting to report them. For these there are no substitutes.

In addition to planning how to begin, the counselor needs also to devote some thought to exact terms he will use in his explanation. Here as in all interviewing it is important to avoid words that have unfavorable emotional connotations. A synonym that has the same objective meaning but does not carry these connotations is more than a euphemism. It is a genuine tool in the counselor's workbox. In his work, bluntness is no virtue. Thus it is usually better not to speak of any counseling test as an "intelligence test." It is always possible to use a more specific term, depending upon what specific test has been used. "Academic aptitude" is one substitute term, but it is somewhat ponderous and technical sounding. Sometimes it is feasible to speak of "vocabulary and verbal skills" or "ability to learn things from books." Obviously this is a touchier point for low scorers than for high. Another family of words it is usually best to avoid consists of terms like *neurotic* and *maladjusted. Masculinity* and *femininity* should in general be placed on the proscribed list. Besides these terms related to spots that are sensitive in a great many people there are individual sensitive areas a counselor will occasionally strike. One student admitted after counseling was over, though he gave no indication at the time, that a reference to personality as a *complex* thing upset him considerably. To him "complexity" had frightening implications.

The need to sense what an individual will take as an affront or a cause for alarm and the impossibility of avoiding such reactions entirely lead into the next general principle governing the reporting of test results: There should always be time and opportunity for the client to express attitudes about the information that has been communicated. No urge to get on with the business and finish what has been started should stand in the way of the client's thinking out loud and thus coming to terms with the facts about himself. If Henry Rowlandson gives some sign of disappointment when he learns that his percentile rank on the college aptitude test is 85, disappointment should be recognized and accepted so that he may analyze it further if he wishes. By saying simply, "You're disappointed that it isn't higher," the counselor can clear the way for such expression. Handling this aspect of the interview skillfully requires good timing and close attention. Too much information must not be thrown at the person all at once. He must be given time to take it in—to realize its meaning. The same perceptiveness, the same knack of feeling what the other person is feeling about things, is called for here as in the rest of the interview.

The statement, "his percentile rank on the college aptitude test is 85," in the paragraph above is a more exact quantitative statement than would ordinarily be given. As has been said before, unreliability makes test scores much less precise than they appear to be. Because of inequalities in the percentile scale it is not possible to make any kind of standard allowance for this inaccuracy. On the other hand, if standard scores rather than percentiles are reported it is practically impossible to explain briefly to a nonstatistical listener just what such a score means. Thus it is usually better for the counselor to make the adjustments for type of score, amount of error, and section of the distribution, and then to put the quantitative fact in simple, qualitative terms. This is most easily done by telling the person in what part of a specified group the test classifies him, as explained in the previous chapter. The less reliable the test or the nearer the middle of the percentile distribution the individual falls, the broader will be the category to which he is assigned. Thus if he obtains percentile scores of 58 and 39 on two tests with reliabilities of .89 he may simply be told that he is within the average range on both and then given whatever information is available from validity studies as to what can be expected of persons at that level. If this percentile is *two*, however, on a test with a reliability of .95, it is possible to be considerably more specific and say something like, "Not more than two or three per cent of the students taking this test score lower than you do." (Naturally what was said above about beginning with something that will not be disturbing and being careful how the trait in question is labeled apply here. But the fact that he is so decisively low is something we should try to get across to him, since it is a fact he must adjust himself to whether he knows it or not. To communicate information like this in a kindly non-disparaging manner is a difficult but very essential counseling task.)

Hard as it may often be to give information without advice, it is this that one should attempt to do. Otherwise the structure of the counseling situation loses its clarity. Even when the advice is nothing more definite and compelling than what is embodied in statements beginning, "If I were you . . . ," or "It seems to me . . . ," the client who has been led to expect that he is to make decisions may sense that pressure is being applied and shift his attitude in the direction of dependence or defensiveness. There are some circumstances, of course, where the final decision actually is not in the client's hands. Public Law 16 cases under the Veterans Administration were of such a nature. For a man to be authorized to enter training it was necessary that the counselor indicate his approval of the plan worked out. In the same category are cases where the counselor's judgment will decide whether or not a student is to be disqualified from further college work. In such instances it should be clear from the beginning that this is how matters stand. The structure of the situation is somewhat different, and the client should realize this.

Before leaving the subject of testing, it might be well for us to consider a few specific questions that counselors and would-be counselors often raise. Should clients be allowed to *see* their test profiles or their scores on specific test blanks? The answer follows from what has been said about the ways in which results are to be reported. It is better to explain to the person in qualitative terms how well he has done than to give him a specific quantitative score and then try to clear up all the possible misapprehensions that may arise from it. Thus it is usually inadvisable to give him his scores to look at. However, there is no invariable rule about this. When a client insists on seeing the scores themselves, it is certainly far better to show them to him than to risk giving the impression that the counselor is concealing something. And for students who are psychology or education majors with some background in testing, practice in applying what they have learned in the interpretation of their own results is definitely helpful.

Should the testing in any one case be done all at once or spread over a period of time with interviews intervening between tests? Some counselors like to give only an interest test after the first interview. Then during the second interview interests showing up on this test are discussed and decisions made as to what further test information is needed to check up on possibilities suggested. Such a procedure is certainly workable and seems advisable in some cases, particularly those in which the person is completely lacking in ideas at the beginning. There are, however, at least two objections to its being adopted as standard routine. For one thing it is more time-consuming than the system of planning the whole test program at once. Furthermore, and probably a more important consideration, it can easily lead to the making of decisions on inadequate grounds. A student may be pleased to find out that the Strong test gives him an *A* as an architect and decide not to take time for any more tests. Thus a mathematics deficiency may not show up until sometime later when failure in a required course makes it painfully apparent. We should try to insure that if a client gets any picture of his interests and abilities at all it should be a well-rounded picture. As has been so often stressed in preceding paragraphs, it is the pattern or total organization of his tested characteristics that a person needs to understand. Taking tests and getting the results one at a time is likely to make it harder to grasp this.

Should some sort of written report be prepared at the conclusion of vocational counseling so that the client will be able to refer to it later? If there is time to make an individual organized synthesis of all relevant data after a case is completed, such a report may have considerable value. A standardized form, however, cannot take the place of this kind of personal summary. Simply to list test results and possible vocational choices may be useless or even misleading. Here again perhaps we can be guided by our client's wishes. Anyone who especially asks for a report should have it, as carefully thought out and expressed as possible. Whether it is given to those who do not request it can depend upon the amount of free time available. Other tasks have a more convincing claim on the counselor's limited hours than has this one.

Probably no other supplementary field has contributed so much to the effectiveness of counseling as has mental testing. Probably also more errors and blunders have been made in this area than in any other. By schooling himself in mental test principles and by keeping clearly in mind the purposes tests serve in the total counseling enterprise, a professional worker should be able to reap the benefits and at the same time to avoid the mistakes.

Research Summary

EFFECTS OF COUNSELING, INCLUDING TESTING, ON SELF-KNOWLEDGE

A number of studies have focused attention on the fact that clients do not characteristically come out of the counseling experience with as much knowledge of their own abilities and interests as one would expect them to have. Froehlich (1957) proposed that the agreement between the quintile rank in which his test score placed a person and his own estimate of this quintile rank for the trait in question could serve, if checked before and after counseling, as a criterion of counseling effectiveness. A group of high school students in a summer high school were counseled by graduate students and compared with control groups of non-counseled students and students counseled without tests. There were statistically significant differences in favor of the counseled group, but the amount of agreement between test evidence and self-estimates was disappointingly low for all groups. In another study in this series Froehlich and Moser (1954) found that ninth-grade students' recollection of DAT scores 15 months after they had been discussed with them was not very accurate. There was a tendency for both high and low scores to be reported as closer to the mean than they actually had been. High scores were remembered more accurately than low ones.

Young (1955), whose subjects were college men in their freshman year, found that a 25-minute interview with a counselor during a three-week period following the first six weeks of classes, using a chart on which the relationship of ability and achievement test scores to college grades was shown, did not produce significant improvement in either self-prediction or grades. A matched non-counseled group was used as a control. Overprediction of grades was common both before and after counseling. In spite of this lack of measurable influence, a large proportion of the counseled group rated the experience as helpful, 89 per cent of them specifically mentioning the value of "knowing achievement test standings."

Berdie (1954) compared the correlations between self-ratings and test scores for counseled and control groups of college freshmen. Self-ratings were made during orientation week and again six months later, after the experimental subjects had participated in the counseling experience. For men, the counseled group showed significantly more increased correlations on the Strong Vocational Interest Blank than did the non-counseled and made a greater improvement in predicting their own grades. There was no trend in either group in MMPI self-estimates.

Robertson (1960) asked 31 prospective engineering students and 31 prospective business students who participated in a three-day precollege counseling program to make self-estimates of their abilities before and after the counseling experience. Although there were some differences between the two curricular groups, neither group showed significant improvement after counseling.

Singer and Stefflre (1954) questioned whether changes in correlations or in mean discrepancy ratings really was an adequate technique for determining whether self-estimates were improving. Working with high school seniors as subjects and the Occupational Interest Inventory as a testing instrument, they obtained self-estimates of interests before and three months after counseling. They compared both means and standard deviations of the discrepancy scores and analyzed male and female groups separately. For males, there was no significant change in means, but all standard deviations decreased, although only for the Mechanical scale was this decrease significant. Females showed a significant decrease in mean discrepancy scores on the Mechanical and Scientific scales and a significant decrease in standard deviation on the Personal-Social and Mechanical scales. The authors interpret the decrease in standard deviation as a trend toward zero discrepancy. In other words, counseling may be helping those persons whose estimates of their own traits are *seriously* in error to become more accurate in their evaluations, even though a moderate amount of inaccuracy persists in everybody. Neither a large overestimate in one case balanced by a large underestimate nor a small overestimate balanced by a small underestimate have any effect on the mean.

Several investigators have tried to analyze self-estimate results to discover whether there were differences attributable to the traits being estimated or to the psychological characteristics of the subjects doing the estimating. It is to be noted that both the Berdie and the Singer and Stefflre studies reported above showed sex differences. H. J. Parker (1957) studied 136 randomly selected veterans who had been given as part of counseling a minimum test battery consisting of an interest inventory, a mental ability test, an aptitude test, and a personality survey. The subjects were asked to recall test results immediately after counseling and one month later. Immediate recall was somewhat more accurate than delayed, and mental ability showed the most accurate and stable recall. The amount of distortion showed no relationship to measured personality traits, intelligence, years of education, age, or vocational aspiration.

Johnson (1953) asked his subjects, 141 clients of a vocational guidance agency, to make self-ratings immediately before and one month after counseling on intelligence, interests, and personality. These were compared with counselor ratings based on the clients' test scores. There were significant increases in accuracy for abilities and interests, but not for personality ratings. Intelligence ratings showed the most improvement. Self-knowledge seemed to be slightly related to intelligence, education, and emotional stability. There was a slight negative relationship between accuracy ratings and the total number of tests individuals had taken. One extra feature of this study was that the subjects were asked to rate their *certainty* about the traits they were estimating in themselves. There were significant increases in these certainty ratings after counseling for all the kinds of traits, including personality.

Tuma and Gustad (1957), like their predecessors, used discrepancies between self-rated and tested abilities and interests but worked out an experimental design that permitted a simultaneous assessment of differences between clients, differences between counselors, and differences in methods of test selection and interpretation. Differences between the three counselors taking part in the study appeared when their clients' self-estimates of interests were analyzed, but client self-estimates of abilities did not distinguish between them. Client growth in self-knowledge turned out to be moderately related to *similarity* between client and counselor in the measured personality traits of dominance, social presence, and social participation.

EFFECTS OF CLIENT-CENTERED TECHNIQUES OF TEST SELECTION AND INTERPRETATION

Gustad and Tuma (1957) in the study described above found no significant differences between groups of clients according to whether client-centered or more directive techniques were used in dealing with test information. L. B. Rogers (1954) also compared groups of clients in two kinds of interview situation labeled "test-centered" and "self-evaluative." The criterion was self-understanding, based on discrepancy between client and counselor ratings of the same trait. No clear difference between the methods emerged when intelligence and degree of participation were not taken into account. It appeared that the high-intelligence subgroup profited more than did the low-intelligence subgroup from the test-centered approach and high participators of all levels benefited more than low participators from the self-evaluative approach. The design of this study, however, did not permit a very clear test of the significance of these interactions.

Kamm and Wrenn (1950) investigated factors related to acceptance and non-acceptance of information about the self. Forty educational-vocational planning interviews recorded by one counselor were rated by three judges on various characteristics. The judgment as to whether self-information had or had not been accepted was made on the basis of post-interview inquiry, and one-month and four-month follow-ups. The detailed data are not given in the published paper but the relationships are summarized. Acceptance of information is related to relaxed attitudes by both interview participants, positive attitudes as expressed by the counselee, readiness for counseling help, relationship to the immediate problem, and whether or not it requires a modification of the self-concept. (Information suggesting a change of plans is less readily accepted than information suggesting their continuation.) Acceptance is unrelated to many factors, including length of the interview, time of day, amount of client talk, academic aptitude, personality pattern, and social status. Seeman (1948b) was especially interested in the question of self-selection of tests by the client. Fifty clients of two counselors using self-selection procedures were the subjects of the study. The criteria as to whether an adequate selection had been made were: (1) the per cent chosen of all tests available for actuarial or clinical prediction of something related to the client's questions and (2) the difference between the frequencies of choice of spatial relations tests by the technical and social science groups. On both criteria, self-selection seemed to work well. Some 93 per cent of all tests available for prediction were chosen, and there was a significant diffrence between the two groups in the choice of spatial relations tests. Client reactions to the procedure differed. There was some indication that indecision about what tests to take was related to indecision in other areas.

Dressel and Matteson (1950) attempted to assess the effect of client participation in test interpretation. They started with three hypotheses: (1) that clients who participate more gain more in self-understanding; (2) that clients who participate more are more certain of their final vocational choice; and (3) that clients who participate more are more satisfied. Forty recorded interviews representing seven counselors were used. All subjects were freshmen who had taken a standard test battery. Interviews were rated by four judges on a client-participation scale, and students took a test of self-understanding and answered questions about their vocational satisfaction and security before, right after, and two months after counseling. Analysis of variance showed significant differences for counselors, students, and raters on the participation variable, with the difference between counselors the most pronounced. Differences between one counselor and another on client participation were related to two of the criteria, self-understanding and vocational security, but not to the third, satisfaction. This was true both immediately and two months after the conclusion of counseling. Differences between clients of the *same* counselor on the participation variable seemed *not* to be related to these things. That is, the counselors who succeed in getting clients to participate more seem to achieve more self-understanding and certainty of direction in them than do those who stimulate less participation. The related conclusion that *clients* who participate more get more out of the situation regardless of who the counselor is cannot, however, be drawn. Again this would seem to point to the importance of the counselor's personality and attitude rather than to the use of a standard technique.

Evaluation

If we base our conclusion on the research that has been done, we cannot assume that an inevitable effect of a counseling experience is to increase the amount of knowledge a client has about himself. The over-all "before and after" and "counseled versus non-counseled" comparisons are somewhat discouraging on this point.

The breakdowns of various kinds, however, point the way to progress in understanding what does happen. Improvements in self-estimates are more striking for some traits than others. It is a universal finding so far that clients do not gain any knowledge of their personality traits through the tests they have taken, but many studies show some gain in knowledge of interests and abilities. Results so far would indicate that differences in counselors have more to do with how much self-knowledge a client gains through counseling than differences in client personality do.

The advantage of any particular technique of test selection or interpretation over others has *not* been demonstrated. General interview climate is more important than specific interview characteristics such as length, amount of client talk, and the like.

What all of these results may suggest is that *communication* is much more complex and difficult than we have assumed it to be and that it would be desirable to study the communication process in counseling interviews far more intensively than it has been studied so far.

CHAPTER EIGHT

The Use of Occupational Information in Vocational Counseling

THE IMPORTANCE OF OCCUPATIONAL INFORMATION

In the short history of counseling as a profession, information about occupations has occupied a prominent position. It was the complexity of the situation a young person confronts when he tries to make an intelligent occupational choice that first made educators aware of the need for guidance. Since the beginning of our century, the vocational guidance movement has grown and flourished. Its principal organization, The National Vocational Guidance Association, is large and influential. Several government departments and dozens of private publishing companies have undertaken to provide occupational pamphlets and other printed material about jobs. Just how does all this activity and this wealth of resources fit into the general counselor's task which we have been describing?

Although there has been a tendency for schools to move forward from narrow vocational guidance services to broader counseling programs designed to meet a variety of student needs, we must never lose sight of the importance of occupational choice. A psychologically trained counselor may be more interested in the intricacies of personal attitudes than he is in facts about jobs, but those facts are just as essential as they ever were to young people planning their futures. He might prefer to leave to a specialist the task of providing clients with information of this sort, but in hundreds of high schools and colleges throughout the country a high degree of specialization in personnel services is impossible.

As the vocational guidance movement has grown, its emphasis has been less exclusively on the dissemination of occupational information. At the beginning it was thought that this was the chief if not the only thing it was necessary to do. It was assumed that a person who saw clearly what various jobs were like, what qualities they required in a man, and what their advantages and disadvantages were, would be in a position to decide without difficulty which one suited him best. Experience has taught us that a person is likely to be as ignorant of his own assets and liabilities as he is of job characteristics, and the testing movement has arisen as a result. More recently the importance of complicated attitudes and emotional factors in even apparently simple vocational decisions has forced itself upon us and much discussion in counseling circles now centers around these issues. What we must be careful of, as we move on to fresh emphases, is not to lose sight of the significance of those that preceded them. The whole problem of wise vocational choice is undoubtedly far more complicated than the pioneer guidance workers thought it was, but the client still needs to be given the relevant information about fields of work in a form that enables him to assimilate it.

The counselor or counseling trainee who sets out to acquire proficiency in the use of occupational materials is confronted with an embarrassment of riches. There are hundreds of books, thousands of pamphlets and leaflets. The flood of printed matter flowing from presses all over the country continues unceasingly. If one could by some superhuman effort read all of the publications available this week, he would find that by next week he was already in arrears, and that some of the things he had covered had become obsolete. This is of necessity a field in which one cannot know everything. The problem is one of selecting and organizing materials and of filing them for ready reference rather than of knowing all their contents.

In this area, as in the broad field of psychological testing, this book on the counselor's task cannot present all of the knowledge a practicing counselor needs about the world of occupations and the many ways in which individuals relate to it. Courses or special reading in occupations and vocational psychology are an indispensable part of a counselor's total preparation. Excellent books, such as those of Baer and Roeber (1958), of Shartle (1959), and of Super (1957), are available. The purpose of this chapter is not to repeat or try to summarize this material about occupations, but rather to show how the counselor makes use of it in his work with individual clients.

PURPOSES FOR WHICH OCCUPATIONAL INFORMATION IS USED IN COUNSELING

Various classifications have been proposed for the uses counselors make of occupational information. If we think of counseling as an experience that leads to choices, decisions, and life plans, we can include most of them under two main headings. The first of these is the formulation of alternatives. What many counselees need more than anything else is some organization of the confusing situation they face that will make it possible for them to deal with it. Some alternative vocational plans may serve to structure the situation enough so that a client can begin to think constructively about what he can do with all aspects of his life, the non-vocational as well as the vocational.

Peter Pyle, for example, may have no ideas at all about majors or careers when he comes to his college counseling service for help. Calling his condition "immaturity" does not help. He must begin as soon as possible to do the kind of thinking he did not do in his high school days. General discussion of interests and attitudes is helpful to such a person, but it is often more helpful to locate some feasible alternative kinds of career to which different college majors might lead. Because he is behind schedule in his "developmental tasks," he probably will not be able to settle definitely on one of these and be satisfied with his decision until he has done much more thinking, but he may be able to make a tentative decision that will guide him in the choices that face him right now—whether to meet his science requirement by taking chemistry or biology, for example. And he learns something in the process about how to do the thinking on which more important choices are based.

In another instance, Everett Johns may come to the counselor with just one question, "Would dentistry be a good career for me?" It is obvious to the counselor almost immediately that this is probably an impractical plan, since Mr. Johns shows a marked deficiency in his ability to handle the mathematical science courses that predental work requires. But to answer his question with a simple "No" leaves the boy all at sea, since at present this is the only idea he has about his future. What the counselor tries to do is to change this "Yes" or "No" structure into one made up of several alternatives with varying degrees of promise attached to them.

The important thing is not that the client ultimately chooses one of the alternatives suggested by the counselor. He is just as likely, if the counseling sessions are productive, to come up with some new alternatives of his own, that would never have occurred to him if he had not begun to do the kind of thinking the first structure made possible.

We can call this search for promising alternative courses of action the *exploratory* use of occupational information. It is often something that the client himself can be encouraged to do between interviews—to browse through some occupational presentations such as those one finds, for example, in the *Occupational Outlook Handbook,* and pick out several possibilities that look more interesting than the others.

It may be part of the counselor's activity in preparing for an interview. In this case he keeps in mind all the objective evidence he has from background records and tests about the client's abilities and deficiencies, interests and aspirations, while he systematically goes through lists or compilations of occupational information looking for possibilities. Volume II of the *Dictionary of Occupational Titles* (U.S. Emp. Serv., 1949) may give him clues, if he turns to the section of the classification system it presents which seems to fit his client's characteristics more closely. Part IV of the *DOT* (U.S. Emp. Serv., 1944) may furnish some leads. Even more helpful may be the newer volume (U. S. Bur. of Emp. Sec., 1956) in which ratings of 4000 jobs according to their requirements in abilities, interests, and temperament are presented. There is a variety of other sources to which he may turn. The kind of empathy or feeling for the inner world of the client is very important here if he is to hit upon job possibilities that can really be seen as possibilities by the person he is trying to serve.

The use of occupational materials for exploratory purposes continues during the time when the client is choosing between alternatives. At this stage, more complete information about each occupation is required. Questions having to do with the prospects for placement in a position when one's training is completed, the areas where one is likely to live and the amount of travel the work requires, the income and chances for advancement, and many other matters often take on considerable importance. What the client needs to do at this stage is to sense with as much clarity as possible the style of life that he will be involved in if he chooses to follow a particular path.

Much of the information of this sort must necessarily be obtained from sources other than printed materials. Although sociological studies delineating career patterns typical of certain occupations have been made, they cover as yet only a small minority of the jobs available to people in our society. Furthermore, such information of this kind as does exist has not found its way into the standard occupational materials, such as leaflets and monographs.

One way for a student to develop some understanding of an occupational life style is for him to talk to one of its practitioners. This is far from being a completely satisfactory method. Any one dentist, for example, cannot be representative of the dentistry profession, so that what Dr. Jones tells Bill Steele may be colored by his own biases and emotional attitudes. In one instance, a young college girl with marked aptitude for science went to talk to a woman chemistry instructor about her work. This woman was a frustrated, embittered individual with a grudge against the world because it had both cut her off from the normal feminine satisfactions and prevented her from rising to the top in her profession. The student came away from the interview confused and unhappy, with the general impression that science is no field for a woman. It is not likely that all women chemists would have put the case this way, although of course there are special problems faced by a woman in a characteristically masculine occupation.

In another instance, a college freshman whose interests and abilities pointed toward law as a suitable profession spent a day with a lawyer friend of the family observing his activities and talking to him about his work. The lawyer almost convinced him that there are now so many people coming out of law schools and attempting to enter the legal profession that the chances for any new person to make a success of it are negligible.

Incidents of this sort lead to caution about depending *entirely* on the information obtainable from personal sources. Career day assemblies, a common practice in some high schools, are subject to the same criticism of possible bias and non-representativeness. But if such information is a part of a counseling program, it has a useful place. During counseling interviews misconceptions can be corrected, and biased information counterbalanced by other facts. The important thing is that out of his counseling experience the client achieves a plan for his life that suits him. Deciding whether any particular plan does suit him is a complex problem, and all sorts of data are useable in solving it.

Another use of occupational information in counseling is in the elaboration of a plan after it has been chosen. At this stage a client needs some detailed factual information to guide him in his decisions about what to do next. If, for example, he plans to become a college teacher of economics, he may wish to consider the relative advantages of several different graduate schools and to find out what their standards for admission are. If he is heading toward one of the skilled trades, he will need information about apprenticeships and about union regulations. If he is a high school senior who plans to become a scientist, it may be important for him to obtain accurate information about scholarship possibilities at various colleges. Any practicing counselor could think of dozens of other specific questions that arise as individual counselees attempt to chart their courses for the future.

KINDS OF OCCUPATIONAL INFORMATION

We have seen how accurate factual information can be useful in helping clients explore, choose, and plan. It is a great advantage to a counselor if reference material of the kinds he will need to use are filed in a readily accessible place, so that his and the client's available time can be spent in assimilating facts rather than searching for them. Let us look at some of the kinds of information available. Some of it is in bound volumes, some in separate leaflets, pamphlets, and monographs.

In classifying the terrifically complex world of work, in his own mind and in his filing systems for printed material, some provision should be made for identifying both the *field* and the *level* that any particular job represents. Generally speaking, all jobs can be arranged in a space marked off by these two dimensions. *Field* refers to special kinds of activity that differentiate one type of work from others, the operation of machines, for instance, from the growing of plants. *Level* is a more complex idea, difficult to define precisely. Almost everyone knows what it means in a general way. Thus in the machine field the man who performs a repetitive operation in a factory ranks below the man who repairs the machines and keeps them in running order. He in turn represents a lower level than the person who installs the machines and organizes the sequence of processes. The engineer who designs them stands at the top of the pyramid. The level a job occupies within any occupational field depends a good deal on the intelligence required for it and the length of time that must be spent in education or special training in order to perform it. In some fields but not others the amount of specialized skill or talent is the deciding factor. The concert violinist probably differs from the average player in an orchestra in the extent to which he is endowed with whatever musical talent is. But the aeronautical engineer probably differs from the mechanic who services planes at the airport not in mechanical ability but in capacity for mastering the abstractions of higher mathematics. Not infrequently level depends upon circumstances and opportunity rather than upon any psychological factors.

The classification system used in the *Dictionary of Occupational Titles* has both field and level aspects. The first digit in the code number represents the level of the occupation in question, except for 2, which covers service occupations of all levels, and 3, which covers agricultural occupations of all levels. The subsequent digits represent differentiated fields. It is this structure that makes Volume II such a helpful tool for the first of the purposes outlined in the previous section, the search for alternative possibilities. As he goes over the material he has about a client, the counselor tries first to ascertain the person's most promising fields and to make an estimate of the level he is likely to be able to attain in each. He can then turn to the sections of the *Dictionary* in which jobs of this nature are listed and examine them in detail. Barney Hinson, for example, has a high clerical aptitude test score, above-average general intelligence, and a marked predilection for white-collar occupations. In view of these facts the counselor turns to the 1 section and runs his eye down over the long list he finds there. Since Barney seems to have shown somewhat more aptitude for working with figures than for working with words, he looks first at subsections headed 1-01, 1-02, 1-06, 1-08, 1-26, and 1-36. He finds some jobs with which he is not at all familiar. He looks them up in Volume I to find out what they are. Then he notices a group that had not entered his mind before, the Timekeepers. How would such a job suit Barney? At the end of this brief survey he has jotted down half a dozen possibilities that Barney has not mentioned and has probably never thought about. Some or all of them will come up for consideration in the next interview.

There have been more recent attempts to construct classification systems less ambiguous than the one used in the *DOT*. The culmination of this line of development is the system proposed by Super (1957). In addition to the two dimensions, *field* and *level*, it makes use of another, *enterprise*, to designate the kind of setting or organization in which the work is done. As such classifications are made available for general counseling use, it may be possible to locate more precisely than is now possible a number of suitable occupational alternatives for a person whose salient characteristics are known.

The concept of occupational level is related to what has in the past constituted one of the most troublesome problems in vocational counseling. Study after study, down through the years, has shown that too many young people aspire to professional careers, too few consider the "blue-collar" occupations. Consequently, a part of the counselor's task has always been to try to make his clients more realistic in their aims. This has been a special challenge with high school and college boys. Girls, and older men in rehabilitation or employment service settings, do not so typically make overambitious choices.

One method a counselor uses for encouraging realistic thinking is to present relevant facts about the comparative sizes of various occupations the person is considering and the number of new openings that occur each year. Another is to make the client aware of occupations at intermediate levels in the areas that interest him. It is a common occurrence for a college boy in academic difficulties to exclaim, "But I've *got* to make my grades and get a degree. I couldn't stand it to be a ditchdigger all my life!" A boy with a passion for airplanes may never have considered any occupation except pilot, although there are dozens of other jobs around planes that demand a high degree of skill and bring in good incomes. The girl who thinks she wants to be a doctor may be just as well pleased with physical or occupational therapy after she finds out something about what such specialized workers do.

It must be admitted, however, that to put a person in touch with intermediate level jobs does not always solve this counseling problem. There are many instances in which the lower-level occupation is *not* as attractive as the higher ones; the more authentic information a person gets the more clearly he realizes this. For example, one of the most attractive of all the professions at present seems to be medicine. Of the thousands of boys who start premedical courses each year, only a minority will complete medical courses and establish themselves as physicians. If those who are not outstandingly successful with the sciences could shift their attention to some other goal at the time they enter college, they could avoid bitter disappointment later and could more intelligently map out their preparation for the occupations they will eventually enter. But to the boy with his mind set on the prestige and income that go with success in the medical profession, any of the alternatives that may be presented are likely to appear dull and undesirable. A less demanding occupation within the medical field itself will look the dullest of all so that it is almost certain to be rejected outright. A career as a male nurse, an orderly, or an X-ray technician is no kind of equivalent for a career as a doctor in the thinking of boys who cling doggedly to their first choice.

This problem, which is perhaps unfortunately called "downgrading," leads us back to an emphasis on counseling situations that facilitate attitude changes. A realistic reduction in ambitions calls for occupational information, but it cannot be achieved by occupational information alone. If all the interviewing is done in a situation rich in acceptance and understanding, so that defensiveness has been minimized and the person has been able to grasp and accept his own limitations, realism and clear thinking may gradually win out over inflated expectations. The word *gradually* must be stressed. It takes time for deep-lying attitudes to change. A young man who insists at the time of his first interview that he will never relinquish his ambition to be a mechanical engineer may be able to modify his self-concept sufficiently so that when a *D* in calculus appears on his grade record he is willing to reconsider the whole matter. A girl with a pretty voice but limited musical talents will almost certainly not give up her dreams of an operatic career overnight, but if counseling releases her from a position where her very integrity depends upon maintaining that choice, she may find herself turning with something like relief to secretarial work or primary teaching. Because it is so fundamental to the success of all the other counseling skills, we have discussed before anything else the use of the interview to create a secure, non-threatening relationship.

During the 1950's, the task of helping young people to lower their vocational aspirations to appropriate levels has been receiving decreasing emphasis. The rapid changes in our economic structure have drastically reduced the need for many kinds of laborers, and tremendously increased the demand for professional, technical, and highly skilled workers of all kinds. We have become far more concerned about identifying talent and encouraging its development than about discouraging the less talented. "Upgrading" has become more important than "downgrading."

This constitutes a major change in counseling attitude, a change that may turn out to have marked effects on counseling theory and practice. It is still true, of course, that a boy with an IQ of 100 will probably not be able to get into a medical school and thus must be persuaded, through counseling or through bitter life experiences, to give up his dream of becoming a doctor. But counselors now see as a more important social responsibility the task of making the bright boy from a poor family and the girl from a family where women have never gone to college aware of the opportunities they have for personal development and service to society.

To discharge these duties successfully, the counselor must be familiar with occupational *trends* and have access to detailed information about them. The basic data for the two principal sides of our knowledge of trends, the size of an occupational field and whether it is increasing or decreasing, come from the census reports. Relative numbers of workers in the various occupations give us the first type of information. Comparisons of percentages decade by decade give us the second, at least in its long-term aspects. Fortunately it is not necessary that the counselor comb the census reports for these necessary facts himself. *The Occupational Outlook Handbook,* published by the U. S. Department of Labor (U. S. Bur. of Labor Stat., 1959), presents them in clear, readable form.

Here again a counselor must differentiate between broad general information in terms of which he habitually thinks and specific facts about specific jobs which he should be able to refer to in order to answer clients' questions. Material included in the first section of the *Occupational Outlook Handbook* is of the first sort, showing as it does what is happening to each of the major occupational divisions represented by the first digit of the *Dictionary* coding system. The professions constitute a numerically small group, but the proportion in them has been increasing steadily from decade to decade. Clerical and sales jobs make up a large *and* increasing division. The group of service occupations is of intermediate size, and the percentage of workers has also shown a steady increase although some subgroups such as domestic workers have declined markedly. Agriculture takes in a very large but constantly decreasing proportion of the country's workers. All of the laborer groups are large, with the skilled just about holding their own, the semiskilled increasing, and the unskilled decreasing. Such major trends can be kept in mind without difficulty. They should be supplemented by knowledge of which kinds of work people stay with longer before retirement, thus limiting replacement needs; how population increases are distributed over the country, thus making for regional differences; and which kinds of work are employing increasing numbers of women. All these main trends are sumarized with exceptional clarity in the *Occupational Outlook Handbook,* along with more detailed information with regard to each main field and industry and many individual jobs within each. It thus serves as both a source of essential general information for the counselor and a reference for both counselor and client when they are in search of specific facts. It is kept up to date by the publication of supplementary reports and periodic revisions.

In this area of knowledge it is not enough to learn the basic facts once and for all. Short-term trends are constantly grafting themselves into the long-term ones in ways which completely alter the outlook for individual occupations. The country undertakes an enlarged defense program, and the demand for engineers increases far more than would have been predicted from census data. Increasing birth rates resulting from wartime conditions create an almost insatiable demand for schoolteachers, whereas a change in selective-service policies curtails markedly the demand for college instructors. The counselor must form the habit of sensing the occupational implications of events as they occur. He must keep up with current materials as they come to him in pamphlets, journal summaries, and periodic reports of research organizations.

So far as trends for specific occupations are concerned, the better pamphlets include summaries of relevant information along with other facts. It is advisable to look for such summaries when choosing materials for the reference file.

The counselor should be thoroughly familiar with the variety and amount of education or special training required by the main kinds of work. Without making a special effort he is likely to know which occupations require a college degree, since he himself has come through that particular channel. By one means or another he must also find out how persons in clerical and sales, agricultural, service, skilled, and semiskilled occupations prepare for their jobs. For what groups do special trade schools function? In which do apprenticeship plans operate? What is the relationship of apprenticeship and trade schools to unions?

We touch on this subject only briefly because most of this material is of a local nature and must be obtained in the community and state where one lives. State departments of education are often prepared to furnish some of the information and to supplement it as need arises. Vocational schools, both public and private, are glad to send catalogs on request. Apprenticeship programs are often directed by a central agency which can give the counselor the facts about the trades in which the program operates and the type of young person it serves. The local employment office can tell him something about what employers are requiring in applicants for various jobs.

Knowledge of local demands and trends is also important. It cannot be assumed that a client will necessarily pass the remainder of his life in his home town or even in his home state, but he should certainly be informed as to which career plans are possible in the region and which are not. Often, too, the availability of training facilities in the area will make a great difference in whether or not a student can finance the kind of educational plan that suits him best.

At the choosing and planning stages of the vocational counseling process, it is important that counselor and client have access to detailed, dependable information about many aspects of the career under consideration—job duties, physical requirements, salary, training, and many other specific facts. To make this possible, counseling centers maintain files of current publications. A relatively small amount of money will procure a considerable quantity of pamphlet material, but care must be taken in its selection, and the file must be culled regularly to keep it free from obsolete information.

The National Vocational Guidance Association has formulated standards that can be used in evaluating printed materials (NVGA, 1939). In general, one considers how recent the facts presented are, how objective and free from bias the presentation is, and how well-organized and readable the pamphlet seems to be. The second of these criteria, the freedom from bias, is perhaps the most important. It can be judged partly from the reputation of the agency or organization issuing the information. Material put out by the Department of Labor, for example, is fairly sure to be accurate. One can judge objectivity also by noting the methods that were used in gathering the data, if this information is given. The texts on occupational information mentioned earlier have good discussions of these criteria and lists of sources from which materials may be obtained.

Besides this factual knowledge about employment outlook, job duties, income, and such matters, the counselor should have some awareness of the ideas and concepts emerging from on-going research in occupational psychology and sociology. As we indicated in an earlier section of this chapter, the kind of printed materials now available do not give a client this knowledge of the needs a kind of work can be expected to satisfy and the roles its practitioners must play in their communities. We have suggested that he try to get this by observation and by conversation with persons in the fields he is considering. It is helpful for the counselor to know that these things are important, so that he is able to set up and maintain an interview situation in which they can be thoroughly discussed.

INTEGRATING OCCUPATIONAL INFORMATION
WITH THE TOTAL COUNSELING PROCESS

This mention of the psychological and social meaning of work in the life of the individual brings us back to a consideration of the counseling process as a whole. Just when and how should various kinds of information be brought in? With individuals as different as they are and possible vocational plans as numerous as they are, we should not expect to be able to set up any one standard procedure; however, there are certain guiding principles that can be applied.

The first of these has to do with economy of the client's time. He should not have to acquire detailed information about occupations that are completely out of the question for him. This means that usually the facts about jobs should be brought in after he has taken the tests designed to get at individual strengths and weaknesses. There are naturally many exceptions to this order. Volume I of the *Dictionary* is often useful in the very first interview for clarifying the meaning of some job label which the client understands only vaguely. As in the case of other specific requests, a client who comes in asking for occupational information should probably be given it without too much delay, unless the thorough-going first interview indicates that the request does not represent what he is really seeking from counseling. The danger in injecting facts about one particular occupation into a case too soon is that a strong mental set in favor of one kind of career plan may be built up and the person be unable to accept later evidence suggesting his own unfitness or to consider alternative plans more in line with his abilities. Aside from this possibility, it wastes the time of counselor and client to spend any part of the initial interview, potentially so valuable for bringing out subtle attitudes, in discussing facts that may or may not have some bearing on the problems.

The question of how best to get pertinent information to those who need it is complicated by the fact that economy of clients' time is not always the same thing as economy in administrative costs. In many high schools and some colleges occupational information is brought to students on a group rather than an individual basis. Courses in occupations or units of this type in group guidance programs are very common. Counselors, of course, must carry on their work within whatever framework has been established, and the integration of counseling with group guidance activities may be a matter of major concern. There are obviously some sorts of information that can be given to groups as easily as to individuals. The main ideas with regard to occupational classifications and trends might well be understood by everyone. Courses to acquaint boys and girls with these important facts about our society can be an important part of general education. Much less, however, can be said for the common practice of requiring each person to make a thorough study of the one occupation in which he thinks he is especially interested. It is at this point that the class takes over a function it cannot discharge satisfactorily. In selecting an occupation for special research, the student is too likely to do casually and lightly something which should be done only after intensive thinking based on a thorough knowledge of his own psychological assets and liabilities. If good career plans could be made as simply as this, the whole vocational counseling movement would be superfluous. Furthermore, by choosing an occupation and learning more about it than he knows of any other, a person may set his thinking in a rigid mold that does not really fit him. Thus the assignment may turn out to have been not just useless but positively harmful. Classes in occupations should not attempt to carry the whole burden of vocational choice. Facts needed by individuals about their own particular vocational plans should be brought into some sort of relationship with individual counseling.

The second principle governing the use of occupational information in counseling is that it should be brought into the interview in such a way as not to break down or confuse the essential structure of the counseling relationship. If the counselor explains the facts in an authoritative way, the client may lose the sense that this is a situation in which he is to make his own decision and see it instead as one in which he is called upon to accept or reject a decision made for him by someone else. Young people are quick to perceive the opinions and biases of those who are in any sort of authority over them. The meaning a boy gets from the clearest objective explanation of the relative advantages of law, teaching, and sales work may be, "He thinks I should be a salesman." Once this has happened the whole climate of the interview is less favorable for a good decision than it was before, whether he decides to agree or to disagree with the recommendations.

The simplest way to avoid this restructuring of the counseling situation is to arrange things so that the client gets his facts from the printed materials themselves rather than from the counselor. This is not difficult to do if the materials are filed according to a clear-cut, easily understood system like the *Dictionary* classification recommended earlier in this chapter. In high schools the files can be kept in the school library. After several occupational possibilities have been discussed, the student can turn to the file and go ahead with his own research on them.

Like many other useful counseling procedures, however, this idea of letting the student read the facts himself has its limitations. Unfortunately the printed materials are often pitched at too high a level of reading difficulty for many clients. Usually the counselor will be aware by the time the information is needed of about how much reading skill the individual possesses. If there is any possibility that his skill is inadequate, it is better not to have him read the information for himself. The alternative is for the counselor to answer the client's questions and tell him what he wishes to know. It is necessary to take particular care not to mix advice with the information but to make it as objective and matter-of-fact as possible. Centering this part of the interview around the client's questions will help to keep the responsibility securely in his hands. For example, pointing to the collection of printed materials the counselor has brought into the office, he may say, "You see we have all sorts of information about the jobs you are interested in. What would you like to know first?"

A third principle in the use of occupational information is similar to one already discussed in connection with tests. There should be plenty of opportunity for the expression of feelings and attitudes. The girl who has been seriously considering social work needs a chance to express the disappointment she feels when she discovers what very low salaries many social workers receive. Otherwise she may not be able to give this factor its proper weight in her decision. The would-be psychiatrist may suffer a rude shock when he finds out that a complete medical course is required before specialization in psychiatry can begin. The expression and clarification of this feeling is an important part of counseling for him. The boy who wishes to be a forest ranger but craves professional security may be thrown into a quandary when he discovers how limited in size the occupation of forestry is and how few new openings there are each year. This conflict must be faced, not ignored or glossed over.

Thus if the first procedure is followed—that of letting the client browse through the files for the information he wants—it is advisable to schedule another interview to be held after he has done this. Uncertainties and conflicts can be aired, doubtful points cleared up, and a tentative final decision made. If the second procedure is followed—that in which the counselor tells the client what he wants to know—expressions of feeling can be recognized and reflected as soon as they occur, even if such apparent detours increase considerably the total time needed for counseling. It is especially important here that the counselor maintain his understanding but non-judgmental attitude. He must not take it upon himself either to justify existing occupational requirements or to sympathize with the client's protests. He may himself be of the opinion that a medical course for psychiatrists is superfluous or that social workers' salaries are far too low, but for him to bring in his own views at this point is to deflect the interview from its purpose, which is not the sharing of views on controversial issues but the facilitation of the client's decision based on acceptance of the situation he must meet.

Whether one is interested in the improvement of our society through the wise use of the talents of its citizens or in positive mental health for the individual through the development of his potentialities, the relationship between people and their jobs is of crucial importance. It is well worth the continuing effort a counselor must make to increase his skill in dealing with the facts and the attitudes, the physical and the psychological aspects of the world of occupations.

Research Summary

EVALUATION OF PUBLISHED MATERIALS

Although there has been a vast amount of occupational material published, there has actually been very little research evaluating its effectiveness in counseling or showing how it can best be used. C. H. Stone (1948) compared 118 students who took vocational orientation courses with 140 who did not, using a variety of before-and-after measures and ratings to show effects on choices and attitudes. The experimental group had more occupational information than the controls and had apparently applied what they had learned in "downgrading" themselves somewhat, since the levels of their choices were somewhat more realistic. When the appropriateness of their choices was rated, however, it appeared that only the students who had had counseling in addition to the course showed a significant improvement. Moreover, those who had both the course and counseling were superior in this respect to those who had had counseling alone. Speer and Jasker (1949) have also reported that the suitability of occupational choices is improved by either work experience or guided reading discussed with a counselor and that the best choices result when both are combined.

Three studies have evaluated published vocational material on criteria closely related to its usefulness to counselors. Brayfield and Reed (1950) used the French formulas to analyze the difficulty level and interest value of 78 pieces of occupational literature selected from the offerings of various publishers. Almost two thirds of them ranked in the "very difficult" or "scientific" levels, and 32 per cent in the "difficult" classification. About the same proportions fell into the "dull" and "mildly interesting" categories on the other variable. Fewer than 5 per cent were at the readability level of our popular magazines. Obviously this is not as it should be. Brayfield and Mickelson (1951) surveyed almost 6,000 references listed in two different indices of occupational materials to discover how adequately the titles covered the various levels of work in our society. They found that the occupational literature is too much concentrated in the white-collar and professional fields. About 44 per cent of the *Occupational Index* titles, for example, and about 31 per cent of the titles from the Forrester list represent professional occupations, whereas only 30 per cent of the former and 37 per cent of the latter titles represent the skilled, semiskilled, and unskilled areas in which the majority of workers must find employment. The authors point out that this unbalanced distribution handicaps the counselor in several ways and helps to perpetuate the tendency of young people to choose occupations above the level of their ability.

Watson, Rundquist, and Cottle (1959) used two readability formulas to evaluate the *Occupational Outlook Handbook* and three other pieces of occupational information selected at random from each of the twelve leading commercial publishers. All had been published since 1954. They found most of the material to be at the eleventh- or twelfth-grade reading level, obviously too difficult for many high school students and rehabilitation clients.

THE FUNCTIONAL OCCUPATIONAL CLASSIFICATION

A reclassification of occupations designed to give prospective workers more of the information they need in considering occupations has been in progress for several years under the auspices of the U. S. Bureau of Employment Security, Department of Labor. The most comprehensive publication to date on this system (1956) lists 4,000 jobs and after each gives information about its requirements in terms of aptitudes, interests, temperamental qualities, physical capacities, working conditions, training time, and industries in which it occurs. S. A. Fine and Heinz (1957) discuss this reference work in a journal presentation.

S. A. Fine (1955) and Fine and Heinz (1958) explain the new numerical classification system that will replace the one now being used in the *Dictionary of Occupational Titles*. There will be a nine-digit code serving to classify occupations by worker traits, by work field, and by product. There are three separate hierarchies of functions for Things, Data, and People. These make it possible to determine the level of any particular job by identifying what the worker does and noting where that operation is located in the appropriate hierarchy.

In a study of Foreign Service clerical workers, Walther (1960) found that the factors that make up the Functional Occupational Classification System did not differentiate one kind of worker from another or distinguish between superior and inferior workers, whereas questionnaire information about family background, hobbies, interests, and school records did. Details of the study are not given in this publication, so that it is not possible to determine whether it really constitutes a serious criticism of the new system.

OCCUPATIONAL INFORMATION
RELATED TO SOCIAL ROLES

Occupational sociology is a flourishing research specialty, but not very much of the information it is turning up has come to the attention of the counseling profession as a whole. Smigel (1954) has pointed out the significance of this material, and Danskin (1957b) has summarized the findings about a wide variety of occupations—physicians, labor union officials, furriers, hotel administrators, lumberjacks, machinists, and many others. Becker and Carper (1956) report an interview study of graduate students in physiology, engineering, and philosophy and make a descriptive analysis of differences between the roles involved.

Research studies are beginning to appear in which the simultaneous effects of sociological and psychological factors are explored. Brophy (1959) tested the hypothesis that congruence between concepts of the person and concepts of the environment should make for job satisfaction. His subjects were 81 Veterans Administration nurses who reacted to several questionnaires and inventories designed to reveal the person's concept of herself, concept of the occupational role, general satisfaction, and job satisfaction. In accordance with the hypothesis, it was found that persons with large discrepancies between self- and job-concepts tended to have lower satisfaction scores than those who saw self and job as more alike. General satisfaction and vocational satisfaction showed a correlation of .50. In a study like this one where the conclusions rest on correlations, it is not possible to determine which variable is cause and which is effect. Does a feeling of satisfaction influence a subject to rate her job and self characteristics in similar ways, or do real similarities produce the satisfaction?

Siegelman and Peck (1960) used a different technique. To start with they formulated personality models that would fit the roles of Chemist, Minister, and Military Officer. They then selected 16 representatives of each of these occupational groups and studied them by means of tests, interviews, and a biographical-data form. They found a considerable number of significant differences in the directions predicted, and none of the differences were in conflict with the predictions. In other words, the personality models seemed to fit.

PERSONALITY DIFFERENCES
BETWEEN OCCUPATIONAL GROUPS

A study like the preceding one is representative of the increasing research interest in the subject of personality differences between occupational groups. The dominant theoretical formulation has been that put forward by Roe (1956, 1957). The principal ideas are that different occupations do require persons with different emotional needs and that these emotional needs with their overlay of feelings, attitudes, interests rest on the kinds of emotional relationships with parents experienced in infancy and early childhood.

Several studies furnish some evidence for the first of these ideas—that there is a relationship between personality needs and occupations. Schaffer (1953) devised a questionnaire for measuring the strength of each of twelve needs. His subjects, 72 young men predominantly at upper occupational levels, were asked to rate themselves in the twelve needs and also to indicate the extent to which their respective jobs permitted satisfaction of each of the needs. A correlation of .58 between job satisfaction and the extent to which the highest needs were satisfied supports the hypothesis. As indicated above, however, there is some ambiguity in correlational studies of this type.

Small (1955) rated 389 students in a two-year institute of arts and sciences for 27 personality needs, on the basis of a special job concept interview with each person. Subgroups of students in the different training programs, Art, Retail, Dental Hygiene, and Medical Technology, differed significantly in their patterns of need strengths.

Merwin and DiVesta (1959) compared college students preparing for teaching with non-teaching majors on scales designed to measure the strengths of certain needs, the extent to which teaching was seen as satisfying certain needs, and general attitude toward teaching. They introduced an experimental variable, a prospective radio program which subjects were asked to evaluate. One form of this communication contained material indicating that teaching *satisfies* the need for achievement. The other form indicated that teaching *does not satisfy* achievement needs. Various differences between teaching and non-teaching groups in original need and attitude scores and in response to the positive and negative communications were explored. Several kinds of differences were in evidence.

The relationship of needs to occupational attitudes was investigated in a different way by Walsh (1959). His subjects, 96 male college students, took the Edwards Personal Preference Schedule, which gives scores purporting to show the strength of different needs in the personality. They also reacted to fictitious job descriptions, each made up of eight statements referring to the way in which the job satisfies eight needs. They were asked to tell which job features should be "played up" and which "played down" in recruiting for the occupation. Correlations in the expected directions, significant but not high, were obtained between measured personality needs and job features emphasized. Minor and Neel (1958) found a sizable rank-difference correlation (rho = .74) between the occupational prestige levels of occupations chosen by 53 male Korean veterans and their scores on Need Achievement, measured by McClelland's projective method.

OCCUPATIONAL CHOICE AND EARLY CHILDHOOD EXPERIENCES

Roe's hypothesis that fundamental personality needs are related to occupational choice is substantiated by much of the research summarized in the foregoing section. Her other hypothesis, that both the personality traits and the occupational attitudes are related to early experience in the home, has fared less well. Grigg (1959) compared 24 graduate nurses (presumably basically oriented toward "persons") with 20 graduate students in physical science (presumably oriented toward "non-persons") on a 15-item questionnaire designed to reflect the parents' attitudes and the child's response to them for each subject. The differences between groups were slight and non-significant.

Utton (1960) used 33 social workers and 26 occupational therapists as a Person-Oriented group, 41 dieticians and 28 lab technicians as a Non-person-Oriented group. Although the two groups did differ significantly on the Social scale of the Allport-Vernon-Lindzey Study of Values, they did not differ on their ratings of childhood experiences.

Hagen (1960) analyzed the references to childhood atmospheres in the case material of the 245 men who participated in the Study of Adult Development at Harvard. The original data on these subjects was obtained during their college years, 1938-1942. Their careers have been followed through 1953 and in some cases through 1956. Rated family atmospheres showed only a chance relationship to career choice in this group.

None of these studies has furnished a definitive test of the Roe hypothesis, since none of the subjects have actually been studied during their early years. But the evidence as far as it goes is negative.

STUDIES OF WOMEN'S OCCUPATIONAL ATTITUDES

It has long been recognized by practicing counselors that most girls do not think about careers in the same way that boys do. The Strong Vocational Interest Blank for Women suggests that there is some sort of basic distinction between career-motivated women and the majority of women whose high scores are confined to the scales for Housewife, Office Worker, and Stenographer-Secretary. Hoyt and Kennedy (1958) divided a class of 407 college-freshmen women into career and homemaking groups, on the basis of a questionnaire dealing with their plans. All subjects took the Strong and the Edwards Personal Preference Schedule. The expected differences were obtained on 14 of the Strong scales. On the EPPS, career women showed higher needs for Achievement, Intraception, and Endurance, and lower needs for Succorance and Heterosexuality.

White (1959) attempted to relate these attitudes to relationships between girls and their parents. His subjects were also freshman girls in college. Each filled out a personal data sheet and the Strong Vocational Interest Blank and, in addition, made Q-sorts representing self, ideal self, and parents' ideal for the daughter. Fathers and mothers made Q-sorts to describe the daughter as she is and as they would like her to be. The Q-sorts of the daughters were more like those of the mothers than those of the fathers. Girls with typical feminine scores on the Strong showed higher correlations than the career girls did between self and ideal, and between self and parents' descriptions. The career girls were more likely to have come from homes where one parent was deceased.

It would appear that these special occupational attitudes of girls, like the general occupational attitudes discussed in previous sections, are tied in with personality needs.

Evaluation

Factual information about occupations is plentiful but pitched at too high a reading level for maximum usefulness. A new classification of occupations based more on worker requirements than on objective features of the job is being put into operational form. It is doubtful, however, whether any of the published occupational materials now available or soon to be available includes enough information about the social roles or the basic personality traits related to each job. A fair amount of research is available showing that both considerations are important. We shall consider studies having to do with the actual process of occupational choice in the research summary following Chapter 10.

CHAPTER NINE

General Use of

Information in Counseling

INFORMATION A VITAL PART OF COUNSELING

In the preceding chapters we have been considering kinds of information that are essential in vocational counseling, the oldest and best-developed branch of our specialty. The principles that have grown out of experience in this particular kind of counseling activity are widely applicable. It is these broader aspects of the use of information to which we will now turn our attention.

The situation in which a counselor works determines the kind of information about which he needs to develop expertness. A school counselor whose clients are mainly students in the last year of high school must be thoroughly familiar with sources of information about college requirements and programs, scholarships, and other financial aids, schedules and fees for College Entrance Board Examinations, vocational schools and apprenticeship programs, and many other specific things with which other counselors even in the same school may have only an incidental acquaintance. Fortunately, a number of excellent reference works in which many of these facts can be found are now available. (See Lovejoy, B. Fine, Feingold.)

A marriage counselor must be able to put his clients in touch with reliable sources of sex information. He must know the divorce laws of his state more thoroughly than the average citizen does. He must be able to distinguish between fact and opinion about the effects of broken homes on children. Although his main task is to help husbands and wives clarify their feelings and explore the possibilities of their relationship, decisions about whether to break it or continue it often involve these and many other kinds of information.

Counselors working with the parents of children needing help must know a great deal about child psychology. They may also need to have more information than most counselors typically do about school resources and about the many agencies in the community that have been set up to serve children. The parents of a feeble-minded child may need to be told as clearly as possible what the functioning level of their child is now and what it is likely to be in the future. The parents of an unusually bright child may need to have the research findings about gifted children summarized for their consideration.

Rehabilitation counseling calls for detailed knowledge of the effects of physical and mental impairments of many kinds on functioning in many specific situations. Pastoral counseling requires theological knowledge as well as many of the other kinds we have been considering. Counselors in agencies dealing with problems of heredity need to know everything possible about the genetic bases of human diseases and traits upon which research has been done. The list of classes of information needed by counselors in specific situations could be extended indefinitely.

INFORMATION DOES NOT MEAN ADVICE

As explained in the historical sketch in Chapter 1, during the 1940's and 1950's the non-directive or client-centered approach to counseling became increasingly influential. As counselors picked up these ideas and began to use them as standards for evaluating themselves and their colleagues, many of them came to believe that the best counseling required that one *tell* the client as little as possible. The belief rested on the assumption that each person has within himself all the resources that he needs to solve his own problems and chart his own course. If this were so, the counselor's task would be to release this knowledge and make it available rather than to impart it.

As time has passed, many distinctions that were not noticed by early adherents of Rogerian principles have become apparent. For one thing, there are differences between kinds of questions with which a counselee may be wrestling. If his efforts center around matters like, "Why can't I study?" "Why am I so moody?" "What can I do to make people like me better?" there is obviously no reference book in which factual answers can be found. But if the questions are about matters like, "Which is the best college for me?" "Shall I give up my job in the insurance office and enter training program for rehabilitation counselors?" or "How does one go about it to adopt a child in this state?" there are sources of dependable information that can reduce the amount of uncertainty the person faces and thus facilitate his thinking.

This distinction leads to a simple rule for a counselor to follow. If a client needs information in order to think soundly about something that concerns him, he should be helped to obtain it. Unfortunately, as indicated earlier, the questions that are brought up first do not always indicate what it is that a client really needs, and to deluge him with irrelevant information is no more helpful than to withhold essential information. A mother whose ostensible reason for coming to the counselor is to find out how she can arrange to have her four-year-old Roger tested so that she can determine whether or not he is really an unusually gifted child may really need to examine her attitudes toward Roger and toward her husband, rather than to be made aware of Roger's IQ. If she is focusing all of her hopes and dreams around this boy, there may be trouble ahead for the whole family whether his IQ is 180 or a bare 100. Students often come to a college counseling center for help with the choice of a career or major when what they really wish to clear up is their relationships with family and friends. As has been said in earlier chapters, if the initial interview is successful, there will be some clarification of what the client is really seeking from counseling before the hour ends.

Another distinction not always recognized by those who insist on following Rogerian principles dogmatically is the difference between information and advice. It is perfectly possible to transmit one without the other. For example, Mr. Girard, Ben's high school counselor, realizes that the boy's plans for a career in engineering are probably unsound, since his high school grades are not high, his mathematics and science grades in particular never having risen above the C-level, and his science percentile on an achievement test with national norms is only 38. It is part of Mr. Girard's duty as a counselor to bring this information about Ben's level of achievement in science to his attention and to make sure that the boy also knows just what pattern of courses is required for engineering programs in college. He may wish also to advise him strongly to change his plans, but it is not *necessary* that he do this in giving the information.

Counselors who are not committed to any one theoretical point of view or technique still consider advice-giving to be indicated in some cases, but they use this technique much less frequently than information giving. The main trouble with advice, practically speaking, is that it is very likely to be ineffective. When the counselor tells Ben what he ought to do, his voice is only one among many. It is likely that Ben's father, his mother, his classmates, and perhaps neighbors, uncles, and aunts, as well, are all giving him advice. Most of them may be saying, in effect, "Why don't you go ahead and try it? If you really work, I know you can get good grades in your courses." It is quite likely that this point of view will appeal to him more than the counselor's does, so that he will adopt it. From then on, the fact that he has not followed the advice the counselor gave him may set up a barrier between them, making him unwilling to turn to him or to some other counselor at a later time.

A more fundamental reason for reducing advice-giving to a minimum even in a situation where a great deal of information of various kinds is transmitted is that basically counseling requires keeping responsibility in the client's hands. Whether one looks upon this as an ethical principle that should never be violated or as a useful generalization that fits in with the kind of service counseling agencies are prepared to give, it leads to the same policy with regard to advice. Regardless of how the counselor means it to be taken, the client is likely to get the impression that someone else has accepted some of the responsibility for his life. Such an impression can lead to a relationship in which he returns to the counselor time after time with questions like: "Now what do I do?" "I tried what you suggested and it didn't work. What do you think I should try now?" There is little if any disagreement among counselors that it is better for the client to see the decision as his own, to accept its consequences realistically, and to deal more effectively with later decisions, because of what he has learned in making this one.

Imparting sound, relevant information without advice tends to accentuate rather than to blur the pattern of client responsibility in the counseling relationship. Giving a person factual information bearing on some complex issue implies that one thinks he has the capacity to make use of it. Along with the facts themselves the counselor communicates to the client that he respects his intelligence, his ability to do realistic constructive thinking. If the counselor's attitude is really sincere (and we assume that he would not have presented the information at this time had it not been), the counseling partnership is strengthened by the communication.

ESSENTIAL CHARACTERISTICS OF INFORMATION

The characteristics information must have if it is to be useful in counseling have been discussed in previous chapters with particular reference to tests and occupational materials. It is the general aspects of these characteristics that are to be brought together here. The first of these is that information must be *accurate* and free from bias. As applied to tests, this means that they should be as reliable as possible and that evidence showing what they measure should be available and known to the counselor. As applied to publications about occupations, this means that they should contain actual facts about the work performed, the salaries, the nature of the training, and so on, rather than generalities or propaganda put out for recruiting purposes. Sex information should consist of what is actually known about the behavior in question, its origins and its effects, rather than moralistic interpretations of it. College information should come from official statements of requirements and policies rather than from someone's impression as to what these are.

One of the most pervasive sources of bias is the client's own wishes and the counselor's awareness of them. For example, it is often very difficult to tell a person that he has scored decisively low on some test he has taken. If Louis Grant has a percentile rank of five on a highly reliable test of college aptitude that correlates even moderately well with scholastic success at the school he is considering, the counselor's duty is to make him aware of his deficiency. It is not enough to say, "Your test score indicates, Louis, that you may have a little difficulty with college work," and reply to his next question by saying, "Well, your score was below the average for students at Blackwood University."

One good way to communicate this information without bias but without advice or pressure is to use expectancy tables and state, "Of students making scores at the level of yours, only ten out of a hundred succeed in meeting the college standards during their freshman year and only five out of a hundred graduate." Whether Louis decides to enter this college or not, this is what he needs to know, and to gloss over the fact of his handicap because we know how much he wishes to go to the college where his friends are going is to be unfair to him.

Any practicing counselor will encounter many situations where this kind of subtle bias—this natural desire to tell the client what he wishes to hear—can operate. The person with idiopathic or essential epilepsy, adequately controlled by drugs so that he is not troubled by symptoms, may desperately wish to be assured that his children will not inherit the epileptic tendency. It is easy enough for the counselor to say, "The evidence is not altogether clear," and leave him free to believe what he likes about it. It is much more difficult to summarize just what the available evidence does show about the inheritance of this condition in a way that the client can grasp and use in making the important decision about whether or not to have children. The man who is enraged about his wife's unfaithfulness may be eager to believe that if he divorces her he can obtain custody of their two children and place them in the care of his mother. It is important for him to know what the laws of his state specify about such cases and what the policy of the courts has been in the past.

Another source of bias is a tendency a counselor may have to rely on his own experience instead of looking up the facts. Jennie Johnson is interested in nursing. Mr. Billings, the counselor, has a wife who is a nurse. What could be more natural than for him to answer the girl's questions by passing on what his wife has told him? There are many reasons why this is not adequate. Training standards and methods may have changed since Mrs. Billings entered the field, and the kind of program Jennie is considering may be quite different from the one the older woman underwent. The way she and her husband see the nursing profession is inevitably colored by their experience with particular hospitals, particular doctors, a particular community. These personal slants on nursing may be helpful to a girl thinking about it, but they should be supplementary rather than total sources of information.

Another characteristic that is essential for information used in counseling is *recency*. In connection with occupational materials, it has been stressed that pamphlets and leaflets are ordinarily more accurate than books, because they can be revised more frequently and discarded when obsolete. Files should be culled at frequent intervals, so that information misleading because it is out of date can be removed. The same principle holds for all kinds of information—college catalogs, books of etiquette, legal opinions, research findings on medical and psychological issues, and a host of others. The student contemplating enrollment in graduate school should compare his score on the Graduate Record Examination with the norms for persons now being admitted to such schools, not with those for persons admitted a decade ago. A rehabilitation client with heart disease must consider what is now seen as a desirable amount of exercise for persons with his condition, not what was considered so by medical opinion in the 1940's. This constant search for the latest information in the areas of greatest concern to the clients with whom he deals is one of the things that makes a counselor's life stimulating.

As well as its accuracy and recency, a counselor must of course consider the *availability* of various information sources. Those to which he can refer the client directly with the assurance that the information needed will appear in an understandable form are of most value. In some areas, standard reference books serve this purpose, at least for clients who are competent readers. College catalogs, compilations of information about schools and colleges such as those of Lovejoy and Fine, and the *Occupational Outlook Handbook* are of this nature. Often the most readily available sources of dependable information are *people* to whom the client can be referred. This is typically the case where legal or medical information is needed. But in some cases it will probably be necessary for the counselor himself to ferret out information clients need. This may require that he look up a journal article in the college library, that he correspond with a colleague in another institution, or that he telephone several social agencies to find out about particular resources they have to offer. It is good policy in a counseling agency to keep the major published sources of information on hand at all times in counseling offices or library. It is also good policy, however, for the individual counselor not to limit himself to such sources, but to use all of the ingenuity he can command to locate the facts required by particular clients who do not follow the common pattern.

PROBLEMS OF COMMUNICATION

One thing that counselors have learned in the course of their work is that it is not as easy to impart information as people tend to think that it is. As indicated in the Research Summary following Chapter 7, a distressingly large proportion of students who have undergone extensive testing of abilities and interests come out of their counseling interviews no wiser about their own characteristics than they were before. It is no surprise to any experienced counselor for a client to ask a naïve question about something that has just been explained to him or to make a comment that shows a serious misconception of some fact discussed in previous interviews. We are beginning to realize how complex the task of meaningful communication is.

To some extent, this difficulty may arise simply from the fact that a person's attention span is limited so that he grasps only a fraction of what is said. But some of the research on the communication of test results would suggest that the phenomenon of selective perception is also involved. A person's expectations and wishes serve as a filter that lets only part of the data through.

The first implication of this state of affairs is that the presentation of necessary information ought to be *planned* very carefully. On the basis of his early interview or interviews with a client and whatever other kinds of background and test data are available, the counselor forms a more or less accurate "working image" of the person. This can serve as a guide to him in planning how to introduce information. For instance, Stan Hillman has been making *C*'s and *D*'s in the chemistry and biology courses his premedical program requires. He is realistic enough to see that his chances of entering a first-rate medical school are negligible and that it would be advisable for him to shift to some other plan now, during his second year in college, rather than to wait until he has graduated. He is considering clinical psychology and dentistry as substitutes for the medical career that appears to be out of his reach. His scores on tests of college aptitude and achievement classify him a little below average for students in colleges of moderate standards. Mr. Sanders, the counselor in the case, knows that the requirements for graduate work in clinical psychology or for professional training in dentistry are just as much out of Stan's reach as the medical school requirements are. How shall he tell him this? To state the fact flatly without any regard for the boy's need for professional status and his present structure of beliefs and attitudes about the fields in question is likely to be an ineffective way of proceeding. Stan will simply close his mind to the ideas presented.

What Mr. Sanders is likely to do is to direct Stan to the catalogs and supplementary information in which the bases for admitting students to the programs in question are clearly set forth. At the same time he will bring up for consideration any other promising alternative possibilities that have occurred to him as he considered Stan's abilities, interests, needs, and attitudes. He will arrange for another interview to take place after Stan has read the material and had a chance to think it over. On this occasion it is likely that the client himself will express doubts about his fitness for psychology or dentistry and devote some attention to alternative possibilities, either those Mr. Sanders has mentioned or some others that have occurred to him independently. What the counselor has attempted to do by this procedure is to modify the structure of Stan Hillman's thinking enough so that the facts he needs can be given a place in it. It is possible that he will still decide to steer his course toward dentistry until he is absolutely certain that he cannot continue in that direction. It is not the counselor's responsibility to make this decision for him. But it is his job to see that the most dependable knowledge available is not only presented but also really grasped and used in the thinking that leads to the decision.

The second implication of the communication problem for counselors is that there must always be opportunity for "feedback" from the client if misunderstandings are to be avoided. Lecture methods, in which a considerable quantity of information is presented in one package, as it were, are out of place here. In the example given above, much of the interview time will be devoted to Stan's response to what he has read. In another sort of situation, where the counselor has decided that the most promising plan is to present a sequence of facts in the interview itself and has decided what that sequence is to be, the procedure may be to take up one of these facts at a time and then ask an open-ended question that will encourage the client to comment on it. Whatever is not clear to him at this point can be repeated in different words or explained more fully. In other instances it will seem best to lay out for consideration several facts that have some relationship to one another and then wait for the client to think out loud about this relationship. There are many ways to structure the information-giving situation, but they all have in common the practice of waiting for client response before proceeding from one step to the next. Needless to say, this response when it comes *may* make all the rest of the plan, as carefully formulated ahead of time, inapplicable. It is of the essence of counseling that the client's needs always take precedence over the counselor's plans.

It also goes without saying that the whole interview atmosphere should be warm and non-threatening, as indicated in previous chapters. It should be evident at all times that the counselor is on the client's side in his struggles for understanding and mastery—that he is not using unwelcome facts as weapons against him. The structure should always be: "These are the facts. This is the reality we face. How can we best come to terms with it?" No amount of preliminary planning or careful structuring of interviews will be effective if the counseling relationship is not solid.

It is increasingly clear to counselors and others who are concerned in some special way with the communication process that meanings can be thought of as successive approximations. This idea applies to many other kinds of communication as well as counseling—conversation, teaching, psychotherapy. Something is said by one participant and partially understood by the other. If conditions for the interchange are favorable, Person Number Two will say, "You mean. . . ." and will proceed to paraphrase Number One's remark. Number One in turn will respond, "Well, not exactly. . . ." and proceed to clarify some part of his former message. After five or six of such clarifications the point Number One was originally trying to make may be completely understood by Number Two. This is not a matter of stupidity or obtuseness on the part of either participant. Because of individual differences in experience and background, I simply cannot assume that the words I say mean precisely the same thing to the listener as they do to me. I must know how he interprets them, and he must know how I interpret them, before we can understand one another completely. In the course of casual contacts between human beings, such effort to communicate exact meanings is not necessary, but in counseling it is.

There is one more aspect of the communication of information in counseling that should be considered. It is not enough that a client understand clearly some facts he has not considered before. He must *assimilate* what he has learned, and this sometimes involves difficulties. The example of Stan Hillman discussed above pointed to one of the counseling skills that is helpful here. If the structure of the client's thinking about some particular question or problem can be modified, the assimilation of new facts will be facilitated. Quite often this modification will be along the lines suggested in the Hillman example. Adding more alternative courses of action to a structure in which the client originally sees only one or two paths open to him makes room for much more knowledge about himself and life situations. Sometimes a shift to another *value* as a basis of organization serves to modify structure. It may be apparent, for instance, that both creativity and social status are important to a college girl. The impasse a broken engagement has led her to in her quest for social status may be less serious if she can focus more sharply on creativity and thus begin to see some possibilities in herself and her surroundings that were not visible when her whole attention was focused on the social goal.

It must also be recognized that assimilation of new information, directly related to one's self and one's plans takes *time*. One cannot expect it to occur during a single interview. The important process is the one that continues after the interview is over, for days, weeks, or even months. Thus it is usually wiser not to insist that a client accept facts that have been presented to him, but rather simply to suggest that he think about them. Another interview at a later time can be scheduled for decision-making purposes. By then he may show a different orientation from the one in evidence now. He will have had time to modify the total structure of his thinking and to explore the effects of the changes in viewpoint on other areas of his life.

Some authorities have defined counseling as *deeper teaching,* and seen it as a skillful, personalized technique of educating an individual in ways not possible in the classroom. Whether or not this definition is adequate to cover the whole circle of counseling activities, it represents a very important sector of it. Sharpening one's communication skills improves the quality of the counseling one does, whether he is a person with twenty years of experience or a novice beginning counseling training. One of the urgent needs in counseling research is the kind of analysis of interviews that would tell us something about factors that facilitate and retard the client's understanding and assimilation of relevant information. Let us hope that the years ahead will provide us with more knowledge in this area.

CHAPTER TEN

Decision-Making Interviews

EXAMPLES OF THE DECISION PROCESS

Much counseling is oriented toward the making of choices and decisions. Sometimes they are large and far-reaching, sometimes they are small and apparently trivial, but always they have some special significance for the person who makes them. For one thing, each decision helps to determine the unique pattern of the individual's personality. Each is to some extent irrevocable, since even if one goes back to the fork in the road and takes the other turning, he cannot eradicate the effects of the experience the first choice has given him. For another thing, there seems to be a *general* skill in the making of decisions, a skill which counseling can help one to learn. Once a person has made a plan for some segment of his life which he is content to abide by, he is better able to make the next one intelligently and without too much hesitation and conflict.

We cannot really single out certain types of interview and say that they and they alone fall in this category of decision-making interviews since any interview may involve some decision-making, regardless of its main purpose. But perhaps we can gain a better understanding of what the process is and how it can be facilitated by thinking about what goes on in three kinds of situation. The first is one in which a school counselor helps a boy or girl decide on a course of study. The second is a vocational-planning interview that follows the accumulation of information about a person and about the jobs and training courses that he is considering. The third is a conference in which a young woman decides what action to take on behalf of her child.

Let us look first at what goes on in the short conference Jim Harris has with his college adviser to map out a freshman program.

JIM: Gee, I'm all mixed up. I certainly hope you can straighten me out.

ADVISER: Pretty confusing business, this registration. I expect you'll be glad when this week is over.

JIM: I sure will! (*He takes out his registration materials and spreads them out on the desk.*)

ADVISER: You know what the procedure is—what you are supposed to do with this blank and these cards?

JIM: Oh, yes. They told us that at the meeting last night. I'm supposed to put down the courses I'm going to take on this card. Then you sign it and I take it around to the departments the courses are in. It's deciding what to put down that bothers me. What do you think I should take?

ADVISER: Perhaps if you told me a little more about yourself—what your general plans are and what you want to get out of college—it would help us decide.

JIM: I've never really thought very much about it, I guess—just took things as they came in high school. I've done all right but haven't been too outstanding in anything. I suppose I've always assumed that I would go into business some day like my father. You probably know my father, Cuthbert and Harris, you know.

ADVISER: Of course. I don't think I've met your father, but I know the store. Is there some possibility then that you will go into your father's business with him?

JIM: Well, that's what he wants, of course, and I suppose that's what I'll do in the end. I probably ought to take a Business Administration course. The only trouble with that is that it says here in the catalog that you are required to take accounting before you can take anything else, and I don't know about that. The boys at the house say that's the hardest freshman course there is. They've got me scared. I'd hate to get some low grades the first term and have to drop out of college.

ADVISER: You want to be sure you don't do the wrong thing. You know probably that the placement test you took yesterday is supposed to tell you how you compare with other entering students in ability to handle college work.

JIM: I've got that score here on this other card they gave me. It says 5. What does 5 mean?

ADVISER: That is just an average rating. It means that there are just about as many freshmen with lower scores than yours as there are with higher.

JIM: That's just about what I thought I'd get. But I was afraid maybe it might be lower. With that kind of score I ought to be able to do regular freshmen courses all right if I study, oughtn't I?

ADVISER: Surely. You're beginning to get a little more confidence about the whole thing!

JIM: Yes, I think I'll try the accounting after all. I'll just plan to spend a lot of time on it, especially this first term. These boys at the house that had it last year will probably be able to help me if I get stuck. What else do you think I should take?

ADVISER: (*turning to the section of the catalog where general requirements are explained*) The University decides some of these things for you. There is the English, the physical education, and the ROTC that everybody has to take. You might put those down and see what it adds up to. (*Jim writes them on the card.*)

JIM: It looks as though I could get in about two more things.

ADVISER: Did they explain these "group requirements" to you? In order to make sure that everybody who graduates has some broad liberal education, the University requires that you take at least one course in each of these groups: the humanities, science, and social science. Here is the list of courses you have to choose from.

JIM: How would it be if I took a history course this year? I've always liked history. I think I'll take this European History. I'd like to know something about that. (*He counts up his credit hours.*) I think I can take one more course, but I'd rather let the other group requirements go until next year. Do you suppose I could take some music? I'd like to go on with my clarinet lessons.

ADVISER: It sounds like a good idea. Well, that just about settles your program, doesn't it? I'll sign the card and then you can work out the times for all the classes from the time schedule yourself.

JIM: Thank you for all your help. I feel as if I were really getting started now.

ADVISER: You're more than welcome. You know where I am now, and I hope you'll come back any time you need my help. Good luck with the rest of your registration.

Let us look next at a section of an interview with Bernice Burchard, a college sophomore who is trying to decide on a career and a college major to correspond to it. This is the third conference she has had with Mr. Lundeen, the counselor. On the first occasion they had discussed her background and general attitudes; on the second they had talked about the results of tests she had taken, and he had directed her to the relevant information about careers. She is ready to think about a definite decision when she comes for this third appointment.

CLIENT: I've been thinking and thinking about the possibilities we talked over last time, but I just can't make up my mind.

COUNSELOR: No single one of them seems exactly right?

CLIENT: The thing I keep coming back to is that my grades and the tests I took show that I get along better in social science than in anything else, and the natural, obvious thing is that I should be a social science teacher. There isn't any real argument against it either. I've looked up what the books say about the opportunities and they seem to be good. The salaries are good now, too—higher than for anything else I could get a job doing. But somehow I just can't see myself as a teacher.

COUNSELOR: There's something about the role you'd be playing that just doesn't seem to fit you?

CLIENT: I don't know. Maybe it does fit. Maybe I'm just not being realistic about myself. I've been trying to figure out what it is about the job that I balk at. I like children and young people and have always gotten along fine with them. I don't think I'll have any trouble with discipline or anything. I never did in Girl Scouts or summer camp. It's more that I hate to settle down in a small town the way you have to do, at least the first job you get.

COUNSELOR: There are things about small-town life you don't like?

CLIENT: There certainly are! I grew up in one, you know. I know all about the narrowness and the smugness and the gossip. And as long as I can remember I've heard my mother complaining about it. She was a music teacher and wanted to go to New York to study voice. But she didn't have any money and decided to teach for a couple of years to save enough to get started in New York. Then of course she married my dad—he works at the First

National Bank—and that was the end of all her plans. She's never even been to New York yet on a visit.

COUNSELOR: Your mother sort of got caught in a small-town life she hadn't planned for herself.

CLIENT: That's just it. I think she's always felt cheated. Between you and me, I don't really think she has such a wonderful voice. She might not have gone very far with it if she had studied in New York. The family gets a little tired of hearing about what she has given up for us.

COUNSELOR: You're not completely in sympathy with your mother's attitude.

CLIENT: No, I'm not. And yet I seem to have been affected by it so that I'm afraid of being caught myself. I can see that I wouldn't need to be. You don't have to marry the cashier of the First National Bank unless you want to, and if you do want to—I probably would if he was like my dad—you shouldn't complain about the consequences . . . .

As a third example, let us consider a portion of an interview Mrs. Ryan, a college counselor, has with Betty Ellison, an attractive divorcee with two children. Betty is completing her requirements for a college degree and working half-time as a stenographer in an insurance agency. Mrs. Ryan had helped her make plans for a new pattern of life a year before when her husband asked her for a divorce in order that he might marry someone else. This had been a great shock to Betty, but she had taken it well. Once she had settled on a course of action she encountered no difficulty in carrying it out. At the beginning of this interview she reports that she has been given a raise because of her good performance on her job and has made the Dean's List for her scholarship.

CLIENT: It's not myself I'm worried about right now. It's Billy. He's my oldest child, you remember, twelve years old now. Marcia, the eight-year-old, seems to be getting along all right, but I don't know what to do about Bill.

COUNSELOR: What is it about him that concerns you?

CLIENT: I think he misses his father, even more than he did at first. He's been terribly moody lately and flares up over the slightest thing. But what really brings things to a head now is his running away.

COUNSELOR: Running away?

CLIENT: Yes. The first time it happened was last month. He didn't come home from school and was gone all evening. I was frantic—called everyone, looked everywhere. At nine o'clock, just as I had the telephone in my hand to call the police, he wandered in. He was cold and hungry and terribly tired—said he had started walking to San Francisco but given it up and come home. I was so relieved to see him that I didn't say much. I fed him and put him to bed and he went right to sleep.

Then yesterday it happened again. Only this time it was worse. I did call the police and they picked him up in Roseburg at about ten o'clock. He had hitchhiked a ride that far. He told the policeman he was going to live with his father in San Francisco.

COUNSELOR: I can see how you feel you must do something.

CLIENT: Yes. I can't have this happening again and again. And the trouble is I can't find out why he does it. He won't talk to me any more. He's sort of sullen all the time, not a bit like he used to be.

COUNSELOR: Is there anything different about your home situation lately?

CLIENT: Well, I've been going with John Harkness. Maybe you know him. He's a lawyer in town. He's around quite a lot, and Bill is especially nasty to him—goes out of his way to be obnoxious. I suppose he does resent him, but it's as I said, he just won't talk about it—to me, anyway. What I need to decide is whether to try to get some kind of outside help for him, and if so where. I don't even know what the possibilities are.

COUNSELOR: What is the situation in the school Billy goes to? Do they have a counseling service?

CLIENT: I think they do. He started just this year at Elwood Junior High, and he did mention a counselor who helped him fill out his program. I wonder, though, how much anybody like this knows. And how serious do you suppose Billy's state of mind is?

COUNSELOR: Would you have any way of finding out how good the counseling service at Elwood Junior High is, and what kind of a man Billy's counselor is—what kind of training he's had, and how much experience?

CLIENT: They're having a Parent's Night next Tuesday. If I go, I may find out something there. One thing about asking this counselor to help out is that it would give Billy a *man* friend. That be good for him.

COUNSELOR: Maybe you will be able to check up on this possibility next Tuesday, then. The other possibility is the Child Guidance Clinic. They are equipped to make a thorough study of a child and plan the kind of treatment that seems most appropriate for him. They may not have any vacancies right now, and you might have to go on a waiting list for a while.

CLIENT: I hadn't heard of this clinic before. Would it be expensive?

COUNSELOR: They do charge fees, but these are on a sliding scale. How much anyone pays is based on his income. I have a leaflet here that tells about the clinic and its facilities. Would you like to take it with you?

CLIENT: Thank you. I'll think this over. Somehow I can't believe that Bill's trouble is serious enough so that he needs psychiatric treatment, but the trouble is, you just don't know. I believe the best thing for me to do is to find out what sort of person Bill's school counselor is, and if he seems to be the right kind I'll talk it over with him. He has a chance to see Bill too. Maybe if things don't improve he could help me decide whether to apply to the clinic or not.

Thinking about these decision-making sessions and others in which we have participated we can identify certain common characteristics. The first thing the client needs to achieve is a sense of the general direction he wishes to go, the purposes that the decision he makes must serve for him. Until this general sense of what he wants exists, there is little likelihood that specific choices will be satisfying. After this or along with it he must consider the limits of the situation within which his free choice operates. These may consist of university requirements, as in the first case above, or his own talents and disabilities as in the second. A multitude of other factors operate in this way—age, financial condition, past record, physical appearance, family commitments, draft status. Knowing what he wants and understanding the limitations that are placed upon him, the individual can narrow down the range of possibilities open to him, thus cutting down on the amount of confusion. He can usually identify more precisely than he could before just what is the factor that holds him back from each of these possible courses of action. In the first example above this turns out to be doubt about ability to handle accounting; in the second it is the influence of the mother's long-continued grievance against small-town life. Once this stage is reached a decision comes fairly easily.

COUNSELING SKILLS FACILITATING DECISION-MAKING

Whether or not the client will have this satisfying decision-making experience depends largely upon the psychological structure of this interview and of the others which have preceded it. The important principles have already been discussed in previous chapters and need only be recapitulated here. There should be an atmosphere completely free from any sort of threat to his self-esteem, an atmosphere of genuine respect and liking. Attitudes should be given the same status as facts. They should be recognized, clarified, accepted, and understood. Dependable information should be readily available and freely used. It should be clear from the beginning that the decision is in the client's hands. The counselor will help him put things together but will not attempt to decide for him.

Along with the general skills previously elaborated there are certain counselor skills specific to the decision-making situation. The first and most important of these is perceptual sensitivity as to whether or not a real decision has actually occurred. Another way of putting this is to say that a counselor needs to be able to distinguish between a genuine decision and a pseudo-decision. This, like so many other special skills, requires the picking up of small cues through which the attitude behind the words can be sensed. Pseudo-decisions are fairly common in counseling, as it is natural that they be in a situation where there is some pressure to decide. A good deal of this pressure comes from outside sources over which the counselor has no control. The university requires that a student state what his major is. Family and friends suggest in subtle or obvious ways that not to be able to make up one's mind is a sign of weakness. No matter how permissive and accepting the counselor is, the client's initial set may be so strong that he assumes that a decision is expected of him before the conclusion of a series of interviews. Furthermore the counselor's own wish to close a case satisfactorily may incline him toward accepting a stated choice too readily and ignoring the hesitation or misgivings that attend it. It is only later when the person returns apparently as confused as he ever was that it is apparent that there has been this sort of error.

What can a counselor do about persistent indecision? In the first place he can accept it as naturally and non-critically as he accepts all of the client's other attitudes. There should be no disapproval, no annoyance. He should remember that it is these very clients who are having difficulty for one reason or another in charting courses for themselves who need counseling service most. By accepting the state of mind in this way he helps to give the client courage to tolerate his own uncertainty during the period of time needed to dispel it.

The second kind of contribution he can make is to help the client with the task of identifying the reasons for his inability to decide. In the examples given at the beginning of the chapter these turned out to be rather simple things—a fear of failing the accounting course, an unwillingness to settle for a unromantic small-town existence. Usually such factors are not so easily pinned down, but there are certain areas in which they tend to cluster. More often than not the attitudes and expectations of other persons in the client's immediate circle are involved. A boy's mother has set her heart on her son's going into the ministry. Because he is very fond of his mother, he cannot bring himself to disappoint her although his religious faith has been weakened and his talents lie in other directions. A girl is interested in nursing but feels that the members of her sorority do not approve of it and will be angry if she leaves after two years of prenursing work to enter the hospital. These deterring influences emanating from family and friends can take innumerable specific forms.

Another cluster of specific reasons for inability to decide on an apparently suitable course of action centers around the fact that an occupation or a college major represents a role one plays, and something about that role can be distasteful even when the activities themselves are appealing. The student who is extremely conservative in his attitudes may not be able to accept a career choice that would involve working for the government. Anything that smacks of socialism or bureaucracy is anathema to him. The young man with an outstanding talent for drawing and painting may shy away from any kind of art career because it suggests effeminacy. The girl whose clerical aptitudes are low may still cling to the idea of taking secretarial training rather than going to work in a store or factory because she pictures herself as a trusted helper of a handsome businessman. Prestige, glamor, financial security, clean hands—all these considerations and many others help to determine which occupations are acceptable and which unacceptable.

Another factor upon which indecision may be based is a genuine equipotentiality along with an unwillingness to narrow oneself down. Among high-ability students it is not uncommon to find individuals equally good at scientific and verbal kinds of work with interest scores also indicating suitability for both areas. But to achieve eminence as a lawyer or writer requires advanced training and experience that cannot be combined with specialized training in chemistry or physics. A person of this sort may have to make his choice in what seems almost an arbitrary way. Once made, there is an irrevocability about it from which he may draw back in alarm. The sense of the inevitable limitations of human life which is one of the chief things distinguishing maturity from childhood may thus come to him all at once and he may need to talk about it at some length in order to assimilate it.

Another complex of factors sometimes standing in the way of decisions is related to what was said earlier about limitations imposed by circumstances. A person can recognize obstacles in his path and walls that close him in without accepting them. A twenty-three-year-old conscientious objector has planned for many years to be a medical missionary. His plans, like those of so many others, have been interrupted by the war. By the time he is free to take up his own life again he is married and has two small children. His wife is unable to work outside the home at least until they are of school age. The eight-year course which would have been difficult enough had he entered upon it when he was eighteen and unencumbered with family responsibilities is now financially impossible. Once he accepts this fact there are other decisions open to him, but until he does there is no way out. We in America have a great admiration for men and women who overcome insuperable obstacles. Every month our popular magazines recite their stories. Perhaps we need to temper this optimistic enthusiasm with the realization that some obstacles *are* insuperable. By maintaining a situation in which a client can look calmly and steadily at his circumstances for as long as he needs to, the counselor helps him accept the limitations that he cannot change.

Once these influences and attitudes that are blocking decisions become clear to counselor and client there are some special ways of dealing with them which may be helpful. Where the attitudes of some other person are strongly involved, arrangements can sometimes be made to explain things to this person. As has been said in an earlier chapter, this should be done with the full knowledge of the counselee himself. The mother who wishes her son to be a minister may not be so disappointed as he expected her to be when she learns of the boy's aptitudes and interests in the field of engineering. The father who has set his heart on a college education for his son, although he proves to be weak in the verbal abilities necessary for advanced education, may change his mind when he is shown that the son's most promising aptitudes are mechanical like his own. These examples point to what is probably the most important characteristic of these interviews with parents. They should stress the client's positive assets in some field other than the one the parent has chosen rather than attempt directly to argue him out of his insistence on an unwise choice.

In the cases where indecision rests upon conflicts in the client himself over roles he is not sure he wishes to play, the most important factor the counselor can utilize to help him is time. This is especially true when the counseling has upset the plans the person has held for some time and given him some new possibilities to consider. The trying on of new roles to see how well they fit cannot be hurried. When Sam Bronson, a boy from a large family that has always been on the edge of poverty, finds out that he has unusual scientific talents and could well plan to continue his education to the Ph.D. level, he will probably need to think the whole thing over for a while before he makes up his mind that this is what he wants to do. Mary Madison, who has set her heart on being an actress, may not be able to grasp all at once the information she is given about the difficulties she would face in getting into this profession, and she cannot be expected to change the picture she has of the Broadway star into one of an unremarkable stenographer instantaneously.

When indecision still exists at the close of an interview in which the client hoped to make definite plans, the natural procedure is to schedule another interview—more than one if necessary. When the sources of his uncertainty are not yet apparent, it is talking the whole thing out in the favorable atmosphere of the counseling room that is most likely to bring them to light. When the uncertainty attaches to one aspect of the situation, some means of resolving the doubt between interviews can often be found. It is here that tryout courses and temporary jobs come in. If Mary Madison cannot quite see herself as a stenographer, a summer office job may clear the matter up one way or the other. She will know when she comes back to school in the fall whether such work suits her or not. If Richard McKenzie is not sure whether he has what it takes to become a successful architect, a year of basic art and science courses in the architecture school may settle the question. When they are planned during counseling, such tryout experiences can be worked out in ways that do not constitute a waste of the person's time whatever his final decision turns out to be.

To accomplish this it is necessary to keep in mind alternative possibilities and second choices. We have already indicated in an earlier chapter that vocational counseling should be thought of as a way of surveying all the alternative choices rather than evaluating one. The same can be said for other choice situations. It often happens that a vocation or a course of study which has been barely mentioned in an interview following vocational testing will come to a client's mind immediately after a failure in some course has shown him that his first choice was impractical. Nels Andriessen wants so much to be a doctor that he decides to go ahead with a premedical course even after he finds out from counseling tests that his college ability is somewhat below average and his science background seriously deficient. This is in September. In January, with a D in chemistry and an F in physics on his record, the alternatives he had barely considered, sales work and physical education, look much more attractive. The tryout has been more effective than anything the counselor could possibly have said in September in confronting Mr. Andriessen with the realities of his situation. An interview now will help him to evaluate himself more soundly and realistically than he was able to before. Similarly, Betty Ellison, in the third example given at the beginning of the chapter, may be more ready to consider psychiatric treatment for Bill next month than she is now, if she finds that his attitude continues to be unsatisfactory, at school as well as at home, and that the school counseling service cannot help him.

INDECISION VERSUS INDECISIVENESS

There is one problem that constantly arises in cases where indecision is a prominent feature. Such cases require the basic minimum of diagnosis to decide what sort of treatment the person needs. The trouble is that sometimes *indecision* with regard to a plan of action represents a general *indecisiveness* growing out of personal problems rather than doubts related to this specific issue. In such instances tryout jobs or courses, occupational information, or additional planning interviews may be futile. They may even be worse than futile since they serve to put off the day when the individual must face his real problems. Meanwhile the unsatisfactory habits of thinking become more firmly established. When a counselor is fairly sure that a client's difficulty in making up his mind is of this nature, it is advisable that he frankly recommend psychotherapy rather than specific ways of attacking the vocational problem. A recommendation of this kind should be put in such a way as not to alarm the client but to make the course of action seem perfectly natural. It might be phrased, for example, "It looks as though the choice of a career or a major isn't really the most important thing on your mind right now. Perhaps that would be easier if you could get some of your other personal problems and uncertainties cleared up. How would you like to make some appointments with Dr. _____ to work on these directly?"

There is another sort of condition besides psychiatric disability that shows up in counseling interviews as indecisiveness. One can call it *immaturity*, although the word does not describe it very precisely. Choices come in sequences, and a person may find it impossible to make a later one if he has not settled the

earlier ones. Thus a college student, faced at the end of his
sophomore year with the necessity for a choice of major, may
reach an impasse because the choice of a general area in which
to function—profession versus business, or science versus humanities, for example—a choice generally made during the high school
years, has never occurred. The general direction counseling
should take in such cases is logically apparent. Somehow help
should be given the person in "making up the work he has
missed," to use a well-known school expression. How to do this
in individual cases is never clear, however. Often circumstances
beyond the counselor's control remove these clients from the
counselor's purview so that he is unable to follow them up, and
thus he does not learn as much about them from his general
experience as he learns about others. Hugh Blake, the immature
sophomore, drops out of college and goes into one of the Services
for a couple of years. Perhaps the experience he gets there serves
as the "makeup work" he needs, but if so his first counselor does
not find out about it since Hugh moves on to a different college
or to a job when he comes out. Research on developmental stages
in choices promises to be very useful to counselors. A good beginning has been made in the study of vocational development. (See
Research Summary.)

There are times when it is necessary that a decision be made
immediately whether a client is really ready to make it or not.
This disabled veteran must sign up for one particular training
plan in order to get his Public Law 16 benefits. This student must
register for four courses this week. In such instances it is well
to make sure that the difference between an arbitrary decision
and a genuine one is clear to the client, so that the way will still
be open for him to work toward a genuine one. The client rather
than the counselor should make this arbitrary decision. In the
first case mentioned above the counselor might say to the veteran: "We seem to have narrowed down the field to teaching
and insurance, but I take it that you are not sure which appeals
to you more. As you know, I have to get something down on this
form for you so that you can start collecting your training benefits. After you get registered we can still talk the whole problem
over until you have completely made up your mind, but what
shall I put down here right now?"

CRITERION FOR EVALUATING DECISIONS

We come finally to the question, What constitutes a *good* decision? It is a question which is not easy to answer even if we confine our thinking to the limited area of vocational and educational choices and omit from consideration decisions about marriage and intricate personal relationships. One criterion which has been used in follow-up studies to evaluate the success of counseling has been the client's acceptance of a plan which the counselor thought carried a good prognosis. We have criticized this approach to the problem in some detail in a previous chapter. The accumulating research evidence that counseling prognoses cannot be made accurately enough to guarantee success or happiness to one who lets himself be guided by them seems to be a serious stumbling block.

In other follow-up studies it has been assumed that an individual has made a good decision if things work out well for him in the future on the basis of it. If his grades improve, if he does well on his job, there is indeed some tangible evidence that the decision he made was satisfactory. This type of evaluation is of little help at the time counseling is going on, however. Furthermore, it would seem that it excludes from the "good decision" category many choices that should be included here. What of the boy who wishes so strongly to be a symphony orchestra conductor that he mobilizes all his considerable talent and energy toward that goal, knowing that the chances are ten to one against his attaining it? Does his inability to get a job as an orchestral conductor prove that the original decision was unsound? What of the journalism student who signs up for courses in physics and astronomy because he wishes to broaden his outlook and understand how scientists think. If his grade average decreases from 3.6 to 2.9 because of this step, does it indicate that he was unwise to take it?

Perhaps the best way out of the dilemma is to say that it is a good decision if the individual who makes it is completely willing to take the consequences. In most cases the counselor would hope that the course a client decides to take is one in which he can make good grades or that the occupation he chooses will be one in which he will find success and satisfaction. But it is quite possible for a person to decide that it is necessary for him to take the risk involved in a field where no certainty exists. If he is willing to face failure if and when it confronts him and is ready to change to a less preferred alternative if circumstances demand that he do so, who is to say that his decision is a bad one? Perhaps we should never have had the prized works of our great composers, artists, and writers had there not been young men who were willing to take such risks. We shall return to this question of what a good decision is in the final chapter.

This single criterion of the soundness of a decision—that the person be ready to accept its consequences—is not entirely satisfactory logically, but it works fairly well in the practical situations with which counseling deals. In abstract discussions of this issue someone is sure to bring up questions like, "Suppose a counselee decides that the best way out of his difficulties is to murder his father?" or "What would you do if the client decided that suicide was the only reasonable course for him?" Perhaps we have not yet faced such ultimate questions as clearly as we might, but counseling experience gives us the conviction that they are academic rather than vital and bear little relationship to the counselor's day-to-day activity. Clients do not in fact decide on murder or suicide in our offices, and the problem of whether or not to try to dissuade them does not arise. We are assuming of course that the kind of differentiation we have discussed in Chapter 3 has been made, and that psychotic and severely neurotic patients have been eliminated from our consideration in connection with this type of treatment.

In all that we have said about the way in which decisions are made there is implicit an underlying philosophy that can best be phrased in terms of concepts developed in Lippitt's often-cited experiment on social climates. Counseling succeeds best when it steers clear of the autocratic attitude on the one hand and the laissez-faire on the other. To apply the democratic attitude to the counseling situation means to view it always as a co-operative venture in which the two participants are making contributions of different sorts. The client alone has the keys which can unlock the inner chambers of his experience. The counselor may help make it possible for him to find and use them but he cannot furnish them. The counselor, on the other hand, has access to much more information of various sorts than the client has. Several such kinds of information have been discussed in previous chapters.

He brings this information into the interview as there is need for it. Out of situations in which these two sorts of contributions are fused in complex ways, decisions come which seem sound to both counselor and client. The fact that something can go wrong, that a client can refuse to do his share or that a counselor may occasionally have to make a unilateral decision, does not alter the fact that this is what the process is like when it is working well.

It may be that when the history of the counseling movement is written and its achievements evaluated, the methods we have hit upon for facilitating responsible decisions will appear to be our greatest contribution to our common life. More research is certainly needed here. A more thorough analysis of what actually goes on in interviews of this type might tell us much that we could use in the many other situations—home, schoolroom, or office—in which we attempt to promote maturity and stability in the lives of ourselves and others.

Research Summary

INADEQUACY OF COUNSELOR PROGNOSES AS BASIS FOR DECISIONS

There have been several studies leading to doubt about counselors' ability to predict outcomes of alternative choices for their clients. Sarbin (1943) asked counselors to predict the grade averages of freshman students they had interviewed. Test results were of course available to them. At the same time an "actuarial" prediction of each student's grade average was computed from a regression equation previously worked out using high school rank and college aptitude test score. The difference in the correlations between predicted and actually obtained grades was not significant when the "clinical" and "actuarial" predictions were compared. What little difference there was favored the actuarial predictions. Summarizing a number of investigations in the armed services, F. B. Davis (1947, p. 57) reaches a similar conclusion: "Subjective evaluation of empirical data appears to add little or nothing to the accuracy with which personnel can be selected on the basis of suitable objective tests." Meehl (1954) has furnished the definitive synthesis of research on "clinical" and "actuarial" predictions.

The inability of psychologists to make accurate predictions even in an area they know well is shown in a study reported by Kelly and Fiske (1951) on the prediction of success in the Veterans Administration clinical psychology training program. Trainees were put through an assessment program which included a large number of clinical techniques such as projective tests, intensive interviews, role-playing and leaderless group situations, in addition to many sorts of objective tests and personality inventories. Unusual care was taken to obtain reliable criteria of success in the clinical activities themselves as well as in course work. The most striking finding was that ratings based on the credentials files and objective tests alone were about as good predictors of clinical success as those based on much larger amounts of material. Although the intellectual aspects of the work trainees did could be predicted moderately well, correlations were low with the criterion ratings on the more specifically clinical aspects of their performance. Few of them were higher than .3, no matter how much information and expert evaluation went into them. If psychologists cannot use their clinical judgment to make valid prognoses about clinical work itself, it seems unlikely that they will be able to make them in areas about which they know much less.

A study at the high school level has been reported by Walker (1955). Twenty-five high school counselors were asked to make job and school predictions for 60 male students, on the basis of tests, grades, and miscellaneous information. These were related to the facts about the students' actual status five or six years after leaving school. Counselors differed quite markedly in the success of their predictions, some scoring worse than chance. Predictions of degree of success were somewhat more accurate for school than for job situations, and they were better for brighter than for duller students. There was a tendency for counselors to underestimate the school performance of duller students and to overestimate that of brighter students.

RESEARCH ON VOCATIONAL DEVELOPMENT

The vocational-choice process has stimulated considerable research interest in recent years. Some of the studies growing out of this interest have been reported in the research summary following the chapter on occupational information because they were concerned with the characteristics of workers and jobs. Those bearing more specifically on the way in which individuals make their choices are summarized here. One source of many of the ideas that are being investigated is the monograph by Ginzberg and others (1951). This study proposed that life stages should be considered and presented some evidence based on comparison of the kind of thinking being done by young people of different ages to support the hypothesis that there was a sequence of such stages in the occupational-choice process. Another source of ideas has been the research-planning report by Blau and others (1956). On the basis of discussions carried on at an interdisciplinary conference, a conceptual framework was set up in which occupational choice is seen as a compromise between wishes and the demands of reality. Super (1956) has proposed that we use the word *synthesis* rather than *compromise* to designate the process.

Super and his associates at Columbia University are engaged in a major research project on vocational development, the Career Pattern Study. A group of ninth-grade boys in a small city has been studied intensively, using tests of all kinds, observations, and interviews with the subjects, their parents, and various townspeople. The plans call for follow-up research tracing successive stages in the development of vocational maturity in these subjects. Super's theory of occupational choice can be found in his text (1957). The specific theoretical ideas upon which the Career Pattern Study is based are set forth in Super and others (1957). In Super and Bachrach (1957) the theory is used as a way of organizing a large amount of material on science careers and suggesting needed research in this area. In the most recent of these monographs, Super and Overstreet (1960) report how the proposed indices of vocational maturity in ninth graders were related to one another in the Career Pattern study. The variable they labeled "Orientation toward Choice" appeared to be the best indicator of the characteristic they were trying to measure.

Another continuing research program is in progress at Harvard under Tiedeman's direction, the Harvard Studies in Career Development. There have been two research reports from this program, and more are to appear. O'Hara and Tiedeman (1959) examined the relationships between self-estimates and measures or scores in five areas—social class, interests, aptitudes, work values, and general values—for more than 1000 boys in grades nine through twelve in a Catholic high school. The results were in keeping with Ginzberg's ideas of a shift from fantasy to reality during this period. There was a general tendency for correlations between self-estimates and all the other variables to be higher for twelfth-graders than for ninth-graders, and the curves for increase in correlation showed different shapes for the different variables. The most definite increase was for aptitude and work values, indicating that twelfth-graders are more likely to consider these things in relation to themselves than ninth-graders are. The curves for correlations with interest measures increased from ninth to tenth grade and then leveled off. Cass and Tiedeman (1960) analyzed choices made by 466 Maine high school students among the six curricula available to them. They attempted to differentiate the six groups using a discriminant function based on 18 variables. There seemed to be three major differentiating factors. The first was sex, the second was college versus non-college families, and the third was based on the interest test. This study agrees with the previous one in indicating that both social class and interests play a part in ninth-grade choices, whereas aptitudes do not. The authors emphasize that their findings are trends only, and that the data show many "misplacements" or exceptions. Borow (1960) gives a good summary of the Super and the Tiedeman research programs and includes some information about similar research being carried on in Japan and in France.

A study by Sinnett (1956) suggest that different kinds of interests mature at different rates. He first asked four counselors to rank Kuder scores and Strong groups as to the temporal order in which an individual acquires realistic perceptions of them and as to complexity. He then ranked the amount of agreement between claimed and measured interests for 500 college men. The two sets of rankings produced a correlation that was significant and fairly high for the Strong, low and insignificant for the Kuder. The implication for a counselor would be that he should take some kinds of interest scores more seriously than others, depending upon the age of the counselee.

A caution against concluding too definitely that the occupational choices of ninth-graders are not "realistic," comes from a study by Stephenson (1957). He presents evidence from 1000 ninth-grade students in four New Jersey communities indicating that they distinguish plans from aspirations, and that the plans are considerably more realistic than the aspirations are. The form of the question put to students has some effect on the answers they give.

OTHER RESEARCH ON VOCATIONAL CHOICE

The part that values play in the choice process was the concern of C. H. Miller (1956) in a study of 180 students who had been classified into three groups: No Choice, Tentative Choice, and Definite Choice. They were asked to respond to a forced-choice scale to indicate their attitudes toward values to be obtained from work—security, career satisfaction, prestige, and social rewards. It was the No Choice group that differed most from the other two, who turned out to be quite similar. They tended to emphasize security and prestige more did those who had made a choice. However, the difference was not clearly significant and interpretation of the findings is complicated by the fact that half of the occupational choices were in teaching fields.

Ziller (1957) applied a stochastic decision-making model to the vocational choice problem. There are three aspects of each choice situation—the prize, the price, and the possibility of success. Ziller assumed that the way in which any individual combines these three depends partly upon his risk-taking tendency, called here *utility for risk*. He attempted to measure this tendency by simply counting the number of guesses each subject made on an ambiguous true-false test. Groups of college sophomores with different career plans did show significant differences on this measure. As was expected, the sales group was highest. The lowest was the Undecided group. This may reflect the Miller study's finding that a greater value was placed on security by the No Choice group.

Evaluation

It is fairly clear from the available research data that counselors cannot be expected to make good enough prognoses of success for clients to safely base decisions on them. There is considerable evidence accumulating that occupational choice is a process, not an event, and that it involves an increasingly complex synthesis of motivation with external reality factors. There is a suggestion that too great a need for some particular value, such as security, may retard the choice process.

What is conspicuous by its absence is any research attention to what actually goes on in decision-making *interviews* or what effects counseling has on the process of choice. With so much of counseling focused on vocational decisions, it would seem very desirable that some research on this aspect of counseling be done.

CHAPTER ELEVEN

Counseling for

Personal Adjustment

THE COUNSELOR'S RESPONSIBILITY IN THIS AREA

Some of the research summarized at the end of Chapter 1 seems to indicate that many people view the process of helping individuals improve their personal and social adjustment as something quite different from the process of helping them make educational and vocational plans. *Counseling*, as we have said, is an ambiguous word. Some define it in terms of one of these functions, some in terms of the other, and many would include both functions in its definition.

There is also some research evidence that college counselors prefer to view themselves as psychotherapists. Casual observation would indicate that the same preference holds for many high school counselors and counselors in a variety of special agencies. This preference may stem partly from the tremendous prestige of psychotherapy in our time and partly from the circumstances of counseling work itself. The cases presenting salient personal problems appear to be more complex and challenging, to require more skill and sensitivity. Whatever the special focus of a counseling service, those who work there are sure to encounter a large number of cases where the difficulty seems to be primarily one of adjustment. To a greater or lesser extent every case presents adjustment problems for the counselor's consideration.

For counselors to increase their skill in helping clients with personal problems is certainly a desirable thing. But the shift in emphasis that accompanies such a change may bring certain difficulties in its wake. For one thing, psychotherapeutic activities are typically more time-consuming than planning activities. The question arises as to whether a school or college counselor is really discharging his responsibility to his institution when he spends 20 hours with one student, if this means that ten other students who need help get no service at all. Furthermore, questions of competence arise. How much special training for therapeutic counseling must one have in order to satisfy himself and others that his efforts do more good than harm? There are some real hazards in long-continuing therapy relationships that are not found in the more typical counseling interactions. Last but certainly not least, when a counseling agency shifts its emphasis toward personality counseling, it may gradually disqualify itself for what was once its major function, helping clients with choices, decisions, and plans, because persons who prefer not to consider themselves maladjusted no longer present themselves as clients.

In this as in so many other uncertain areas, synthesis of opposing views is possible. Counselors do concern themselves with general adjustment problems of clients and must continue to do so, since the situations and emotional attitudes that produce adjustment difficulties are present everywhere and may crop up at any time. But they must not tie up too much of their time in dealing with such problems and must not neglect what this writer sees as the more important task of facilitating optimum development for each individual through wise choices. The synthesis recommended here is to include in one's counseling repertory, skill in what can be called *minimum-change therapy.*

Very often in general discussions of the psychotherapeutic process, it seems to be assumed that its aim is bringing about the largest possible change in the personality of the client. (As indicated in the research summary at the end of this chapter, the evidence that large changes in personality occur under any system of therapy is not very solid.) In the kind of therapy we are considering, the opposite assumption is made. Its aim is to enable the person to make some *small* change in the *direction* in which he is moving. Difficulties he is experiencing are taken as indications that he is headed in a direction wrong for him or that he has at some former time made a bad choice and turned into a blind alley. All of this may of course have happened without his conscious awareness. The counselor attempts to create a situation in which the person can become aware of directional shifts that are now possible for him and in which he can be sure that someone will see him through what may be a difficult "rotation of his axis."

This is a procedure that fits in very well with the purposes of counseling as a whole—to enable individuals to further their own development, to "make something of themselves." And because of its emphasis on small changes, it takes much less time than therapy designed to get at the roots of all difficulties. It involves no great change in the interview procedures we ordinarily use. Let us examine it in more detail.

GENERAL FEATURES OF MINIMUM-CHANGE THERAPY

In place of the kind of diagnosis that often precedes therapy, the initial stages of minimum-change therapy include a process that might be called *exploration of resources*. The counselor pays little attention to personality weaknesses that are adequately controlled or neutralized. He notes what difficulties are actually blocking the person's forward movement but is on the alert for the possibility that even these may be bypassed rather than attacked. What he is most persistent in trying to locate are ways of coping with anxiety and stress, already existing resources that may be enlarged and strengthened once their existence is recognized.

Though there is much current interest in ego processes and positive personality traits, we do not as yet have tests we can use with confidence to measure them. We are more likely to become aware of a person's resources by observing things he does than by asking him questions. Meaningful behavior of this kind often occurs in the interview situation itself. For example, when Mary Hart flashes a sudden smile as she is struck with the amusing aspects of a particularly humiliating social experience she is recounting, the counselor knows that she possesses an asset that may be of considerable use to her. Call it a defense if you will, but in social situations and in personal emotional adaptation to the vicissitudes of life her ability to laugh at her own predicament will be a valuable resource. Other assets frequently showing up even in interviews where hostility, doubt, guilt, and anxiety are the main themes include moral principles of which the person is absolutely certain, demonstrated courage in the face of adversities, loyalty to those he loves. Whether or not it is advisable for the counselor to reflect or interpret such expressions at the time they occur is another question. But he can make a mental note of them.

We are more likely to become aware of a client's personality assets if we have some knowledge of his life outside the counseling room. In small or moderate-sized colleges, the counselor is likely to encounter his clients here or there—on the street, in the student union, at concerts, plays, or games. The growing practice of placing psychologists on the wards in mental hospitals serves the same purpose of permitting the kind of observation that positive diagnosis is based on. Conversations with a client's family or friends is another resource, but as has been said before, it should not be used without his knowledge or permission. It is the characteristics he *knows* the counselor has had a chance to observe— the things they can talk over together—that are grist for counseling's mill. In the last analysis, it is the client himself who must make the positive diagnosis we have been talking about if it is to be effective in his life.

A second point of emphasis in minimum-change therapy is the way in which the situation is structured for the client. The counselor must take into account *his* expectations and goals as well as his own. To a person profoundly dissatisfied with the way his life has been going, the only thing that really looks good is change—complete change. What he may have read about psychotherapy in popular magazines or seen in movies leads him to expect or at least hope that some fundamental change will occur. True, the experience of countless therapists has shown that such a person will hang on to his unconscious defenses and fight every sort of change at every step of the way. But if anyone *tells* him at the beginning that small shifts of direction rather than larger changes in total pattern are to be expected he is likely to reject the whole undertaking. He thinks he wants to be made over.

It is in this connection that some explicit verbal distinction between counseling and therapy may be useful. Instead of trying to fight the person's wishful dreams about miraculous effects of therapy, one can simply explain that he is a counselor rather than a psychoanalyst and that his job is to help a person find out what his personality is like and decide how he can use the assets he has and get rid of the obstacles blocking his progress. If the client accepts the situation on these terms, therapeutic counseling can proceed within the framework of the very broad general question, "What kind of person are you?" Anything he wishes to bring up can be considered, but the counselor has not committed himself to an analysis of all the client's problems and innumerable childhood experiences out of which they may have arisen.

A third essential feature of minimum-change therapy is the use of the counseling relationship to reduce the client's anxiety enough to allow him freedom to consider new possibilities. This, of course, is nothing new or at all peculiar to therapy of this type. It seems to be the one common denominator linking together all sorts of diverse procedures. Some would classify this whole approach as just another variety of supportive therapy. There would be no quarrel with that idea if we were not so prone to discredit support and to think of it as a superficial palliative measure to be used when more powerful methods are impractical. The idea of support should not be devalued in this way. Obviously support does not mean inspirational pep talks, shallow reassurance, or the encouragement of dependence. What it does mean is the act of lending one's own strength to the client for the period during which he needs it, so that he can be certain that his world is not going to fall apart if he moves. It may be that this is by far the most important thing we do for our clients, whatever our special theoretical predilections are. It is the crucial factor that enables his own development processes to operate.

If the counselor is not working for insight or drastic restructuring of client self-concepts, he may furnish such support without using time needed for other clients. Once the client has established a new direction for himself, regularly scheduled interview hours, a month apart, may be enough to maintain his courage and confidence. It is the quality of the relationship rather than the amount of time spent in the counselor's presence that constitutes support.

FIRST STAGE: GENERAL EXPLORATION

During the first stage the counselor's aim is to encourage the freest possible expression of everything the client is able to talk about. In other words, counseling follows the pattern character-

istic of initial interviews for a longer period than it would if attention were focused on one particular question or problem. The
counselor's main job is to listen. What he says is not very important except as it facilitates or hinders the communication.
Open-ended questions or remarks showing that he has not quite
grasped the client's meaning are appropriate. But perhaps the
most generally useful means for encouraging the client to continue
to try to express what is on his mind is the technique called
"reflection of feeling" in non-directive or client-centered counseling. Regardless of whether or not one adheres strictly to the
system formulated by Rogers, he will find this a good procedure
in handling exploratory interviews. Let us look at an example[1] as
a basis for discussion.

MR. S.:   It often seems to me that I just can't go on. I get up at
               five o'clock every morning and work a six-hour shift at
               the power plant. Then I go to my classes in the afternoon.
               Sometimes I'm so sleepy that it's just torture to keep
               awake during a lecture. In order to get my studying done
               I have to stay up till after midnight. I never get enough
               sleep. I'm getting more and more tired. I just can't stand
               this much longer—but I've *got* to stand it.

COUNSELOR: You're driving yourself to the very limit of your endur-
               ance.

MR. S.:   Yes, but the worst of it is that it affects other people
               besides myself. I'm giving my wife a bad time. I'm tense
               and jumpy and irritable at home. My little boy Jimmy
               gets on my nerves so that before I can stop I'm shouting
               at him and knocking him around. I know what it's doing
               to him. I was treated badly enough when I was a child
               so that I know what a terrible thing this is. But I can't
               stop.

COUNSELOR: It's disturbing to see yourself as a person who ill-treats his
               own child.

MR. S.:   That's not the only disturbing thing either. Two weeks
               ago I rammed my car into the back of a truck. The truck
               stopped just ahead of me and I didn't notice it at all.
               It's going to cost me two hundred dollars for repairs.

---

[1] This is not an actual case, but rather a synthesis of several from the
author's experience. A considerable number of actual interviews is now
available in printed form. It is expected that the student will study this
material in connection with the present chapter.

Why was my mind wandering that way? Why didn't I know what I was doing? If I'm going to have lapses like that, anything can happen! It scares me to think of it.

COUNSELOR: You wonder sometimes if you're beginning to crack up.

MR. S.: That's what I'm really afraid of. There is some insanity in my family. My grandmother spent ten years in an asylum before she died. I've been worried that I might be like her as long as I can remember. Now I often wonder if it has already happened—that I'm out of my mind but that people haven't realized it yet. Oh I know it sounds silly, but I can't help thinking it.

COUNSELOR: You wonder sometimes if you've really lost control.

As has been suggested in an earlier chapter, a counselor concentrates on feelings rather than content and responds to what appears to be the most significant part of each complex sequence. One of the reasons it is difficult to learn to do this is that it requires us to set aside some of our most firmly established conversational habits. For example, after the client's first speech in the foregoing example it would be natural to say: "There just aren't enough hours in the day for all you are trying to do" or "You are really working hard for your education." Neither of these replies shows that the counselor understands the intense strain, the feeling of imminent catastrophe that pervades what has just been said. Counseling is concerned with that strain rather than with the facts. We have also learned through years of practice in conversational good manners to react to the less disturbing parts of what a person has said. After the client's second outburst, the counselor might have replied, "You hate being so irritable at home." Had he done so he would not have faced the most unsettling fact at all. It is the possibility of psychological damage to the child around which the strong guilt centers. It is just such matters that need to be faced steadily without flinching. We have mentioned before that in expressing the almost intolerable feelings of a client, the counselor must be careful about the words he uses. It is better to say "ill-treats a child" than "is cruel to a child," for example. However, in the effort to use a word which will not deliver too much of a shock we must not minimize or gloss over the emotion. To say, "Your father's attitude annoys you sometimes," when the client has been expressing furious resentment fails to show real understanding. What we aim at is an expression which is right quantitatively as well as qualitatively. It goes without saying that it is not easy to achieve this. It is not even possible under all circumstances, since words do not mean the same thing to everybody.

If there seems to be a conflict between what is being said here about reflecting negative feelings and the previous emphasis on positive rather than negative personality traits, it is an apparent rather than a real contradiction. What is meant by positive personality traits is not freedom from conflicts and anxiety but the ability to cope with them. No useful purpose is served if either client or counselor denies the existence of unhappy states of mind or circumstances. One must face them in order to deal with them.

Partly because it is impossible always to reflect feelings accurately, regardless of one's skill and experience, it is better to think of the whole process as one of communicating to the client your understanding of his experience rather than acting as a mirror for it. A counselor cannot be a faithful mirror. He too is a human being and his own particular areas of acuteness and obtuseness will inevitably distort the picture. Furthermore, experience has shown that the progress of counseling is not seriously impeded by some failures to reflect feelings correctly. If there is a sound counseling relationship and if the counselor is following the client's words with intelligent attention, showing from time to time that he understands, a response that is wrong will simply lead to further elucidation of what was really meant. Of course if there is too much of this failure to comprehend, the client may give up the attempt to explain how he feels, but a fair amount will be tolerated in the ongoing stream of self-expression.

This point is emphasized because of its implications for the student-in-training. To be too conscious of the importance of saying the right thing at every pause is a state of mind that hampers the counselor's work. It cannot be stressed too much or too often that the basic skills are perceptual, not verbal. If the counselor's whole attention is given to understanding what the other person is trying to tell him, things will usually work out all right even if what he says is hesitant or inept. It is better to begin with good relationships and attitudes and then gradually perfect and polish the verbal skills than to work on the verbal skills first and ignore the human realities. It is quite possible for a client to be acutely uncomfortable in a situation which would look in a typescript like a perfect example of counseling procedure.

Fortunately this skill, the knack of listening for the meaning behind the words, does not have to be learned entirely in interview situations. Conversation, although it is different from counseling in several important ways, is like it in that both content and feelings are expressed. Thus it is quite possible, whenever one is in or near a group of people talking together, to practice listening for the emotional attitudes underlying the words and trying to sense imaginatively another person's state of mind. This ability is very much worth developing, not only because it is crucially important in counseling but because it has so much to contribute to the richness of life in general.

In communicating his understanding to a client, the counselor needs to be aware of the difference between "reflection of feeling" and "interpretation." To interpret is to go beyond what the person has actually said and make some comment on the sources of the feeling or its relationship to other things. In the example given, had the counselor said after Mr. S.'s second speech, "Because you were a rejected child yourself you show a tendency to reject your own child even when you don't wish to," he would have been interpreting rather than reflecting. During this first stage interpretation is likely to be unwise. At best it is of little value; at worst it generates defensiveness that may bring counseling to an abrupt end. It is plain that the response just cited shows the counselor thinking as a psychologist rather than as Mr. S. He is classifying the problem in accordance with certain theoretical concepts rather than understanding the experience of the man stating it. But this is a rather extreme example. There are many borderline instances where reflection and interpretation merge into one another so that it is impossible for experienced counselors to agree which a remark is. This is because when we respond to feeling rather than content we tend to give to what the person has said a somewhat broader reference than he himself gave it, thus adding something to his meaning. Therefore no hard-and-fast rule can be laid down to distinguish reflection from interpretation. The best course for the beginning psychotherapist to follow is to give first importance to the habit of adopting the client's frame of reference and seeing things as he sees them. Such an attitude will head off interpretations of the disruptive sort.

One supplementary problem that often arises is that of direct questions. Dogmatic followers of the non-directive method try always to reflect questions rather than answer them. This can lead to ridiculous results, highly exasperating to the questioner:

"How do I get to the Registrar's Office from here?"

"You'd like me to tell you where the Registrar's Office is."

"Yes, where is it? That's all I want to know."

"You're a little annoyed because I did not show you the way to the Registrar's Office. . . ."

It is obvious to common sense that it would have been better in this case, admittedly an extreme one, for the counselor to tell the student in the first place that the Registrar's Office was on the next floor. But again most real counseling situations are not so clear-out. There is a danger that if the counselor starts answering questions as the client brings them up, the structure of their relationship will solidify into a question-and-answer pattern quite different from the one he wishes to create. A satisfactory way of dealing with such situations is for the counselor to answer any question of fact if he knows the answer but to comment at the same time on the feeling that prompted the question if he can sense what it is. Thus:

CLIENT: What time is it?

COUNSELOR: It's a quarter to eleven exactly. You're wondering if the hour is almost over?

CLIENT: Yes. I feel as though I were running out of things to say . . . sort of running dry. Yet I don't like to leave early and waste time that's been assigned to me . . . I do so want to get something decided . . . and soon.

COUNSELOR: There's a kind of urgency about the whole thing for you.

By answering the factual question the counselor does the simple, natural, friendly thing that heads off resentment. But by adding the remark about the motivation, he keeps the emphasis where it belongs—on the person's state of mind. When questions do not have to do with factual matters, he can explain briefly that he does not know the answer and again go on to recognize the feeling that is involved:

CLIENT: What do you really think is the matter with me?

COUNSELOR: It would be nice in some ways if personality were simple enough so that one could answer a question like that, but it just isn't. It seems to you that it would be a relief in some ways to have someone tell you straight out what is wrong?

CLIENT: That's really what I came for. Like when you go to a doctor he decides you have appendicitis. He takes out your appendix and then you feel all right. I guess I knew all the time that it wouldn't be like that but I still sort of hoped it would.

In these situations where direct questions are asked the guiding principle is to deal with each in an honest way but in a way that keeps the structure of the counseling situation intact.

The first stage of minimum-change therapy merges into the second at the time when a pattern of what this client is really like begins to take shape in the counselor's mind. This is a pattern of development rather than one which reflects the client's present status only. It involves an awareness of the directions in which the person's growth has proceeded and in which further growth is likely to occur. As the counselor begins to see, even dimly, some of these things that perhaps the client himself does not see, he begins to take a somewhat more active role in the relationship.

SECOND STAGE: CLARIFICATION

Because of the ambiguities in the meaning of the term *interpretation*, which were mentioned in the previous section, it seems advisable to use another term for the specific process involved during the second stage of minimum-change therapy. *Clarification* will be used to refer to this process, since what the counselor attempts to see are possibilities of forward movement rather than origins of symptoms and problems. What the client needs to see clearly are things he may be able to do in his own behalf.

The emphasis is on the person's *values*—what he wants, what he prizes, what seems important to him. There are several reasons for this emphasis. The main one is that the kind of directional change in the person's orientation to life that we are trying to facilitate is more likely to be brought about by a decision to work toward some recognized value than by insight into hitherto unconscious needs. Another less cogent reason is that statements about values typically generate less resistance than statements about deep-lying personality needs, and thus are more likely to be considered by the client.

In the personality theories dominant in our time, there has been much more emphasis on needs than on values. Only recently has there been a noticeable trend in the other direction. It seems to this writer that a number of things quite different in their character from the basic needs for food, water, and air have been labeled "needs" and that thus some important distinctions may have been lost. One can as readily speak of *valuing* success as of *needing* achievement, for example. The term *need* has a connotation of compulsive force about it that the term *value* does not carry. One can *choose* among his values, and it is such choice that counseling should facilitate.

Concretely, what the counselor does as he tries to help the client clarify his values is to make statements like: "Your ideal is the creative, truly original person," or "You place a high value on independence." Typically the client will go on from such a statement, elaborating it, recognizing a conflict between this value and some other he has expressed, or exploring the anxieties and uncertainties about himself that have prevented his acting in accordance with the recognized value. The person whose regard for creativity has been recognized may talk about his doubts as to his own talents, his fear that he may not have it in him to be original. The person who values the approval of others may do some thinking about whether it is really necessary to have *everybody* like him or whether he could develop some tolerance for opposition and ill will. The girl to whom independence is so important may see without having it pointed out the possible conflict between this attitude and another almost as strong wish to be close to her family and intimate friends. The counselor can often point out such discrepancies, such conflicts between different values that have been expressed.

It is advisable to keep the discussion close to the specific material brought out in interviews rather than to use general psychological terms or broad philosophical concepts. The question is always, What does this person really want? and it can be answered in specific as well as in general terms.

The outcome of the discussion at this stage should be some alternative things the client sees that he might do. These may be steps as decisive as ending an intolerable marriage, getting out of an intolerable work situation, or leaving a church with which he has been closely identified for many years. They are more likely, however, to be small steps the significance of which would not even be noticed if their relationship to values had not become apparent. The unhappy wife may see the possibility of talking to her husband and trying to break through the wall of misunderstanding that has been built up between them. The unhappy worker may start taking a course or two to qualify him for some other line of endeavor. The person whose ideals are out of line with the beliefs of his church may join another organization and gradually transfer his major loyalty to this non-religious center.

It cannot be emphasized too much that this clarification of values leading to action cannot be done superficially if it is to succeed. Platitudes and general inspirational talk have no place in it. The only actions that can really make a difference in all of his subsequent personality development are those based on what a person really is. Unless one can get down to this bedrock, the effects of counseling will be slight.

THIRD STAGE: REINFORCEMENT

Once the client has taken some step, however hesitant, in a direction he is sure he wishes to go, the counselor can let his own words and behavior become reinforcing influences to facilitate the learning process. Some kinds of remarks that are to be avoided early in the course of a counseling relationship, such as approval, encouragement, and helpful suggestions, can now be made in responding to things the client says during the interview. When 18-year-old Chris, who has come to realize that he must get over his shyness if he is to experience the close human relationships he sees as a major value, reports that he has asked a girl for a date and been accepted, the counselor shows that he is pleased. When Lucille, who has not handed in an English composition paper for five weeks, reports that she kept doggedly at the task until 1:00 A.M. the previous evening and produced a theme for the course, the counselor in some way puts his stamp of approval on the thing she has accomplished. When Lew Landon, whose communication with his wife has been deteriorating steadily for three years, reports that the two of them had a long talk the night before and got some of their misunderstandings cleared up, the counselor shares his satisfaction in his achievement.

When it is clear from the client's actions and reports on his behavior outside the interview room that a change of direction has occurred and is at least partly stabilized, it is time for counseling to end, even though there are many emotional complexes still unexplored, many personal problems still unsolved. It may well be that at some future time some of these deficiencies will turn out to be serious handicaps, but if they are not at present impeding the client's progress toward the goal he has chosen, they need not be dealt with now. An implicit assumption underlying the kind of therapeutic process outlined here is that further counseling at a later time will be available if it turns out that the person needs it. It is no more essential that a counselor produce personalities with a lifetime guarantee than that the physician turn out perfect physical specimens who will never again need to see a doctor.

THE USE OF LIMITS IN PERSONALITY COUNSELING

At all the stages of personal counseling it is advisable to have clearly defined limits set and maintained. They are important in defining for the client what he must learn and in enabling the counselor to create a situation in which learning can occur. There is no general agreement as to just what these limits are, and they may vary somewhat from case to case, but some basic general principles can be formulated.

The first of these principles is concerned with time limits and is based on the obvious and simple fact that there is a limited number of hours in the counselor's day. It is usually impossible for the counselor to allow one client to run over his allotted time without either depriving the next person of his rights or depriving himself of time he needs for other duties. These same practical considerations usually limit also the number of interviews to be scheduled with any one person in a single week. It is important that the counselor look ahead farther than the next hour or even the next week. At the beginning of a school term he might find it possible to see John Jones for three two-hour sessions a week, but if he gets the pattern set this way he may be in serious difficulties by the third or fourth week when ten other John Joneses are claiming his attention. The student serving his apprenticeship in a counseling agency may be so eager to get experience that at the beginning he is quite willing to devote a large part of his time to the one client with whom he is working. Later he will find that things do not go as well as he gets into the thick of the year's work and needs time to study for examinations and gather data for a thesis. The counselor's aim should be to work out at the beginning a schedule that will not become cluttered and confused as time passes. To adhere to such a schedule unless there is some special reason to depart from it is the only reasonable procedure.

Ordinarily it is not too difficult to make time limits clear to a client in the early interviews when he may have a tendency to disregard them. To glance at one's watch about five or ten minutes before the hour is up and mention that it is almost over is usually all that is necessary. If no timepiece is visible in the room it is sometimes a good idea to lay the watch on the desk so that the client himself can see how he stands. Bringing the subject up a few minutes before the time actually runs out enables the person to complete one line of thought instead of having it switched off in the middle and prevents any sudden feeling of rejection at the last minute.

But should no client ever be allowed to continue for a few minutes even if he is not intruding on someone else's time and even if he is expressing feelings of great significance? Most counselors would not like to answer this question with a dogmatic "No." If an extension is given, however, it is probably good policy to limit it by some such remark as, "Our time is up, but I can spare another fifteen minutes if you would like to stay that much longer."

To change the time limits in even this limited way, however, is to risk certain undesirable developments in the counseling relationship. An understanding of what they are constitutes the second principle which can be applied to problems of limits in general. It is, briefly, that clients should not get any sort of reinforcement for attitudes of overdependence on other people or habits of manipulating them. In some persons such attitudes are at the very heart of the problems which have caused them to seek counseling, although they may be quite unconscious of the presence of these attitudes. The counselor does not condemn a person for having them; it is a part of the therapeutic process that they be accepted and understood. A boy with a father who tries to make up for neglect of his children by giving them things and a mother too weak to hold out against any persistent demand could scarcely have learned anything else about basic human relationships. Naturally he goes around attempting to force his associates to give him things or to give in to him. It is the only kind of human tie he knows how to create, and if it does not bring him love and satisfaction, it is at least some sort of substitute for them. The most important thing such a person needs to learn is that friendship is more than favors and that one need not dominate people in order to be safe with them. We cannot tell him this in words; we can only set up situations in which he can find it out. For him the apparently trivial matter of exceeding his time limit by five or ten minutes may be a real deterrent to learning the new ways for it may mean that he has forced the counselor into the same mold as the other adults he has known.

This principle of avoiding the perpetuation of unsatisfactory basic attitudes applies to other less common situations. It is usually inadvisable for a counselor to lend a client money although he may have a strong impulse to dispose of some of the person's problems in this simple way. Ordinarily he should not take action on the client's behalf—clear up a misunderstanding with an instructor, petition for an exception to academic regulations, or get him a job. Again, such acts shape the counseling relationship for an overdependent client into the familiar pattern in which he manages to get along, though not very successfully, by inducing people to take care of him. It is precisely that pattern which the counselor is attempting to enable him to break away from.

Obviously not all clients who show a desire to overstay their time limits are persons who need to dominate or extort favors, and not all who ask for help to get out of a specific academic difficulty are overdependent. It is the essence of the procedure we have been setting forth that the counselor continuously direct all his efforts toward understanding the client's words and the feelings that underlie them rather than toward diagnosing the structure of his personality. For this reason, in early interviews he is likely not to know how strong such tendencies are in a given individual, and the safest procedure is to work within limits that will hold them in check if they are there.

Still a third principle related to the function of limits in the counseling situation has been discussed very little but may well be at least as important as the other two. The counselor himself needs limits to safeguard the important attitudes upon which the success of his work is based. Self-sacrifice is a virtue whose stock is rapidly falling on the present-day psychological market. As we have come to understand better the deeper recesses of personality, we have seen that a person cannot renounce his own wishes too completely without carrying along some resentment against those for whom the renunciation is made. It follows from this that if a counselor allows his free time as well as his working hours to be invaded and if as a result he has to forego tasks and pleasures that mean a great deal to him, it may be impossible for him to maintain the active good will that is the essential atmosphere of the counseling room. The main reason why physical attacks are not allowed in play therapy is that it is very difficult to love a child who is beating you or kicking you in the shins. This factor, along with the others, is involved in the specific situations we have discussed and in many others besides. If, somewhat against his better judgment, a counselor allows a client three interviews a week when he can really only spare time for two, he saddles himself with some doubt about the wisdom of the decision and some hostility against the person for being so insistent. If he allows an individual to exceed his time limit knowing that work planned for this hour must now be done in the evening, a similar unwelcome change in his own attitude may follow. If he permits calls outside of office hours and a call keeps him from going to a play or a concert he has looked forward to, his feeling for the client is not likely to remain unchanged. Psychotherapy that required men and women so dedicated to their calling that all of their own desires were completely merged in their work would have to be given up entirely. Such people do not exist. What the therapist can do is to show toward his own nature enough of the same acceptance he gives other human beings so that he does not hesitate to use limits to safeguard the soundness of his own feelings.

In applying this principle, however, we are forced to recognize that inevitably the counselor will feel differently about different clients. This means that limits will vary somewhat from one case to another. There are persons he would be genuinely willing to see every day in the week if it seemed advisable, even if it meant giving up other enjoyable activities in order to do it. (Usually this would not be advisable anyway, as we have said, for other reasons.) At the other extreme are clients to whom it would be hard for him to guarantee an accepting attitude for more than one hour a week. Moreover, in treating an anxious, discouraged client it may actually *add* to the counselor's peace of mind if he gives the person permission to call him at any hour of the day or night. As we have said before, although all counseling relationships have common features, they are not alike. Because of this, some limits vary from case to case, depending on the nature of the particular relationship between two human individuals. The more sensitive a counselor is to the patterns of these relationships, the better he will sense the limitations that go with the pattern. It is a matter of recognizing in each instance how much of himself he is completely willing to give.

Student counselors often protest against limiting an interview to the time scheduled for it saying: "But he had only just begun when the hour ended. He was beginning at last to talk about things that were really important." In this connection we must always remember what has been stressed in this chapter—that counseling is a process of change in a person, not just a series of topics discussed in interviews. The mental activity going on when the hour ended does not cease when the client leaves the office. It reverberates in his own brain. Its effects may be significant and permanent even if they do not take place under the counselor's eyes.

At the risk of appearing repetitious, we emphasize once more in connection with maintaining limits the importance of showing the continuous warmth and kindness which are counseling's most essential ingredients. The client must not see any limit as a rejection. Again there is no certain way of guaranteeing success here. An imaginative grasp of the other person's feelings is required. Ending an interview rather than letting it run on indefinitely may call for nothing more than going to the door with the person and saying, "I'll see you next Tuesday then," with a tone of voice and manner that shows plainly that you are glad he is coming back. But in the case of a girl who knocks on your door at eleven o'clock at night and explains tearfully that she has just left her husband, more than this is obviously required. In such a situation it may be a matter of allowing a little time for her to calm down, perhaps giving her some coffee, bringing up quietly the question, "Is there anywhere you can go for tonight?" and driving her to the place she decides upon.

THE USE OF THE COUNSELING RELATIONSHIP AS THERAPY

If constructive change of any sort is to occur during the counseling process, it is not enough that the counselor know what he is trying to accomplish and use appropriate techniques at each stage. He must be willing to let himself become an important part of the client's life—to use the counseling relationship itself as therapy. What the client experiences is "learning by doing." What goes on is not just thinking and talking about life. It is in a very real sense life itself.

We have stressed the fact that the counselor's fundamental attitude is acceptance and that from the client's point of view the feeling that must exist at the beginning or come into existence as time passes is *confidence*. He must be sure that he is dealing with a person who will never under any circumstances let him down or turn against him. As we have considered various other topics, we have touched upon things the counselor does to create and maintain such confidence. He avoids accepting for therapy any person toward whom he does not genuinely feel friendly. He works within limits to insure that he will not be confronted with situations which would prompt him to reject the person or show irritation at his behavior. He refrains from talking to anyone about the things he has been told. He scrupulously keeps his appointments and safeguards the individual's time from interruptions. These things all help to make genuine confidence possible, although they are not essentially what produces it. They are not techniques, skills, or methods, in the narrow sense. Rather they are expressions of the fact that he *is* a person to be trusted.

Besides these vital ingredients, the acceptance on the one hand, the confidence on the other, every individual counseling relationship has in it a complex mixture of all sorts of things. The counselor needs to be able at all times to sense the pattern and the way it is changing as therapy progresses. He knows, for example, that Henry Harmon still distrusts him to some extent but that in spite of temporary ups and downs, confidence is growing. Mary Gleason is more dependent than most girls and is trying to use the counseling relationship as something to lean on, but there have been some signs of more mature participation. Janice Bailey desperately needs a man to love her and is trying to cast the counselor in this role. Peter Johnson has not done very well in his graduate courses in psychology and shows signs of resentment against the counselor because he has succeeded where Peter is failing. All these things and many others a therapist may sense in the attitudes toward himself of the persons he is interviewing. They do not dismay him. He accepts them in the same spirit as he accepts all other expressions of the personality. He knows that through the gradual approximation process that occurs in the interviews, each of these people will be able to reshape his concept of the relationship into something closer to what it actually is. And if he can come to perceive this one relationship clearly in all its individuality, he will be better able to see the others in which he is involved with similar clarity.

The counselor communicates his understanding of what the counseling relationship means to the client in the same way as he handles the other less personal feelings. When a boy says, "My mother used to do her hair the way you do yours. You look something like her too," the counselor replies, "I remind you of your mother." When a client says in a joking manner, "I'll bet I'm the most neurotic student you have ever talked to," she replies, "You'd like to feel that you were special for me in some way." When a young man explains, "I think perhaps I should see a psychiatrist. I don't suppose psychologists know much about problems like mine," an appropriate reply might be, "You're doubtful whether you have come to the right place—whether I am the person who can help you." (The context and tone of voice are of course important in all these instances. In some settings and with some expressions they would not mean what they are taken to mean here.) The most common mistake that inexperienced workers make is to avoid the recognition of these personal feelings. Here again habits of polite conversation stand in his way. Counseling requires that the counselor learn to face feelings toward himself as steadily and objectively as he faces the other kinds of feelings.

There is another side of the counselor's careful observation of his relationships with his clients. He must sense his own subtle attitudes in each situation. The woman who reminds Clarence so strongly of his mother may realize that she has in fact found him an exceptionally appealing boy and may have been showing tendencies either to protect him or to manage him. To recognize such a tendency is usually all that is needed to correct it. A counselor thinking back over an interview just completed may realize that there was some irritation woven into his attitude toward Mr. Rolfe, the client, that day. "Why was that?" he asks himself. "Why was it there today and not before?" He goes back over the sequence of discussion topics and realizes that the irritation started when Mr. Rolfe began talking about his gambling debts and the anxiety they were creating. "It was his blaming his father for keeping him on too short an allowance and never even considering the possibility of going to work himself that rubbed me the wrong way," he says to himself. As he thinks it over he realizes that some old resentments he had thought dead still show a surprising vitality. His own college days had been a period of unceasing struggle. He had been completely self-supporting. Naturally he had at the time felt bitter toward the playboys who dashed around the country in bright-colored convertibles and seemed to have the best of everything. It now seems a long time ago and not very important, but here is this evidence that when he is caught off guard the old feeling can flare up again. In this case, too, recognizing the source of the trouble is really all that is necessary to take care of it. Since this old resentment has nothing to do with Mr. Rolfe as an individual, it need not affect their relationship in any important way. The remedy is of course for the counselor to adopt for the time being Mr. Rolfe's frame of reference instead of his own. This he finds not too difficult to do. The experience as a whole has been valuable to him in that it has increased his awareness of his own vulnerability.[2]

A counselor can accept unwelcome attitudes in himself as he accepts them in others because he understands the complexity of

[2] It might be said that this is an example of one's need for personal psychotherapy before undertaking to counsel others. We will take up this question in the next chapter. It seems likely, however, that this kind of situation can arise regardless of how thorough one's personal preparation has been. Theodor Reik, in *Listening with the Third Ear*, Chap. VIII, discusses this problem from the psychoanalytic viewpoint.

the ties by which humans are bound together. Knowing that his basic feeling for each client is liking and respect he knows also that a few threads of anger, impatience, resentment, jealousy, sexual attraction, or paternalism woven into the pattern will not distort it too much *if he recognizes them.* The whole counseling venture calls for as much honesty as human beings can command. To say to oneself, "I have the same attitude at all times toward all my clients and this attitude is one of high, unselfish helpfulness free from any admixture of less noble feelings," is to start down the path toward self-deception. Along this way there is no growth for others or for oneself.

It is plain that the skills we have been considering require *practice.* They can never be acquired by reading about them. What has been said in this chapter should be regarded as a guidepost showing what to practice. As has been suggested, the basic perceptual skills can be developed to some extent in ordinary conversation. Interviews of various sorts which do not have special therapeutic aims can contribute to facility in expressing understanding. Role-playing situations help to enable students to develop their abilities. The would-be counselor will be on the alert for opportunities to practice what he wishes to be able to do well. It is only after considerable competence has been achieved that a person should take upon himself the responsibility for the lives of others that therapeutic counseling brings. The best controls the trained counselor has for what may be profoundly disturbing procedures spring from his own psychological knowledge and ethical convictions.

The purpose of this chapter has been to construct a framework within which counselors who are not primarily psychotherapists can serve the many persons who come to them for help with personal and emotional problems. It is an approach consistent with counseling's central emphasis on individual development through choices. The techniques involved are not new nor extraordinarily difficult. And a considerable amount of this kind of counseling can be done without encroaching on time needed for other essential counseling duties. There is perhaps some danger that the framework will appear too clear, too simple. In practice all sorts of uncertainties arise. In some cases no pattern of values ever seems to take shape. The client remains caught in his net of conflicts and symptoms, and the counselor begins to realize that this is a case of a severe neurosis that should not have been accepted for this kind of treatment. In other cases clients do initiate some actions that seem likely to change the direction of their lives, counseling is terminated, and they then experience relapses in their new efforts and give up trying. There are all sorts of variations on these themes.

The counselor must be ready to cope with such complications as they arise and not become too discouraged in the process. There is much that we do not yet know about therapy and the whole vast area of personality. Any one worker can only do his best to meet the particular challenges he encounters.

Research Summary

HOW EFFECTIVE IS THERAPY?

Research on psychotherapy has become so voluminous that it is impractical even to think of summarizing it all. All that will be attempted here is to bring together the studies bearing on the questions with which general counselors are most likely to be concerned and to refer to sources where other studies have been summarized.

The over-all question of how much good psychotherapy of any sort actually does is important to counselors to the extent that it affects their decisions as to how they should spend their time. As indicated in Chapter 1, there is some evidence that college counselors, at least, prefer psychotherapy to such other activities as helping students with vocational and educational choices. How certain can we be that therapy is effective enough to warrant this emphasis?

Eysenck (1952) directly challenged the common belief that psychotherapy was the cure for psychological ills. He brought together the data from twenty-four reports making up a total of some 8,000 neurotic cases and classified the outcomes under four headings: (1) Cured, or Much Improved; (2) Improved; (3) Slightly Improved; (4) Not Improved, Died, Discontinued Treatment, and so on. The percentages in the Much Improved group run from 39 to 77 with an average of 64. His conclusion that psychotherapy has not been demonstrated to be effective rests on a comparison of this figure with the percentages reported in two of the papers for cases to whom no treatment or a bare minimum of treatment was given. This proportion of cures was actually *higher* than the general average, 72 per cent for patients given custodial care in state hospitals, 72 per cent recovery after two years for patients with disability claims who had been treated only by general practitioners. Reports from psychoanalysts show the lowest percentage of cures. Whether or not we accept Eysenck's conclusions, it is plain that if we are going to attempt to do psychotherapy we need to understand the process better in order to cut down the number of failures.

A similar survey of reports from child guidance clinics was published by Levitt (1957). In seventeen studies where outcomes had been rated, the average improvement rate was 75.22 per cent. For control cases, consisting of clients who had applied and been placed on a waiting list but did not follow through, the improvement rate was 72.5 per cent. This is a small and not very significant difference. In a criticism of Levitt's survey, Hood-Williams (1960) calls attention to the fact that the studies showing the higher percentages of improved cases were almost all reported before 1940, and those with the lower percentages almost all since World War II. Levitt (1960) replied to some of Hood-Williams' criticisms but did not mention this point. It has a number of possible interpretations, but one of them might be that before 1940 various kinds of counseling and environmental manipulation were being used more extensively than psychotherapy.

Studies reported since Eysenck's survey show about the same proportion of successes as his figures indicate. Some of the reports on non-directive or client-centered counseling give such figures. Bartlett (1950) reports a six-month follow-up of 498 veterans given personal counseling under the Veterans Administration program. Of this group 38 per cent were rated by their training officers Much Improved, 44 per cent Improved, and 18 per cent Not Improved. Nothing is said in the report about a possible bias in the ratings which might have operated, since presumably at least some of the referrals for personal counseling were made by the training officers who did the ratings, and they would hardly have recommended this treatment had they not *expected* improvement. Cowen and Combs (1950) reported a follow-up study of 32 cases, for 27 of whom they had before-and-after Bernreuter scores for comparison and 20 of whom were available for interviews. They classified 60 per cent in the Success category, 30 per cent in the Progress category. Haimowitz and Haimowitz (1952), who followed up 10 cases one to one and one half years after therapy was completed, reported that only 6 out of the 10 showed significant improvement in Rorschach scores. If we equate the Success and Improved categories to Eysenck's Cured or Much Improved, the proportion reported is very similar to his average figures for all methods.

Watt (1949) evaluated non-directive counseling in the treatment of delinquents, comparing 11 experimental subjects with 11 controls matched with them for age, intelligence, grade placement, and previous records. Statements made in the interviews indicated that 6 of the counseled subjects had attained the therapeutic objectives of free expression, insight, and decision and action. Significant differences between the groups showed up in gains on some of the MMPI scales, *Hs, Pd, Pt, Sc,* and *Ma.* No significant differences appeared in the other measures, the California Test of Personality, and the Haggerty-Olson-Wickman behavior ratings.

WHAT KIND OF PERSONALITY CHANGE DOES THERAPY PRODUCE?

Of recent years, attention has shifted away from the question of whether therapy does any good and focused instead on attempts to evaluate the changes it produces when it is successful. The client-centered group has been especially active in this research area. A large-scale investigation is reported in the book edited by C. R. Rogers and Dymond (1954). A variety of personality measures were used to compare clients with controls matched for general background characteristics and, for some of these clients, to compare changes occurring during the therapy period with changes during a non-therapy period while they were waiting for the process to begin. The results are too detailed to be reported in full. In general it can be said that all measures based on *self-reports* showed more change as a result of therapy than behavioral measures or test scores did.

Factor analyses of correlations between various measures of change were reported by Gibson, Snyder, and Ray (1955) and by D. S. Cartwright and Roth (1957). Both studies indicated that there are at least three change factors fairly independent of one another.

Studies by Rosenman (1955) and by R. D. Cartwright (1957) both suggest that the major changes client-centered therapy produces are in self-concepts. The self is, of course, a key concept in the theory based on this therapy. An annotated bibliography of research and theory construction in client-centered therapy has been published by D. S. Cartwright (1957).

Ewing (1954) has contributed some further evidence about the effects of personal counseling on self-concepts. Thirty-nine college students were asked to check adjectives at the beginning and the end of counseling, after several different sets of instructions. In general, the results showed that in Improved cases all the kinds of self-descriptions were more alike than in Unimproved cases. The actual self, the culturally approved self, the ideal self, and the self as seen by parents and by the counselor tended to converge.

Some investigators are convinced that the measurement of actual behavior changes as a result of therapy is essential. In this there are many methodological difficulties, and nothing can be said with certainty about what kinds of changes are to be expected. A good survey of the attempts to develop behavioral criteria has been made available by Zax and Klein (1960).

An important summary of the major research efforts to study therapeutic outcomes and process is to be found in the volume edited by Rubinstein and Parloff (1959).

HOW DIFFERENT ARE THERAPIES BASED ON DIFFERENT THEORETICAL SYSTEMS?

One of the reasons the writer has felt free to combine features of client-centered and more directive methods of personal counseling in the present chapter is that research seems to indicate that therapists of different schools do not differ very much from one another in attitudes and behavior. Using Stevenson's Q-sort technique, Fiedler (1950a) has shown that experts representing Freudian, Rogerian, and Adlerian theories show a high degree of agreement on the ideal therapeutic relationship. In another paper (1950b) he reports that when therapy interviews conducted by persons representing these three different approaches are judged for the characteristics entering into this concept of the ideal relationship, there are higher correlations among *experts* of the different schools than between expert and novice in the same school.

Strupp (1955, 1958) has compared the responses to patient statements made by client-centered and psychoanalytic therapists. The only difference that stood out was the tendency of Rogerians to use the "reflection of feeling" response more than the analysts did. The experienced Rogerians, however, used it significantly less than the inexperienced did.

There have been some results, however, which suggest that it is an advantage for the counselor to show an understanding that goes a little beyond pure reflection. Dittman (1952) based his analysis on typescripts of the first thirty of a series of recorded interviews of one patient by one therapist. Ratings were made of the therapist's "participation level" (degree of attention) and "depth" (on a continuum running from "superficial" to "deeply interpretative"). Responses to be rated were categorized into response to feeling or response to interpersonal behavior provided that it was in a section of an interview in which responses to both had been occurring. It is evidently a good thing for a counselor to try to pick up both kinds of attitude. There appeared to be an advantage in responses slightly deeper than pure reflection so far as therapeutic progress was concerned.

Keet (1948) set out to test the relative value of interpretation and reflection by setting up an experimental counseling situation. For each of his 30 subjects a word having reference to some area of disturbance was located by means of a word association test. Later a learning situation was devised in which retroactive inhibition would produce a failure to recall this traumatic word, thus setting up an emotional problem and a need for therapy. About half of the 25 subjects who failed to recall the traumatic word were given "expressive" therapy, half "interpretive" therapy. Recall of the word on a subsequent test served as a criterion for the effectiveness of the therapy. Keet's results showed significant differences in favor of the "interpretive" procedure. Some doubt has been created, however, by the inability of other investigators, Merrill (1952), to repeat the study, because their subjects failed to show differential forgetting of traumatic key words. Final judgment as to the meaning of the results will have to await more evidence as to why the procedure worked with one group of subjects and not with others.

In a similar study by Wiener (1955), stress was induced in 90 undergraduates by giving them reports on their Rorschach scores. A single session of counseling seemed to have a significant effect on performances impaired by stress, but there was no difference between groups in which counseling involved reassurance and interpretation and groups in which it involved catharsis and reflection.

Evaluation

There is some danger that an evaluation of the research studies presented here may be misleading, since they constitute only a small proportion of the published material that might have been selected for comment. It seems to the writer, however, that the following summary statements are warranted:

1. No kind of therapy has been clearly demonstrated to be more effective in actually "curing" neurosis than the miscellaneous processes of time and experience are.
2. The most clearly demonstrated changes produced by client-centered therapy are changes in self-concept. There is little evidence for consistent behavioral changes.
3. The difference between therapy situations depends more on the skill and experience of the therapist than on the theoretical position he represents.

CHAPTER TWELVE

The Counselor as a Person

REASONS FOR CONCERN WITH THIS TOPIC

Counseling is an intensely personal sort of activity. Again and again the results of research studies comparing methods, techniques, or theories run up against the fact that differences between counselors are greater than any of these systematic differences in procedure. Successful outcomes seem to depend as much on what a counselor *is* as on what he says or does. Thus more and more attention is being focused on the study of these personal factors. What kinds of people should be encouraged to go into this kind of work? What should they know? What sorts of experience should they have?

Attempts to answer these questions are complicated by the great diversity within the counseling professions. A wide variety of men and women with all sorts of backgrounds are now doing a wide variety of things. By a proper selection of cases, one could show, for example, that a school counselor should get his basic training as an insurance broker, a musician, or a football coach, since persons from all these areas are functioning effectively as counselors. Similarly, many rehabilitation counselors were trained to be businessmen, engineers, or teachers. However, it would probably not be a very good idea to base our selection and training procedures on a job analysis of what persons in the profession are now doing; it might well perpetuate bad practices along with good ones and thus stand in the way of progress.

In situations of this kind, the decision can best be made by pooling the ideas of those who are in the best position to judge what is needed. It is through the deliberations of committees representing professional organizations, certification boards, and

selection and training committees of colleges and universities
that policies take shape. As years pass, these are modified to
keep pace with changing social needs, but there is enough continuity to maintain stability in the profession.

THE TRAINING OF PROFESSIONAL COUNSELORS

There is more agreement as to what constitutes desirable
training for counselors than on what criteria should be used for
selecting them. Committees of several national organizations representing counselors have studied the training problem and there
is substantial agreement in their findings.

It has been necessary to recognize different levels at which
counselors function. The standard level of training for the largest
proportion of practicing counselors is the Master's degree. In
many institutions, the degree is based on a two-year graduate
program that includes field work or supervised experience in
addition to academic course work. We shall call this Level 2.

Many psychologists are convinced that more education is
desirable for counselors and favor the Ph.D. rather than the
Master's degree as standard preparation. Although it has not been
possible to fill all counseling positions with persons at this higher
level of training, there are considerable numbers of counseling
psychologists and persons with Doctor's degrees in education,
social work, rehabilitation, or other specialized areas, who constitute a very influential part of the total counseling professional
group. We shall call this Level 3.

There is still another group of workers who have *less* training than the standard Master's degree. They tend to function as
part-time counselors in schools and other agencies. Many highly
competent high school teachers who get along well with students
are assigned to counseling duties for one or more periods a day.
Although there is widespread agreement among counseling
authorities that it would be desirable for all workers to obtain
the standard training, it is often necessary for training institutions to arrange to make the most essential knowledge and skills
available to such part-time workers who never intend to become
candidates for a counseling degree. We shall call this Level 1.

Let us look first at what the training for the middle or
standard level should be. The discussion here will be based on the

formulations of a committee representing Division 17, the Division of Counseling Psychology of the American Psychological Association (APA, 1950). They have classified the essential kinds of preparation needed by the psychological counselor under eight broad headings. The first of these is *Personality Organization and Development*. This includes a number of separate courses and makes up as much as a fifth of the individual's total graduate training program. Specifically he should know well (*a*) the current *theories* about personality, (*b*) the *developmental* patterns of perceptual, conceptual, and social behavior, (*c*) the psychological characteristics of *deviant personalities*, and (*d*) the relationships of personality to *cultural determinants*. The courses a student in a particular institution will need to take in order to give him this background will depend upon how things are organized there. He may, for example, need to take Child and Adolescent Psychology in the College of Education, and the work on cultural determinants in the Sociology or Anthropology Departments. The kind of credit a course carries is not important. The content and the capability of the instructor are.

The second heading is *Knowledge of Social Environment*. This includes such things as information about community social agencies and the kinds of help they are equipped to give, occupations and sources of information about them, marriage and family patterns and the heterogeneity of subgroup attitudes toward them. The psychologists allocate less than a tenth of the person's graduate training to this area. To the other groups who have considered counselor preparation, its importance bulks larger and they tend to assign it a more prominent place in the total picture.

The third heading is *Appraisal of the Individual* (*Theory and Practice*). The suggested subdivisions here are: (*a*) measurement and individual differences, (*b*) the administration and interpretation of individual intelligence and aptitude tests, (*c*) informal methods of group and individual appraisal such as interviews, autobiographies, questionnaires, records, and observations, and (*d*) projective techniques. This work is seen as requiring about a sixth of the total training time. Here again some of the specific courses through which the knowledge is obtained might in many institutions be found in education rather than psychology departments.

The fourth heading is *Counseling Theory and Practice*. This includes both courses setting forth processes, procedures, and theories of counseling and a considerable amount of supervised experience. Altogether this area should make up something like a third of the individual's total training program, including as it does an internship which should extend over at least a third of a year.

The fifth heading is *Personal Therapeutic Experience*, but the committee did not wish to specify that this be required of all trainees. Since it falls outside the framework of course planning with which we are primarily concerned at this point, we will postpone the consideration of it until later in the chapter.

The sixth heading is *Research and Statistics*. The objective for Level 2 counselors would seem to be a clear understanding of principles essential for the interpretation of tests and the evaluation of research rather than skill in using the techniques and carrying out research studies. This is the heading under which the differences between Level 2 and Level 3 are most marked.

The seventh heading is *Professional Orientation*. This includes such things as professional ethics and an understanding of the administrative patterns within which counseling functions.

The eighth heading is *Diversification,* and constitutes a miscellaneous category leaving room for the particular needs which individuals are likely to show.

Statements issued by other professional groups about training for particular counseling specialties are similar to this in most respects. They all stress the same broad background of psychological and sociological knowledge, the same skills in appraisal and counseling. In addition they include the specialized information of the particular group with whom they are concerned. Vocational guidance workers place more emphasis on occupational information. Rehabilitation workers include somato-psychology and information on the medical and legal aspects of rehabilitation. School counselors include some material on the organization and administration of guidance services and recommend courses leading to certification as a teacher in addition to the work in the counseling area.

Not all undergraduates steering their course in this direction realize how almost universal this teaching requirement is for school counselors. In the states that now have special certification for school counselors, some teaching experience, usually two years, is one of the specifications (Kremen, 1951). In other states where no special counselor certificate is given, the hiring of counselors from among the ranks of teachers is the accepted practice. Since these rulings ordinarily apply to junior colleges as well as secondary schools, they cover a large proportion of the positions available in school counseling and practically all of those available to persons trained to the Master's degree level.

This means that a young person who decides while he is an undergraduate that he would like to be a school counselor needs to set as an intermediate goal the obtaining of a teaching certificate valid in his state. This will ordinarily require that he take a certain prescribed minimum of professional education courses, including practice teaching, and that he acquire a reasonable proficiency in some field of subject matter which forms a part of the secondary school curriculum. It is best that he defer the specialized training in counseling that we have outlined until his graduate years, although he should get a general background in psychology if he can. Courses in biological and social science and in the humanities should also be a part of his undergraduate experience, since they help to produce the broad, tolerant, flexible view of human individuals which is so important to a counselor's work.

For a large number of part-time workers who are now doing counseling as an outgrowth of the work in which they started, the training problem is complex and in many ways more difficult. In the first place, a person in this position may find that the responsibility for securing further training rests on himself alone. When a small high school sets up a counseling program by transferring Miss Hawkes, a popular, successful English teacher, into a counseling position, the administration feels that the problem is solved. No one in the school system is in a position to say whether or not Miss Hawkes is doing an adequate job except Miss Hawkes herself. It is a tribute to the sense of responsibility of teachers in this position that so many of them reach out for summer and extension courses that will increase their knowledge and sharpen their skill.

It is evident that the same core of material in psychology, sociology, and education should constitute the solid foundation of the training of the experienced as of the inexperienced. But it may well be that the sequence in which the different parts of it are taken up should not be the same. The decision as to what should come first can be made on the basis of direct applicability to the daily tasks with which the working counselor is confronted.

When we apply this touchstone, we find in most cases that it is knowledge about the counseling process itself that is most urgently needed. The one thing counseling always involves is interviewing. The interviewing skills we have discussed in previous chapters do not spring full-blown into existence when a person takes on a counselor's role, and they do not develop as an offshoot of teaching skills. One needs to learn them. Fortunately, in a school situation the teacher-counselor will have plenty of opportunity to practice them once he understands what they are. Thus the first course the working counselor should take may well be one in counseling techniques and procedures.

As has been stated before, it seems advisable for counselors not to use tests until they are thoroughly familiar with their characteristics and limitations. Since it is a considerable advantage to be able to bring tests into a counseling program, the next of the principal areas to be covered probably should be *Appraisal of the Individual.* This may need to be preceded or supplemented by course work in the theory of mental measurement and statistics, depending upon the organization of the institution offering the courses.

The more general fields listed first for the inexperienced trainees, personality theory and abnormal psychology, will often come last for the experienced, not because they are of little importance but because the other information is more urgently needed. Individuals doing counseling will probably have had at least some of this more general material as part of their background for teaching. The learning process, growth and development of children and adolescents, and mental hygiene are often included as part of the work in professional education.

Under the provisions of the 1958 National Defense Education Act, some new and imaginative ways of educating partially trained high school counselors have been attempted (Tyler, 1960). Because the stipends paid to enrollees made full-time participation possible, the institutes set up under this program have been able to break through customary patterns of courses and stress the specific kinds of knowledge and skill most needed by counselors. Lectures and readings about psychological concepts, cultural and sociological information, principles of mental measurement, and many other kinds of knowledge are combined with small group discussions and supervised experience in actual counseling. The aim is to increase the level of competence of part-time counselors and to encourage as many as possible of them to continue their training to the Master's degree level.

Counselor education at the Ph.D. level includes the same general areas we have been discussing, adding both depth and breadth. The longer program usually includes work in other special fields of psychology, such as learning, perception, and motivation, and perhaps more work in philosophy, anthropology, and sociology. Students obtain more supervised experience with a wide variety of human problems in the normal and the abnormal range. They also undergo a more intensive and thorough training in research methods and perhaps some preparation for supervisory and administrative activities (APA, 1952). A one-year full-time internship is a standard requirement of Ph.D. programs.

There is still a considerable amount of confusion in the counseling professions. Undoubtedly many persons consider themselves counselors and function in that capacity with little or none of the kind of preparation we have been outlining. But standards are gradually taking shape in one specialized counseling field after another. The three-level pattern discussed here is the shape that the counseling profession is beginning to take.

PROBLEMS OF SELECTION

The problem of selection for the profession is much more difficult than the problem of training. It is generally agreed that there are personal characteristics related to counseling success, but just what these characteristics are is not so generally agreed. The research on this question that has been done so far has not settled the issues.

It may be that we have been approaching the problem from the wrong direction. The assumption that there is a certain combination of personal characteristics which is optimum for counseling may be unsound. It seems possible now that men and women of a wide variety of personality types can function successfully in this situation. If we give up the belief that there is *one* standard relationship that should be created in every case, we can relinquish along with it the requirement that the counselor be any *one* type of person. Logical-sounding reasons have been given for emphasizing certain personality traits, but often reasons with just as much logic can be advanced for their opposites. One can say, for instance, that a counselor should be a very stable, well-adjusted individual himself so that the help he attempts to give others with their problems will not constitute a case of the blind leading the blind. It can just as well be said, however, that a counselor should have experienced anxiety, conflict, and indecision in his own life so that he can understand it in others. Some would hold that a counselor should be an extrovert responding easily to other people. Others would expect him to be an introvert with the capacity to enter another's thought world imaginatively. Perhaps it would be better if we all assumed that any personality pattern which permits rich and deep relationships with other human beings to develop is satisfactory. Just as there is no one kind of personality essential to the husband or wife, mother or father, lover, neighbor, or friend, so there is no one kind essential to the counselor.

In the discussion of tests in a previous chapter, the point was made that it is often possible to set up negative predictors—indicators of probable failure—with more accuracy than one can set up positive predictors. This statement seems to hold for counselor selection also. First of all, there is an intelligence requirement. Graduate training at the Master's-degree level requires that the student have the intellectual capacity to comprehend the abstract concepts he encounters in such areas as educational philosophy, personality theory, and statistics. Work toward the Ph.D. requires a still higher level of the same ability. A student who does not meet this requirement will not be able to qualify himself as a professional worker, regardless of the other personal qualities he possesses. This can be put in academic terms. It would not be very inaccurate to say: For the Master's degree, only B or A students need apply. For the Ph.D., the applicant must be capable of making A's in academic courses.

It is probably true also that there is a basic minimum of general emotional stability necessary for counseling. The common view that the persons who go into counseling, social work, and the other helping professions are those whose own adjustment is unsatisfactory has nothing but anecdotal evidence to support it.

It may be true that persons who have come through periods of personal emotional stress make good counselors once their own difficulties are resolved. Unless or until they are resolved, however, such persons should probably not be accepted for training as counselors. It is apparent that this limit is not nearly so definite as the intellectual limit discussed above. We have as yet no way of measuring emotional stability accurately enough that we can set some definite "cutting score" with regard to it.

One particular personality trait is generally considered to be more of a handicap than any other in counseling. It is the one we characterize as *rigidity*, although we are not able to define it very precisely. A person who has strong convictions about many things and feels compelled to win others over to his point of view often has difficulty in comprehending what clients are trying to express. This does not mean, of course, that counselors should have no convictions of their own. But they must be able to distinguish between more and less important values and to recognize the validity of different value systems. They must be able to shift points of view so as to see things as others see them.

Another thing rigidity sometimes means to those who discuss it in relation to counseling is the inability to tolerate ambiguity and uncertainty. Persons with too much of this kind of rigidity need to have things settled one way or another. They need to be sure that they are using the "right" technique and they expect their clients to respond in specified ways. That one can never be sure that one is using the right techniques—that indeed, perhaps, there is no right technique—and that clients are continually behaving in unexpected ways lead to continual frustration for such persons.

The doubtful issue with regard to *selection* on the basis of personality qualities is the extent to which traits can be modified during training for the profession. Each personality shows both stability and change as the months and the years pass. If we could be sure which characteristics of an individual are likely to change under favorable circumstances, we could deal with selection problems more intelligently.

The qualities most essential for counselors are the basic attitudes that make it possible to accept and understand other people. These are difficult to evaluate with any precision and are to some extent subject to change with experience.

As we have repeatedly emphasized before, the greatest handicaps to counseling are hostility (or in milder form indifference) and obtuseness (or a tendency to oversimplify). The man or woman who plans to make counseling his life work should do everything possible to avoid or eradicate these traits, and keeping himself free from them will be a continuing responsibility long after his training period is over.

The necessity for keeping basic attitudes sound is closely related to the question of whether or not personal therapy of some sort should be a part of every counselor's training. Practically all those who have given the matter any thought consider such experience valuable; they differ mainly on whether it should be compulsory. Besides the part it can play in producing accepting attitudes toward people, it can be recommended for other reasons. It helps the counselor to know where his own biases and sensitive areas are, so that he can be prepared for complications that may arise in some counseling situations and relationships. Furthermore, his willingness to take such a step indicates that he does not place himself in a category different from or superior to his clients. He accepts his own human weaknesses in the same way as he accepts theirs.

If personal therapy is to become an accepted part of the experience through which men and women learn to be counselors, the graduate schools giving training will need to provide for it in the arrangements they make, and individual trainees will need to know of its availability. It will then be the responsibility of the person himself to evaluate his own attitudes and decide what he wishes to do. In the light of the knowledge we now have, these arrangements seem preferable to a rigid requirement with regard to it. Psychotherapy is not the only method for achieving the sound, constructive attitudes toward others which counseling demands. It may be that for some kinds of people long walks in the country, participation in the arts, or conversation with trusted friends serves some of the same purposes. It is the goal that is important, not the means one takes to reach it.

Once we really take seriously the fundamental importance to counseling of attitudes toward others, we realize that modifications of some of our traditions in graduate and professional training are called for. It would seem self-evident that the experiences through which a student passes on his way to professional status as a counselor should not be productive of frustration and hostility. One of the strongest arguments for a fairly rigorous preliminary selection on an intellectual basis is that it insures that those undertaking difficult graduate courses will be persons who *need* not feel overly anxious about their abilities, defensive about their performance, or too conscious of competition. It is then the responsibility of those planning training programs to think in terms of attitudes as well as skills and to organize class work and practicum experiences in such a way as to keep morale high and minimize anxious, hostile, competitive motivation.

In friendly, stimulating surroundings where insight and self-acceptance are encouraged, much selection can be *self*-selection. A woman whose underlying motive for going into counseling is a desire to manage other people's lives may see herself more clearly as time passes and decide that counseling does not constitute for her the absorbing interest she thought it did. The boy who assumed unconsciously that he would get rid of his own crippling sense of inferiority by putting himself in a position of looking down on persons with problems will have less need to pursue this course if his inferiority feelings decrease. All sorts of complex motivations underlie decisions to become counselors (and all other types of work, of course). The most skillful clinician would not be able to analyze accurately what these motives are at the time a candidate applies for admission to graduate training, but the individual himself may be able to face them and deal with them a little later.

As he concludes this section the reader may be conscious of a feeling of incompleteness, a sense that he has not been told what he would like to know. "I'm still not sure as to whether I am the sort of person who should go into counseling," he may well be saying, "and I still haven't a clear idea of what sequence of courses I should take if I do." The most that can be said in response to such doubts is that this is the way things stand at present. The task of the counselor is being gradually clarified, and there is more and more agreement as to training programs and procedures. But as yet there is no certainty. Our thinking about these problems fifty years hence may be quite different from what it is today. When one chooses a profession of this new variety, a profession which has not yet settled into any kind of a rigid mold, he accepts both the assets and liabilities that go with such a choice.

PROFESSIONAL RESPONSIBILITIES

It is easy to talk glibly about "professional" status without considering what participation in a profession really involves. We do not achieve professional status just by claiming it. We must create it through our own behavior.

The word *professional* implies first of all the possession of special abilities, skill, and knowledge, based ordinarily on advanced intensive training in the field of specialization. It is the responsibility of the counseling profession as a whole to see that all of its practitioners obtain such training. This involves the considerations that have been discussed in the earlier sections of this chapter and a number of other things as well. It is a matter of some importance to the whole profession what the certification requirements of a state include. It is also important to promote policies of employing only adequately trained counselors in schools and other agencies. As professional people we must be willing to contribute some time and effort to these undertakings that affect the profession as a whole.

Another thing the word *profession* implies is a code of ethics governing the conduct of its members. We cannot expect those who employ us or the communities in which we work to decide for us what ethical counseling practice is. The central core of the counselor's code is concerned with the safeguarding of the counseling relationship. In previous chapters problems that may arise in connection with maintaining confidentiality have been discussed and an attempt made to clarify what the ethical principles are that apply here. Other important ethical issues sometimes arise in connection with decisions as to whether to continue with a case or to refer it to someone else. Still others have to do with the use of tests in a manner that results in misinformation for the client. The most detailed consideration of the ethics of helping relationships is the one developed by the American Psychological Association (APA, 1953, 1959).

Still a third implication of professional status is the participation in organizations set up to represent the profession as a whole. The organization serving the largest number and the greatest variety of counselors is the American Personnel and Guidance Association. Its divisions are as follows: Division 1—American College Personnel Association; Division 2—Association for Counselor Education and Supervision; Division 3—National Vocational Guidance Association; Division 4—Student Personnel Association for Teacher Education; Division 5—American School Counselor Association; and Division 6—Division of Rehabilitation Counseling. The journal of this organization, *The Personnel and Guidance Journal,* is one of the best sources of current information about counseling theory, research, and practice.

Counselors whose training has continued to the doctoral level are likely also to belong to Division 17, The Division of Counseling Psychology, of the American Psychological Association. Through its committees, issues of importance to all counselors, issues having to do with research, training, relationships to other professions, and so on, are considered and resolved.

There are also many community, state, and regional associations representing counselors. They are often in a better position to work on local problems than the national associations are and thus more likely to gain the support of workers in the area.

What many beginning counselors do not realize, however, is that a strong national organization should be supported even though one is unable to attend conventions and can read the journal in the library. Particularly during our present period of rapid growth in the profession, it is advantageous to have people who can speak for all of us when crises arise. The APGA was in a position, for example, to give Congress the information that led to the guidance provisions in the National Defense Education Act. It comes to the defense of members subjected to unjustified attacks, legal or otherwise, for situations that arise during the exercise of their professional duties. A national professional organization provides a common voice and machinery that can be used for carrying out the common will.

RELATIONSHIPS TO OTHER WORKERS

Counseling is more than a profession. It is a point of view. Important as it is to develop skill in the use of various techniques, it is still more important to keep in mind the purpose of the whole undertaking—the welfare of the individuals for whom the program exists. But since there are other people with that same aim, counseling inevitably involves some concern with their work also and an effort to strengthen the relationships within the larger organizations.

For counselors who work in school settings at either the high school or the college level, this means that they must fit themselves into the total student personnel or guidance program. The large high school or college has a considerable number of specialized personnel workers. Some are concerned with selecting and admitting students to the institution or to its various curricula or programs. Some carry responsibility for the development of students' social life in desirable directions. Some furnish services related to housing, food, or health. These are only a few of the aspects of student welfare with which someone must concern himself if the purposes of education are to be accomplished. Most or all of them involve some counseling.

It is generally recognized also that teachers do a considerable amount of counseling. Long before the days of specialized personnel services, warm-hearted teachers were showing the kind of constructive, friendly interest in individual students which is the essence of counseling. It is still true that a boy or girl may feel much more at home with a favorite English or science teacher than with the person designated by the administration as a counselor.

School counselors must also take into consideration the work being done in other community agencies. Good relationships with workers in various specialized community agencies are even more crucial for counselors in non-school settings such as hospitals and rehabilitation services. For the client's welfare it is necessary that these services work together harmoniously rather than at cross-purposes.

To achieve good working relationships is more than just an administrative problem. A student personnel director can, of course, construct a chart that shows clearly just what role each kind of worker plays in the total undertaking. Similarly a community survey can delineate clearly what the aims and the resources of each agency are. But the relationships that count are constructed of human attitudes and feelings which no organization chart can produce or even include. The counselor, because of his trained sensitivity to attitudes and human relationships is in a good position to work toward the development of genuine co-operation.

Such co-operation must be built on mutual *respect*. The counselor who considers the work of other guidance people to be "superficial" or the psychologist who needs constantly to insist on his superiority to social workers cannot achieve enough understanding of what the people in the other positions are doing to generate this respect. Our first task, if we really wish to co-operate with others, is to understand them. This involves personal contacts of many kinds, such as social conversations, committee work, and consultation on cases.

Even in situations where such respect exists constant attention must still be given to problems of *communication*. In the relationships between different kinds of student personnel workers, for example, difficulties can grow out of a counselor's insistence on not making decisions for his clients, unless he explains his attitude to faculty advisers, housing directors, or deans, who occupy positions in which they *must* make such decisions about students. If a faculty adviser telephones a college counselor to ask whether or not he should allow Ed Sandstrom to drop Chemistry 10 from his program, it is not very helpful to say simply, "Ed must decide things like that for himself." It is better for the counselor to explain that he and Ed are working on the task of determining what is really best for him to do and that in order to stimulate the kind of thinking that needs to be done, he must refrain from making a recommendation. He can also indicate, however, that he knows the matter has to be decided one way or the other and can show that he is not going to be critical of the decision. To deal with each situation that arises in such a way that neither his relationship to his client nor his relationship with other members of the school staff is jeopardized is one of the counselor's responsibilities.

Similarly in interagency relationships much of the communication occurs in connection with particular problems, situations, and cases. Each time one of these is handled constructively, the links of co-operation we are trying to forge are strengthened. Simple as this sounds, it is often neglected. One Veterans Administration vocational adviser used to dispatch a memorandum to any member of his staff who failed to fill out a required form correctly, even though the man was only three doors down the

hall from him. Nothing could be more remote from the attitude
of friendship and mutual confidence at which we are aiming.
A telephone call is much to be preferred to a memorandum; a
personal conference is better than a telephone call. If a counselor
thinks it important that referrals be made in one way rather than
another, his obvious course of action is to talk the matter over
with the persons concerned. If he is asked for information he
considers confidential, he should not just refuse to give it. He
should explain his reasons to the person who has asked for it
and try to clear up their relationship so that from this time on
they can co-operate without friction. Personal relationships of a
constructive sort do not spring up by themselves like weeds; they
are garden plants requiring careful cultivation.

Communication is facilitated also through joint staff meetings of various kinds. Sometimes these are organized around
individual cases. One participant presents the information he has
about a client and outlines the problems that he sees, the questions that might be raised. Others who know the individual in
other capacities bring their specialized information into the total
picture. General discussion follows, as a result of which the persons present attain a deeper understanding not only of the client
but also of each other. This method is widely used in training
programs for counselors. It is an indispensable part of the procedure in "team" undertakings, such as those that go on in
comprehensive rehabilitation centers.

Through the cultivation of mutual respect and the development of communication channels, counselors and other kinds of
service workers can learn to co-operate with one another. Good
working relationships do not come about in a day, a month, or
even a year. They must be a gradual growth over a long period
of time. And they can never be established once and for all.

It may be that in the long run the indirect results of such
co-operation and common concern with community needs may be
fully as important as the specific undertakings out of which they
grow. School personnel workers talk a great deal about the
"personnel point of view" and its desirability in education generally. There is no reason why the same concept should not be
applied to the larger community surrounding the school. It is a
difficult term to define with any precision but it is not so difficult
to recognize it in operation. It means that each person is seen

(Counseling) to respond to 22 incidents in which loyalty to the client conflicted with loyalty to society. There were some significant differences between groups in the positions they took on the issue. Industrial psychologists were most likely to stress the social responsibility; clinical psychologists, most likely to stress responsibility to the client. Counseling psychologists took a position between the other two. All differences were small, however, showing more similarity than difference in the three groups. All agree that confidential information the client has given should be divulged if there is a clear and imminent danger to society, such as murder, suicide, or treason. Where they differ is in their judgment of how clear and imminent the danger represented in a situation is.

Evaluation

One comes through this survey with a feeling that we have barely scratched the surface of knowledge in these areas. The studies showing that there are differences in personality and motivation between counselors and other people, and that some traits are related to successful performance, can be thought of as pilot studies pointing out directions in which it might be profitable to proceed. The clarification of ethical principles to maximize their applicability to individual cases and situations is another research area where much remains to be done.

CHAPTER THIRTEEN

The Evaluation
of Counseling Effectiveness

EVALUATION RESEARCH AS A
BASIS FOR COUNSELING PROGRESS

After most of the preceding chapters, research summaries have appeared which bring together the accumulated evidence relating to the counseling practices considered in the chapters. Some of the most important research in the counseling areas has been of this nature—the study of the special kinds of contribution made by separate parts of the service, such as interviews, tests, and occupational information.

There are, however, other important questions which have led to research. These have to do with the service as a whole. The first and most obvious of these is simply, Does it do any good? Do persons who experience counseling get along any better in their later lives than those who were not given any help of this sort?

The second kind of question that needs to be answered is, What is counseling good *for?* Many aims and objectives have been stated during the half century counseling services have been in existence. Many kinds of clients with diverse needs and problems have been served. It is quite possible that counseling is helpful in some situations but not in others.

Still a third kind of question has to do with differences between various methods or theories. This approach can be combined with either of the first two kinds of question. We can ask whether one specified theory and technique of counseling produces better results in general than does another specified theory and technique, or we can ask whether the two approaches differ in their applicability to different kinds of problems or clients.

It will be apparent to the reader when he finishes this chapter that we have scarcely begun to formulate satisfactory answers to these questions. If we are to plan wisely for the future of our profession, we must obtain such information. Otherwise thousands of counselors may spend precious counseling time working with clients who are unlikely to obtain any benefit whatever, while others who have needs that could be met go uncounseled. Training programs may focus on ideas and skills that are of little or no importance instead of on those that are basic in carrying out purposes counseling can accomplish. Even in its present incomplete form, evaluation research suggests directions in which the counseling professions may move forward.

DIFFICULTIES AND PITFALLS IN EVALUATION RESEARCH

Whatever particular question a research worker sets out to answer, he encounters several rather serious difficulties. These have been well analyzed in papers by Williamson and Bordin (1941a), Froehlich (1951), and Travers (1949). In the first place, there is the question of whether the criterion of counseling success should be satisfaction or adjustment. It can be argued with some conviction that the basic evidence as to the satisfactoriness of the service rendered is what the recipient thinks about it. If he is pleased and feels he has been helped, we can consider our efforts successful. Although most research workers would agree with this way of thinking to some extent, they can see reasons for going beyond it. There are certain social conventions that make for positive findings in studies planned this way. When anyone asks a person whether he feels better or worse as a result of some experience, it seems to be more natural for him to report an improvement than a decline. It is easy enough to get evidence favorable to counseling by this method. The trouble is that the same sort of evidence can be obtained for the success of fortunetellers, phrenologists, and faith-healers.

If we decide, then, to rest our case on adjustment rather than, or in addition to, satisfaction, we face some new problems. Should we use objective or subjective evaluations of this adjustment? The objective criteria such as grade-point changes and dropout rate for students, number of job changes and earnings for workers, are definite, clear-cut, and convenient to use in statistical computations. But it is easy to see that any one of them can be misleading in an individual case. If we use dropout rate in a counseling group as our criterion, we are loading the dice against ourselves to the extent that our group contains low-ability students for whom persistence in academic work is an *unfavorable* rather than favorable indication. If we use grade-point changes, we are not taking into consideration a large number of bright but unhappy students whose grades are likely to *drop* somewhat when their social adjustment improves. There are many instances when giving up a job is a healthier thing to do than clinging to it. In spite of these qualifications on using such objective criteria, there still is a place for them. On the whole, we might expect *averages* of counseled and non-counseled groups to differ on these things, even if there were numerous individual exceptions to the general trend.

The alternative subjective methods involve the use of some-one's rating of the degree of adjustment achieved in each individual case. Sometimes the raters are given case material to read; sometimes they base their judgments on follow-up interviews. These methods are subject to the same difficulties and limitations as all other types of ratings. Some degree of reliability can be attained by using two or more raters and clarifying for them the nature of their task. Their judgments will still, of course, represent whatever attitudes they have as to what constitutes success and adjustment in our society, attitudes which may not be appropriate in all individual cases. However, this method also has a very definite place in follow-up research. If *both* objective and subjective criteria are used, each tends to correct the defects in the other.

Another puzzling problem has to do with the use of a control group with which the counseled group can be compared. It would seem, as in all research which assesses changes, to be important to make provision for a control group in one's experimental design. Whatever our criterion, we know that changes occur in individuals in the absence of any identifiable influence that has been brought to bear on them. Unless changes produced by counseling are more marked than such spontaneous changes tend to be, we cannot be sure that it has been effective. For instance, in a high school study, the fact that a group of seniors shows a higher level of adjustment than they showed a year earlier might indicate simply increasing maturity, the influence of a particularly helpful homeroom teacher, a change in academic regulations, or an improved extracurricular program—or something different from all of these. The only way we can be sure that counseling produced it is to compare the gains with gains made in a similar group where no counseling was given. To find suitable control groups is not easy. Where counseling is voluntary, the very fact that an individual seeks it out shows that he is different in some aspect of his motivation from another person who seems to be like him in age, intelligence, and circumstances. Thus the practice, common in many research fields, of pairing each member of the control group with one member of the experimental group, works less well here. We do not know how to match the pairs on this motivational characteristic which may have a more important bearing on our particular problem than does any other trait. The obvious solution from the standpoint of methodology, to give counseling service to only half the applicants for it and use the other half as controls, is difficult to justify in a service agency. Investigators have solved this problem in various ways, and most of their solutions are not altogether satisfactory. In some cases it has been possible to compare the results of a new program with those of a program already in existence and thus evaluate the significance of the features that have been added.

There has been one study directed specifically to the problem of developing good criteria of counseling effectiveness. Froehlich (1949) located 279 former clients of the State Consultation Service, Richmond, Virginia. The subjects were interviewed according to a rather detailed interview schedule yielding information on many specific items having to do with occupational and personal adjustment. Relationships between these items were analyzed statistically. Clusters of related answers having to do with occupational adjustment, personal adjustment, and attitudes were found. The change-of-status criteria seemed not to be related to the others. In this report Froehlich made no attempt to tie up these criteria with any aspect of the counseling clients had previously received, but they should constitute useful tools for subsequent research. Clear-cut criteria of counseling effectiveness have been badly needed.

EVALUATION OF GUIDANCE PROGRAMS

The first group of studies we shall discuss are attempts to appraise a total *guidance* program. Such programs, of course, include many services besides counseling, so that evidence of their effectiveness cannot be related to counseling alone. Kefauver and Hand (1933) compared an eleventh-grade group from a city having an outstanding program with an equivalent group from a city having very little guidance emphasis. No difference showed up in the percentage of students with vocational choices, in vocational information, or in measured adjustment. In the group with the good guidance facilities, however, the average IQ of those planning to enter the professions was more in line with professional requirements (117.5 as compared to 104.2 in the non-guidance group) and students had more knowledge of college requirements. Remmers and Whisler (1938) reported changes in measured attitudes toward five occupations following a guidance program consisting largely of talks and self-analysis. Cole (1939) in 1936 followed up two matched groups of 100 boys each who had been members of Worcester Boys Club in 1931. One group had been counseled, the other not. Counseled boys were significantly higher on all criteria—persistence in school, job level, freedom from delinquency, and so on—but since we are not told on what basis counseling was given to them and not to others, the possibility of motivational differences between experimental and control subjects remains. Hutson and Webster (1943) compared a group of eleventh graders who had experienced a special guidance program the year before with the previous group of eleventh graders who had not experienced it. The emphasis in the experimental group was on *self*-evaluation. Relationships between success in specific courses and various predictive variables were emphasized. The students in the guidance group planning to go to college were higher in previous grades than were college-goers among the controls, and the distribution of occupational choices was more like the census distribution although still warped somewhat toward the white-collar end. Experimental subjects also made higher grades in elective courses, which would seem to indicate wiser choices. No statistical significance tests are given, but the numbers are large enough so that differences are more likely to be significant than they are in some other reported studies.

Probably the most important series of studies evaluating total guidance programs is that which Rothney and his students and associates have been carrying on over a period of years. Rothney and Roens (1950) compared a guidance and control group of 129 students each. The counseled group had had the benefit of guidance services during a five-year junior and senior high school period. They were divided into a college-going subgroup and a vocational subgroup, and a variety of criteria were used in comparing counseled students with controls. In both subgroups significant differences in favor of the counseled group were obtained.

In a later study, Rothney (1958) followed up students in four representative Wisconsin high schools five years after graduation. In the four schools, 870 students were randomly assigned to experimental and control groups during their sophomore year. Counseling was provided for the experimental students by members of the university staff, and generally accepted techniques of testing and information gathering were used. No systematic counseling was provided for control students. Here as in the previous study, a number of criteria were used in comparing groups at the time of follow-up. Differences, while small, were quite consistently in favor of the experimental group. Reports of separate parts or aspects of this Wisconsin study have been made by Kaczkowski and Rothney (1956), Caravello (1958), and Merenda and Rothney (1958).

Another long-range study designed to evaluate a guidance program has been carried on in Flint, Michigan. The first report on this project was that of Worbois (1947). The ninth-grade class was divided into two *equated* halves. Controls were given only the regular school guidance; experimental subjects were given intensive individual guidance over a three-year period. At the close of this time 24 from each group were tested by the Luria technique, which is a method of using involuntary motor responses to a word association test as an indicator of emotional disturbance. The experimental group was significantly more stable by this criterion than was the control group. The use of the objective criterion of emotionality rather than some type of self-report, as well as the comparability of experimental and control subjects, makes this study stand out.

In 1953, ten years after the students in this study had graduated from high school, a follow-up study was made. Cantoni (1955) reports the results. Of the 234 students in the experimental group, 140 graduated from high school, as compared with 119 of the 234 controls. The follow-up investigators were able to locate 121 of the graduates in the experimental group, 119 of the graduates in the control group. There were significant differences in favor of the counseled subjects on general adjustment (measured by the Bell Adjustment Inventory), cultural status, educational achievement, and occupational status.

Turney and Morehead (1954), comparing two Kansas high schools, one of which had a guidance program, reported similar differences. Gribbons (1960), in a much less ambitious study, interviewed eighth-grade students before and after a group-guidance unit using the material published by Educational Testing Service entitled *You: Today and Tomorrow*, designed to develop continuous self-appraisal as applied to decision-making. Interview responses were scored for the different components of vocational maturity as outlined by Super and others (1957). There were highly significant changes in this variable.

In general, then, it can be concluded that guidance programs are having desirable effects on students.

CLIENT ATTITUDES TOWARD COUNSELING

Although we have questioned whether client attitude is a sufficient criterion of counseling effectiveness, it merits some consideration as a partial criterion. It is hardly necessary to consider in detail the reports that have been made by Paterson and Clark (1943), Hawkins and Fialkin (1935), Anderson (1949), Gaudet, Carli, and Dennegar (1950), Glazer and England (1949), Barnette (1950), and J. R. Ward (1948), since there is a remarkable consistency about them. Of the subjects who send in questionnaire replies, from 80 to 90 per cent report full or partial satisfaction with the service. The consistency with which the percentage in the 80's shows up is especially interesting in that a variety of types of subjects are represented in the above-mentioned studies—

college students, unemployed men and women, industrial workers, and veterans. Unfortunately, none of these investigators succeeded in getting all of his subjects to return their questionnaires, so that we are left in doubt as to the attitudes of the non-respondents. Furthermore, the impossibility of getting a control group for this type of study keeps it from being conclusive. We cannot ask people who have not received any counseling to report on whether it has helped them. This constant figure *may* represent only the proportion of favorable answers one is likely to get to any sort of question about influences on one's life. It is interesting to note that an early study from Australia reported by Mirk (1931) also gives comparable figures.

During the 1950's studies of this kind have continued to appear. Blum and Sullivan (1953), Porter (1957), F. W. Miller (1952), and Raplus (1956) obtained predominantly favorable reports on counseling from students. Bloom (1952) collected even more favorable comments on the helpfulness of counseling from former Air Force officers counseled at Lackland Air Force Base. Skyne (1960) asked former clients of a social agency giving service to disturbed adolescents to comment on the counseling they had received. About 82 per cent of the comments were at least somewhat favorable, a figure that was considerably higher than the social workers who had dealt with these clients had expected it to be.

The unanimity of the results in all these studies suggests that no more evidence of this over-all sort is needed to demonstrate that clients like counseling. It would seem more profitable to design research that would permit comparisons of subgroups and identify factors related to degrees of favorableness of reaction. One such study is that of Nelson (1956). In this follow-up of 88 former clients of a university guidance center, subjects were classified as vocationally *mature* and *immature* on the basis of their previous thinking about occupations, as evidenced in the preliminary interview. Although the general response of the group as a whole showed the typical 74 per cent who were satisfied with counseling, the breakdown indicated that maturity is an important factor here. Of the mature clients, 83 per cent were satisfied, as compared with only 59 per cent of the immature clients. The same kind of difference was found when the maturity classification was based strictly on age, one group consisting of clients who were 19 or over, the other of clients 18 or younger.

EFFECTS OF COUNSELING ON SCHOOL ACHIEVEMENT

One of the first and largest of the studies on this problem involved almost 700 students counseled at the University of Minnesota during 1933, 1934, 1935, and 1936. Williamson and Bordin (1940) compared a group of 405 freshman counselees with a control group matched with them for class, age, sex, size and type of high school, high school percentile rank, college aptitude test score, and English test score. Ratings on "progress toward adjustment" were made after follow-up interviews by staff members not involved in the original counseling. Significant differences in favor of the counseled group were found for both adjustment and scholarship. The only doubt this study leaves centers around possible motivational differences between the counseled and non-counseled cases, carefully matched as they were for the other variables. In another report (1941b) the authors attempted to relate rated adjustment of the whole group of 693 students to various factors for which there was evidence in the case records. Some 83 per cent of the arts college students and 86 per cent of the general college students (a lower-ability group) were rated as satisfactorily adjusted. This would seem to show that counseling was as effective with lower-ability as with higher-ability students. The degree of co-operation with the counselor, which was also rated, was significantly related to adjustment. There was a higher proportion of adjustment among those who had come with vocational problems than among those whose problems had been of a personal nature. Adjustment was not related to whether or not the counselor confirmed the student's original vocational choice. The reported material having to do with the number of interviews and the time over which the case extended is less clear-cut in its implications. Partially adjusted cases seemed to be highest in number of interviews but lowest in time.

Blackwell (1946) compared changes in grade-point average for a group of 40 University of Texas counselees and a control group matched with them for ACE level and amount of previous college work. There was a significant difference in points gained between the two groups, but again our inability to be sure that they are motivationally similar leaves some doubt.

Faries (1955) compared 140 students entering City College of New York in 1947 and 1948 who took advantage of the counseling offered during an orientation class with 140 controls matched with counseled subjects for high school decile, entrance test scores, date of entrance, and degree field. Seventy-seven per cent of the experimental group graduated from college, as compared with 51 per cent of the control group, a significant difference. Again interpretation is hampered by the fact that the two groups may have differed in original motivation.

After World War II there were a number of studies attempting to evaluate Veterans Administration counseling centers here and there. J. R. Ward (1948) showed that a group of counseled veterans at the University of Oregon averaged slightly higher in subsequent scholarship than a group of matched controls but showed less favorable attitudes toward the whole college situation. Because of the impossibility of matching them for motivational factors in the first place this difference cannot be interpreted. Kirchheimer, Axelrod, and Hickerson (1949) compared improvement in grades from one semester to the next for four groups of University of California veterans classified according to whether or not they had received counseling and whether or not they had changed their course of study. The only significant improvement was in the "Counseled-Change" group. In general, counseled groups made more improvement than non-counseled.

Several studies have reported the percentages of groups of veterans still in training for a specified objective six months or more after counseling was completed (Brown, 1948; Condon, 1947; Lipsett and Smith, 1948; Long and Hill, 1947). Of the cases on which they report half or more seem to persist in the pursuit of the objectives chosen, but since there was a high percentage of non-returns in all these studies and since we lack any baseline against which we can evaluate the figures, it is hard to make use of them.

There have been a number of studies which attempted to check on the effect of interviews alone on scholarship. In general, they suggest that this personal attention has some value in itself. Although Williamson (1936) found that students advised by a faculty counselor did no better than those not advised, Toven (1945) and Walthers (1932) at the college level and Adams (1932), Lund (1931), and Newland and Ackley (1936) at the high school level reported favorable results. Cowley (1933) reported that the number of freshman athletes remaining eligible was greatly increased by a counseling program, but since his procedure constituted a more intensive effort including tutoring where needed, it is impossible to attribute the results to counseling alone.

A suggestive study of a somewhat different sort was reported by Sherriffs (1949). Thirty-four general psychology students out of a class of 257 were given a personal interview with the instructor after the first mid-term, at which time he rated them on tension and needs for achievement, affection, and praise. The interviewed group made a significantly greater improvement on the second mid-term than did the rest of the class. The differences on the final examination were in the same direction but not so great. The effect of the interview was greatest for students rated highest on tension and the need for affection and praise.

Hoehn and Saltz (1956) in a similar study found the same kind of improvement. Moore and Popham (1960) compared three groups, each consisting of 25 students, drawn form an introductory educational psychology class. Those in the control group were not interviewed. In one of the experimental groups, students were given two extra class "student-centered" interviews, while those in the other experimental group were given "content-centered" interviews. Although the "student-centered" group showed a significantly greater increase than the other groups on the Borow Inventory of Academic Adjustment, neither experimental group differed from the controls in final course grades.

The evidence on the question of whether having someone take an interest in him tends to improve a student's academic performance thus seems to be somewhat ambiguous. Perhaps attention from the teacher of the course is more effective than attention from others.

Guthrie and O'Neill (1953) compared three groups of college students who received different amounts of dormitory counseling and found no difference between them. Scarborough and Wright (1957) made a follow-up study of 188 students who attended a four-day counseling clinic before entering De Pauw

University. They did not differ significantly from matched controls in grade-point average or in proportion graduating from college. Patterson (1957) found no difference in either grades or persistence in the training program between counseled and non-counseled veterans in an industrial school.

One group of students for whom special attempts have been made to improve scholastic achievement through counseling consists of those whose aptitude for college work is marginal. The available evidence here is not altogether consistent but in general suggests pessimistic conclusions.

Ross and Boyd (1936) reported a significant difference between the grades of counseled freshmen in the lowest fifth of their class and non-counseled controls of the same ability levels, but since they used group-counseling centered around a discussion of entrance test scores, the results may show the value of the self-understanding that tests can bring rather than of counseling itself. The most thorough analysis of the effects of counseling on low-ability college freshmen was done at the University of Iowa. It was begun in 1925-1926 by A. C. Lemon and reported several years later by Holaday (1929) and Freeman and Jones (1933). The first results gave the advantage to the counseled group, as compared with their non-counseled controls, both in grades and in persistence in college. The final follow-up, however, showed that only 14 out of the 106 actually graduated from college as compared with 13 of the controls. The grade-point average for the graduates in the two groups was almost identical. Since the net effect of counseling for students of this ability level was to get them disqualified late rather than early in their college careers, the authors concluded that it had been unprofitable. Of course the conclusion applied to students in the lowest decile on the college aptitude test, not to the whole ability range.

A much more recent study at Iowa (Goodstein and Crites, In press) produced even more negative results. The subjects were college applicants who had been informed that they must register for summer work and demonstrate their capacity before they could be admitted to college. They were in the lower half of their respective high school classes and had scored in the bottom 30 per cent on placement tests. Some of them were invited to make use of the counseling service and the others used as a control group. Although the *N*'s are small, the differences are clear-cut and significantly in favor of the group *not offered* counseling. This was true for both summer and fall term grades and even when the effects of differences in academic ability were removed by covariance procedures.

Several other studies have concerned college students who had been placed on probation. (Hackett, 1955, Richardson and Perry, 1956, Kulick, 1953, Klingelhofer, 1954). They differ in the particular questions asked and methods used but agree in the general conclusion that counseling does not significantly increase the proportion of cases showing recovery from academic difficulty.

There is one other special group in which there have been attempts to improve scholarship through counseling. This is the group usually labeled *underachievers*, bright students whose performance does not measure up to their abilities. Results in this area so far are conflicting and difficult to interpret. At the ninth-grade level Broedel, Ohlsen, and Proff (1960), who carried out an unusually well-designed study in which group-counseling techniques were used, found that although experimental subjects improved more than controls in acceptance of self and others and in rated behavior, there was no improvement in grades, either immediately or after an 18-month follow-up period. Baymur and Patterson (1960) compared three methods of assisting underachieving high school students, two of them involving individual counseling and one involving group counseling. Between groups given different kinds of treatment, there were no significant differences on any of the criteria used, but those who experienced group counseling showed some superiority to the controls in grade-point average.

Studies reported by Serene (1953) and by Stasek (1955) at the senior high level and by Calhoun (1956) at the eighth-grade level present clear positive evidence for the value of counseling to underachievers. One factor that may warrant some consideration is that in both the Serene and the Calhoun studies the procedure was more definite and highly structured than it ordinarily is in counseling. Students were presented with the evidence for their underachievement and encouraged to analyze its causes and plan ways of correcting it. It may be that in connection with this particular problem such methods have a more direct effect than those in which the focus is on the more subtle aspects of motivation and personal relationships.

EFFECTS OF COUNSELING ON
VOCATIONAL ADJUSTMENT

Some of the most important of the evaluation studies in this area have been summarized at the end of Chapter 6. They are the investigations made in Great Britain of young people who left school and went to work during the 1920's. They showed conclusively that those who had experienced counseling based on test information were more successful than the others and that the tested clients who took jobs in accordance with the counselor's recommendations were more successful than those in "non-accordance" positions.

Many evaluations of vocational counseling have been carried on in the United States also. From the beginning of the so-called "scientific" vocational guidance movement, considerable emphasis was placed on follow-up studies which would show how successful the programs were. In reading these reports from previous decades, one is conscious how much our attitude has shifted away from authoritativeness and counselor decision-making. The feature of the guidance situation that is apparently being evaluated in most of these studies is the counselor's clinical judgment as to what is best for the individual. Thus one of the most essential comparisons is between those who followed the counselor's advice and those who did not. Viteles (1949) reported a follow-up of 75 out of 91 cases seen in the University of Pennsylvania Guidance Clinic during 1923-1924. The numbers of cases in the subgroups were too small for significance tests, but the trend of the differences suggested that there was more school failure among those who did not follow the advice received than among those who followed it. Non-followers were making higher wages than followers, but this might easily have resulted from their being more likely to enter blind-alley jobs.

In 1935 a series of bulletins was published evaluating the Adjustment Service in New York (American Association for Adult Education, 1935). This agency was in operation for a period of about sixteen months during the depression years of 1933 and 1934. It was an emergency organization, and the staff consisted of persons with a great diversity of background experience, none of them highly trained counselors at the beginning. A well-planned in-service training program helped to make good this deficiency, however. Altogether they took care of more than 15,000 clients, most of them unemployed white-collar workers. The most searching of these follow-up studies is the one reported by Seipp (1935). Case records on 100 randomly selected clients were studied by two reviewers three months to a year after the completion of counseling. Questionnaires were then sent out, and unusual care was taken to obtain complete returns, only 4 out of the 100 remaining finally unreported. The criteria of adjustment were also carefully defined: (1) whether the client had formulated an objective, (2) whether he had taken steps in accordance with the plan, (3) the extent to which steps taken seemed to mark progress toward the goal, and (4) satisfaction and hopeful outcome. Fifty-seven were rated as satisfactorily adjusted. Whether this is high or not cannot of course be determined in the absence of a control group.

Webster (1942) obtained questionnaire returns from 81 out of 125 clients rather diverse in age and schooling two to five years after counseling. He considered that his judgment had been correct if the follow-up indicated either that a subject had entered a recommended field and found it satisfactory or that he had entered one not recommended and found it unsatisfactory. This method of classification gave him a score of 80 per cent correct predictions for vocational cases, 84 per cent correct for educational.

One interesting report by Lorimer (1944) has to do with a follow-up of 397 Columbia College students counseled by Dean Herbert E. Hawkes. He seems to have used what we would now call a rather directive technique based almost entirely on Strong scores. Results, however, are more impressive than in the other studies. The 87 per cent response after an interval of from two to over nine years is a notable fact in itself. All but 43 of the subjects agreed with the results of the conferences and not one student who followed the advice given expressed dissatisfaction or unhappiness. In spite of its limitations this study does focus our attention on one variable that is largely ignored in the others—the personality of the counselor himself.

Patterson and Fotiu (1953) checked on the status of 155 clients counseled under the Veterans Administration program 6 to 22 months after counseling had been completed. Of those who had followed the counselor's recommendations, 71 per cent were making a satisfactory adjustment, as compared with only 39 per cent of those who did not follow the recommendations made.

Kaess and Long (1954) reported less favorable results. They compared a counseled and an uncounseled group with the same educational background. All were engineering students at City College of New York. The groups did not differ in scholarship or job satisfaction.

Most of the studies cited have evaluated counseling which involves both interviews and tests. The Birmingham studies seemed to indicate that this combination produces more favorable results than do interviews alone. The question of the value of counseling interviews without tests in vocational counseling has had very little attention. One such study has been reported by C. H. Stone and Simos (1948). The subjects were applicants filing at a public employment office, who were counseled in 1941-1942. Occupational recommendations were made in the same way for both experimental and control groups, but the former were given a counseling interview, the latter a summary letter. Six months later a questionnaire was sent out to all subjects and an 80 per cent return obtained. There was little difference between the groups, quite favorable reactions coming from both. The counseled subjects did report that the interview was a help before talking to employers and their rating of the general helpfulness of the service was somewhat higher. This study is of course subject to the general criticism made earlier of the use of client attitude as the only criterion.

There is an apparent paradox in some of the research cited here and following the chapters on tests and on decision-making. The studies of E. L. Thorndike and others (1934), Latham (1951), and R. L. Thorndike and Hagen (1959) seem to indicate that vocational aptitude tests do not predict vocational success to a significant extent. Studies by Sarbin (1943) and Walker (1955) indicate that counselors' predictions are not accurate. Yet the studies cited here seem to indicate that if young people follow the recommendations of counselors who base their judgments on tests, they are more likely to achieve success and satisfaction than if they do not. How shall we reconcile these different kinds of results?

One important consideration has been mentioned in the discussion of the aptitude test studies following Chapter 6.

Although the tests do not *correlate* significantly with success within each occupational group, they do *differentiate* occupational groups from one another. The counselor's judgment as to what is suitable for a person may rest mainly on such evidence. He may be able to see where a person belongs with much more clarity than he can see just how successful he is likely to be.

There is another factor to be considered also. One thing that differentiates subjects in the Birmingham studies of vocational guidance from subjects in the Thorndike and Hagen study of vocational tests is whether or not a counseling experience occurred. This may be a place where the whole is more than or quite different from the sum of its parts. When it seems that a client has simply accepted the recommendation or prognosis the counselor has made, it may well be that he has actually participated in a decision-making experience that is deep and far-reaching. The important thing may not be the accuracy of the counselor's prognosis but the satisfactoriness to himself of the individual's decision. The value of tests would seem to be that they contribute to the self-knowledge underlying these satisfying decisions rather than that they predict what a person will do well some years hence. (An exception to this generalization needs to be made for tests of scholastic aptitude and any occupational criteria that are related to length of schooling. *All* studies show that this *educational* variable can be predicted.)

We should note here also that this conclusion as to the function of tests applies equally well to occupational information according to the report by C. H. Stone (1948) previously cited. It is only when the facts about jobs have been incorporated into counseling that they lead to more appropriate choices. They too would seem to be effective insofar as they facilitate the decision-making process we have been postulating.

One other aspect of these studies perhaps deserves a little more attention than it has received of recent years when concepts based on non-directive therapy have dominated counseling philosophy. This is the clear-cut evidence that favorable outcomes follow upon counselor recommendations that are carried out by clients. In this field where much specialized knowledge must be integrated into complex judgments, it may be that the counselor's trained skills are more likely to produce workable syntheses than inexperienced clients' methods of attack on the problem are. It has been recommended in earlier sections of this book that counseling be viewed as a partnership, a *democratic* rather than a *laissez-faire* undertaking. If he looks at it in this way, there is no reason for the counselor to hesitate to use his special knowledge and skill in the formulation of occupational objectives for the client to *consider*. The client's freedom is not curtailed so long as the decision rests in his hands.

EFFECTS OF COUNSELING ON PERSONAL ADJUSTMENT

In the Research Summary following Chapter 11, some of the more important therapy-outcome studies have been summarized. As indicated there, comparisons of counseled individuals with controls have given rise to considerable doubt as to whether more significant personality changes occur with therapy than without it. Any changes that do occur are more likely to show in self-reports than in behavior.

There have been several outcome studies in counseling centers that have evaluated personal counseling in various ways. Yates (1951) arranged a follow-up study of 38 clients at the University of Missouri. It was judged that satisfactory progress had been made in 18 of these cases, little or no progress in the other 20. In keeping with the previous findings on the difference between self-reports and other evaluations, clients themselves were better satisfied with their progress than the judges were. Love (1958), however, did find some favorable changes in personality test scores and reports from outside sources for a group of individuals who had been counseled as opposed to a control group who expressed a need for personal counseling but could not arrange it because of geographical location.

Martinson (1955) compared a counseled group with a "delay" group, using George Kelly's REP Test. The counseled group showed a significant increase in the number of positive dimensions, indicating a growth in ability to describe or evaluate others in ways which would contribute to good interpersonal relations.

Jesness (1955), on the other hand, did not find differences between 31 counseled college freshmen and 29 "wait" controls on any of nine variables having to do with personality change.

Both groups gained during the period of the study, but the difference between them was not significant. It is interesting that a difference did appear in the specific area of vocational planning. Sixteen of the experimental group, as compared with 7 of the controls, changed to new goals more appropriate to their aptitudes and interests.

One of the most comprehensive studies of the effects of personal counseling in the college setting is the research program at the University of Minnesota reported by Berdie (1958). The characteristics to be measured were decided upon after an exhaustive survey of the counseling literature and extensive staff discussion of counseling behaviors. The three main variables were Anxiety, Defensiveness, and Personal Problem-Solving. The carefully-worked-out experimental design involved 80 subjects counseled by eight counselors and 20 control subjects who were placed in a "wait" group until one month after their matched experimental subjects had completed counseling. Of the 33 specific hypotheses with regard to treatment effects that were tested, *none* were substantiated. What seems to have occurred is different kinds of movement in different cases. Specific problems were solved even though general personality change did not occur.

A much earlier study of college students indicates that guidance that goes beyond counseling to stimulate actual participation in college activities has desirable effects. Aldrich (1942, 1949) divided a group of freshman girls who made low scores on inventories of social adjustment into two equivalent subgroups. The controls were given only the regular counseling for which they had applied. Girls in the experimental group were given a special interview and personally introduced to activities in which they expressed some interest. Evaluation at the end of the school year indicated that the experimental group had improved significantly more than the controls on both inventory scores and ratings of adjustment and participation. A recheck of activity records several years later after all of the subjects had left college showed that throughout their college careers the experimental group had engaged in a larger number of campus activities, been on more committees, and held more offices. The controls, however, had made slightly better grades and a slightly higher proportion of them married.

There are also a few studies that indicate changes produced by counseling at the junior and senior high school levels. Working with seventh-graders, McLaughlin (1956), found significant differences between his 50 subjects and their matched controls on effort rating (report card), number of disciplinary referrals, and peer-group status. Caplan (1957), working with a group of junior high school boys in a series of ten group-counseling interviews, found significant changes in self versus ideal self correlations and in the number of classes in which "poor citizenship" grades were given. The boys showed a slight improvement in scholarship also. The Broedel, Ohlsen, and Proff (1960) study previously cited found significant improvement in self-attitudes and rated behavior in ninth-graders.

Taken as a whole, these studies do not lead to optimistic conclusions about the amount of personality improvement that can be produced by counseling in the typical school or college setting. The fact that the results of different studies at the college level are somewhat conflicting suggests that there may be many aspects of the complex situation needing separate analysis. The fact that the few studies carried on with high school groups report more striking changes than college studies do suggests that difficulties may be more amenable to treatment in younger subjects. However, no conclusion has been established with any certainty except that more research is needed.

COUNSELING IN REHABILITATION SETTINGS

During the 1950's the participation of counselors in the rehabilitation of physically and mentally handicapped persons has been vastly increased. Several evaluation studies have been carried out in this area. Stotsky, Daston, and Vardock (1955) compared 14 schizophrenics with 14 matched controls. The experimental subjects participated in group and individual counseling sessions leading to planned work activities in the hospital. The counseled group showed significantly more change than the controls on things relating to work characteristics, such as grounds privileges and trial visits, and on Q-sorts reflecting self-concepts, but not on group Rorschach scores or psychiatric symptom ratings. Stotsky (1956) had previously shown that such patients do not see psychotherapy as useful to them, in comparison with other hospital activities. It would seem that even chronic hospitalized patients can learn to make more use of the capacities they have without undergoing marked personality change.

Kir-Stimon (1956) showed that psychoneurotic veterans counseled under the Veterans Administration program were able in many cases to make a good work adjustment whether or not they had been given therapy in addition to the vocational counseling. Seventy per cent of them were judged to have made a good adjustment at the time of the follow-up study about six years after the counseling had occurred.

New ways of combining counseling with actual training in work attitudes have recently been getting considerable attention. Gellman, et al. (1956) reported that of 102 clients who completed an eight-week experimental workshop, 48 per cent were rated successful at the time of the follow-up a year after the experience (meaning that they had worked steadily throughout the year) and 21 per cent were rated partially successful (meaning that they had worked half or less than half of the year). The thing that makes these results seem remarkable is that all of these subjects were persons considered to be "hard-core unemployable" clients of the agencies referring them for treatment. As in the previous studies, the changes were not in basic personality but in work habits and interpersonal relationships. Feintuch (1954) also indicates that an integrated program combining counseling with training in a sheltered workshop can increase the employability of clients.

What these studies are suggesting to those who work with the disabled is that counseling and training designed to enable individuals to make use of their assets can be effective even in cases where serious personality difficulties persist uncorrected.

THE RELATIVE EFFECTIVENESS OF
DIFFERENT KINDS OF COUNSELING

During the 1950's there has been a growing interest in group counseling. Three of the studies reported in earlier sections of this chapter, Broedel, Ohlsen, and Proff (1960), Caplan (1957), and Gribbons (1960), used group rather than individual methods in their attempts to answer particular counseling questions. The Baymur and Patterson (1960) study on underachievement previously cited compared both group and individually counseled subjects with controls. The differences between the two counseled groups were not very striking.

In another study at the high school level, D. A. Davis (1959) found that both group and individual methods of counseling produced significant improvements in students with low citizenship grades and that the group was somewhat more effective than the individual treatment.

The one comprehensive college study that has been reported on this topic, that of D. P. Hoyt (1955) showed no difference in the amount of increase in certainty, satisfaction, and realism in vocational choice produced by group and by individual methods. The subjects in this study were 60 freshman boys who were uncertain of their vocational choice at the beginning of the year. There were significant gains under both treatment methods.

So far as present evidence is concerned, the outlook is promising for group counseling. It seems to be about as effective as individual counseling in producing some kinds of desirable effects.

The other kind of comparison of counseling methods which has found a place in a number of special studies has to do with different techniques, theories, or philosophies. In previous Research Summaries it has been indicated that counselors and therapists representing different schools or theories do not differ as much in their actual interview behavior as it is commonly believed.

There have been several evaluation studies in counseling settings in which comparisons of directive and non-directive counselors have been made. Carlson and Vandever (1951) divided 46 students into three approximately equal groups labeled directive, non-directive, and control. Six interviews were scheduled with each individual in the two counseled groups, and the TAT test, scored according to the Murray system, was given at the beginning and end of the study to evaluate changes. The results showed no differences between the groups in changes on Need and Press ratings. The study is inconclusive because of doubt as to the adequacy of the counseling either group received and doubt as to the suitability of the TAT test for this purpose.

Barahal, Brammer, and Shostrom (1950) report what looks like more satisfactory evidence of the superiority of what they call "client-centered" procedures over those used by the Veterans Administration in vocational counseling. (Since their experimental procedure included an orientation interview and numerous special forms for presenting occupational information and facilitating client thinking about occupations, it is not strictly comparable to methods used by Rogers and his co-workers.) The investigation was carried out at the time when Stanford University was about to shift over from a Veterans Administration Guidance Center to some form of student service. The subjects were 100 male, non-veteran freshmen, divided into two groups comparable in age, scholastic aptitude, socioeconomic status, and previous counseling. For the first four weeks of the study, the control group was processed according to the standard VA procedures. After an interlude of a week during which the three counselors reviewed and practiced the new "client-centered" procedures upon which they had previously decided, the experimental group was counseled using these new procedures. In every case an evaluation interview was recorded the night after counseling. The man who did those interviews was not one of the counselors participating in the study. He rated each person on over-all feeling tone, and afterwards the three counselors made ratings from the records on the same variable. They obtained significant differences on this characteristic in favor of the "client-centered" group. Experimental subjects seemed to be more enthusiastic about all aspects of the service—testing, library, attitude of the personnel, counseling, and sureness as to future plans.

Unfortunately for the conclusiveness of these results, one crucial point seems to have been ignored. The questions which were asked in the course of the evaluation interview would have indicated beyond a doubt the group to which the subject belonged. Questions 14 and 15 referred specifically to procedures which were not used in the control group (Barahal, 1950). Thus the raters who based their judgments on these interview recordings could hardly have avoided a bias growing out of their counseling philosophy and their preference for the procedures they had originated. Forgy and Black (1954) did a follow-up study of these same subjects three years later at a time when most of them were graduating from Stanford. Exceptional care to get as complete returns as possible resulted in an 87 per cent response to their questionnaire. Ratings of satisfaction with the counseling based on responses to some general questions did *not* differentiate experimental and control groups, and there was a practically zero correlation between these ratings and those obtained from the evaluation interviews three years before. The one factor that did differentiate significantly between groups on these follow-up ratings was an *interaction* factor between counselors and procedures. What this seemed to show was that one counselor obtained better results with the VA procedures than he did with the experimental procedures, whereas the other two showed differences in the other direction. This is especially interesting in view of the fact that all three of them had a strong philosophical loyalty to client-centered ideas. This finding may have important implications for the planning of evaluation studies and for our thinking about counseling methods in general. Different personalities inevitably produce differences in the way in which any specified counseling procedure will be used. Two counselors who are attempting to use the same technique may not be producing the same psychological effect at all.

A number of later studies have reported similar results. D. P. Hoyt (1954) compared outcomes for Rogerian and eclectic counselors on a number of outcome variables. Most differences were not significant, but here as in the Forgy and Black study cited above, significant interaction effects were found.

A long-term research program at Pennsylvania State University (Snyder, 1957) seems to be demonstrating that differences between *reflective* and *leading* methods are not significant but that the interaction between therapist and method is. A detailed report of some of the studies that have come from this program of research can be found in the monograph by Ashby and others (1957) and the paper by Baker (1960).

Some of the most decisive evidence on the question of whether theoretical differences affect counselor behavior has been contributed by R. L. Wrenn (1960). Excerpts from counseling interviews were chosen by experienced counselors in such a way that they might be expected to *maximize* theoretical differences. Fifty-four counselors from 23 institutions representing a variety of theoretical orientations responded to the last client statement in each of these excerpts. Their responses were then analyzed using categories proposed by Bales and dimensions proposed by Robinson. Of the many comparisons made of frequencies in these categories, there was only one difference that was significant for counselors of differing orientations. Psychoanalytically oriented counselors were lower than the others on *reflection* category. (This is the same difference that Strupp found in the study previously cited.) The principal differences were between excerpts representing different *situations*. Sensibly enough, it would seem counselors of all orientations vary their counseling behavior according to what is being discussed.

In the light of all this evidence, there would seem to be no reason to perpetuate the directive, non-directive distinction in discussions of counseling. Its principal consequence may be to induce inexperienced counselors and counseling trainees to behave in an unnatural way during interviews.

There is a little evidence that clients tend to prefer an eclectic approach. Grigg and Goodstein (1957) made a follow-up questionnaire study of 288 University of Iowa clients, based on a 57 per cent return. Subjects were asked about their satisfaction, about counselor technique, and about their reactions during counseling. Reports of favorable outcome tended to accompany answers indicating comfort during counseling and active participation rather than passive listening on the part of the counselor. Sonne and Goldman (1957) began with the hypothesis that more-authoritarian clients would tend to prefer eclectic techniques, whereas the less-authoritarian would prefer client-centered techniques. The subjects in this study were not themselves counselees but high school seniors listening to recorded interviews of counseling sessions. The hypothesis was supported to some extent, but a more striking finding was that all groups, whatever their level of authoritarianism, tended to prefer the eclectic.

IMPLICATIONS OF EVALUATION RESEARCH

Incomplete as the evidence is on a number of questions, it can serve as a guide in decisions about practice and about future research.

So far as practice is concerned the studies cited would lead to several tentative conclusions:

1. that long-range guidance programs have substantial effects on the development of students and are to be preferred to "one-shot" counseling experiences;

2. that counseling leads to more satisfactory vocational adjustments and more adequate self-concepts, but that its value for improving school achievement and for changing undesirable personality traits is not very great;
3. that counseling efforts expended on college students with doubtful intellectual capacity for college work are largely wasted;
4. that group techniques where applicable are as satisfactory as individual techniques;
5. that differences in theoretical orientation have little effect on counseling behavior or outcomes.

These conclusions have real implications for practicing counselors who must decide how best to use the limited time they have available for counseling. Group procedures can often be substituted for more time-consuming individual procedures. Clients for whom not much can be done on the basis of present knowledge can be given a minimum of attention and others whose needs are more likely to be met by counseling allotted more time. Objectives related to specific problems or particular decisions are more likely to be attainable than objectives related to general personality improvement.

Such conclusions would make a real change in the structure of many counselor's jobs. In some high school and college settings, counselors spend most of their time with students who are failing and whose abilities are definitely limited. In other places, prestige considerations lead the most highly trained and experienced counselors to spend most of their time with clients seeking "therapy" and very little with those who need limited help in planning their own futures. Neither the administrative structure that underlies the overattention to low-ability students nor the attitudes that underly the overattention to the maladjusted can be justified by existing research findings.

Probably the most important implications of evaluation research, however, are for the planning of further research. It is plain that we do not need any more studies in which former clients are simply asked how they feel about the counseling service they received, although some further analysis of the reasons why a minority are dissatisfied might be illuminating. We do not need any more studies in which directive and non-directive approaches are compared. We do not need studies that show that clients who follow counseling recommendations about occupational plans get along better than those who do not.

What we do need is research of a more analytical nature that would enable us to understand why results differ from case to case. Why do some underachievers work harder and do better school work after counseling while others do not? Why do students seek vocational guidance and then *not* follow the recommendations made? Why do clients think that their behavior and personal relationships have improved as a result of counseling when objective evaluations do not indicate any improvement? How can individuals handicapped by personality deficiencies be helped to get themselves into situations where improvement is likely to occur?

These are just a few of the many questions still unanswered around which interesting and useful research could be organized. A sound research foundation has been laid for at least some of the work we are now doing, but much must be learned if we hope to do it more skillfully and more intelligently.

CHAPTER FOURTEEN

A Conceptual Framework
for Counselors

THE GENERAL PROCESS OF DEVELOPMENT

The basic science for counselors is the body of knowledge that has been built up as man has studied the laws that govern his own development. Development is a complex field of study that ignores boundaries we are accustomed to set up between subjects or disciplines. We know that it is *biological* and that intricate chemical processes govern the person's progress through his life cycle. We know that it is *psychological* and that changes in thinking processes, emotions, and attitudes accompany visible changes in bodily structures. We know that it is *sociological* and that at each stage a person is imbedded in social patterns both narrow and broad.

Development involves *general* principles universally applicable and *individual* characteristics unique for each person. For some purposes and in some contexts we focus on the universality; for other purposes and in other contexts we focus on the individuality. But always, whatever our particular concern with the developmental process, we must keep both aspects in mind.

It is possible to view the whole developmental process in an individual as a single unbroken line extending from the moment of conception to the moment of death. Patterned change is continuous and inexorable. Today is not yesterday. Tomorrow one will not be exactly the same person that he is today.

Those who study the developmental process have, however, found it useful to break it up into successive stages, each qualitatively somewhat different from the one preceding and the one following. But there is no unanimity about how this should be done. The beginning of a stage can be based on biological events, such as the coming of puberty. It can be based on psychological events, such as the resolution of the Oedipal conflict. It can be based on social demands in a particular culture, such as starting to school.

One of the most useful ideas for stimulating research thinking about developmental stages has been the concept of developmental tasks, as formulated in different ways by Havighurst (1953) and by Erikson (1950). This is primarily a sociological or cultural concept; a developmental task is a challenge to be met, something to be learned or mastered, if a child or a man in a particular culture is to move ahead with his capacity to meet future challenges unimpaired.

In this framework, adolescence, the stage with which so many counselors are concerned, is the period when the young person must attain economic independence, expand and change the quality of his social relationships, channel his sex impulses into a mold sanctioned by society, sort out his values and organize them into a coherent philosophy of life. In Erikson's terms, he must establish his *identity*.

As a background for counseling at any stage, it is desirable for the counselor to know what the other earlier and later stages are. An outline the writer finds useful, based on discussions by a number of people, is the one given below. A more detailed account of each of these stages can be found in Goodenough and Tyler (1959).

1. *Infancy.* The main developmental task is to progress from complete dependence to relative autonomy. The stage lasts for about the first two years.
2. *Early Childhood.* The main developmental task is to attain *initiative*—to learn to take responsibility for one's own actions. The stage comprises what are usually called the preschool years from 2 to 5.
3. *Middle Childhood.* The main developmental task is to achieve *competence* in the many kinds of physical, mental, and social skills considered essential in a culture. The stage comprises the elementary school years.

4. *Adolescence.* As indicated above, the many developmental tasks to be mastered during this period can all be subsumed under the attainment of an individual *identity* as a mature human being. The stage lasts from the age of 12 to approximately 20.

5. *Adulthood.* The main tasks are those of *establishment* in work, family, and community, and the attainment of the kinds of emotional relationships Erikson calls *intimacy* and *generativity*, a close personal concern for others, especially those in the oncoming generation. The period extends approximately from 20 to 40.

6. *Middle Age.* The developmental tasks can be described as *maintenance* of the way of life one has established and the consolidation of one's values into a durable *personal philosophy.* The period can be considered to last from about 40 to 60.

7. *Old Age.* The developmental task is primarily the *adaptation to decline* and change of status. In many ways the challenges are more acute than they have been since adolescence, since they often call for the reorganization of life activities around some new focus. The years from 60 on are usually considered to make up this period.

We are just beginning to see that counseling of some sort might help with all these successive tasks and challenges. It is likely that in the years to come, counseling activity will not be concentrated so heavily in the adolescent period. Service to the aging and to handicapped adults in all the different periods is increasing rapidly. The extension of school counseling services downward to the elementary school period is being widely recommended. Counselors need the perspective that "life-span" psychology gives.

From a broad social point of view, the whole developmental process is one of *socialization.* This has its universal and its individual aspects. All persons growing up, working, and growing old in a particular culture must have certain standards of behavior, certain values and attitudes internalized if the society as a whole is to survive. Just as important as this universal side of the socialization process, however, is its individual side. Persons must develop in ways that will prepare them for particular *roles*

in the total complex pattern of the culture. Of 100 children born
this week, a few must grow up to be professional men, a larger
number to be tradesmen and industrial workers, a sizable fraction
to be clerical workers. Artists, homemakers, and community
leaders must somehow emerge from the group as the developmental process runs its course for all.

If one looks at this process solely from the point of view of
the society as a whole, one can see it as an enormously complex
machine in which lives are shaped to built-in specifications. But
when one looks at it from the psychological point of view, one
sees choice, decision, selection going on. A person is not really
molded by his culture. He *reacts* to its pressures and *selects* from
its many alternative possibilities those that best suit his emerging
self.

It is this selection process in which the counselor plays a part.
It is this that he must understand in its largest outlines and in
its minutest details if he is to do his job well. One of the main
values of the research that has been done on the development of
vocational choices is that it affords us a means of studying this
choice process as it applies to *all* of life. This is one of the main
reasons why counselors should not abrogate their historical concern with vocational guidance. The process of choosing an occupation is a process of establishing an identity. It is not the only
way this can be done, and increasingly counselors will probably
have to be concerned with other kinds of choices that have this
identity-fixing quality. But occupational choice is perhaps the
most common challenge of this sort with which individuals in our
society are confronted, and it has been the most carefully studied.
We shall use it in subsequent sections when illustrations of
abstract ideas are required.

THE TRANSFORMATION OF POTENTIALITIES
INTO ACTUALITIES: TWO DIFFERENT PROCESSES

Let us take a rather abstract look at what goes on during any
developmental stage. In the broadest sense, what is accomplished
is the transformation of the *potentialities* that exist in the beginning into *actualities*. The earlier the stage is, the larger is the
number of potentialities. The act of conception rules out a tre-

mendously large number of egg-sperm combinations that might have occurred before one particular combination takes place. A newborn infant has an almost infinitely large number of possibilities for personality development that might occur under different kinds of family situation and cultural environment. All these diverse potentialities are quickly lost when he begins to develop in the one family to which he has been born. At the age of one, a child has potentialities for fluent expression in several thousand languages. By the time he is two, most of these potentialities have been lost because he has had the mark of one language stamped upon him for life.

This part of the process of development is, then, a *narrowing* or a *limiting* process. At first it is accomplished through selection carried on consciously or unconsciously by forces and persons outside the individual's own control. Increasingly, as he grows older, the individual himself participates in the process, setting his own limits through his own choices. There are large individual differences in the extent to which this taking over of responsibility for one's own development occurs. Some persons live out their lives at the mercy of chance circumstances and other people's decisions. A few are to a considerable extent really "self-made" men. Most of us are somewhere in between, selecting potentialities for actualization partly on the basis of circumstances and pressures, partly on the basis of our own decisions. But it is important to remember that in one way or another the selection process *must* occur. Each person has only 24 hours a day at his disposal and lives only a relatively small number of years. The complete actualization of all potentialities is impossible.

The narrowing process described above is one thing going on at any developmental stage. In addition, there is another process, just as universal, the phenomenon we call *learning*. Sometimes this works in a direction opposite to that of the limiting process, creating new potentialities from among which selections can be made. More often it complements the limiting process, strengthening and enriching the particular trends that have been selected for actualization. Always the two processes work together in some way, forming a pattern that a counselor or anyone else who hopes to understand an individual life must try to understand.

THE PLACE OF COUNSELING IN DEVELOPMENT

With these concepts, a counselor has a basis for studying systematically any individual life at any given stage of its development and for deciding how to use his influence to facilitate future development. He will look first at the limits as they exist for his client at the beginning of the stage he is in. These are of several kinds. The first class consists of those that are set by circumstances, such as family financial situation, accessibility of schools and colleges, geographical factors. The second class consists of those that are set by relatively permanent physical or psychological characteristics of the person himself. It includes physical handicaps of all kinds, intellectual limitations, basic temperamental qualities, and things like sex, race, and age. The third class consists of limitations based on what has and has not been learned at previous stages, or, in other words, on the success or failure the person has experienced with his earlier developmental tasks. The fourth class consists of attitudes, values, and concepts about self and the world.

Once the counselor sees these limits clearly, he is in a position to be helpful in one or more of a number of ways. Probably the most common one is to assist the person in choosing from among the alternative courses of action that are within the limits discussed above. This is the standard situation in vocational and educational guidance. For any particular college freshman boy, possibilities of choice are limited by all of the four kinds of factors, but a number of majors and careers are still open to him. By clarifying both the limits and the possibilities, using all of the sources of information and all of the interview skills discussed in previous sections of this book, the counselor helps the person to make a good choice. What he decides now will constitute an important limiting factor at the next stage. Thus it is important that the decision be a good one.

In saying that a decision is good, we make a value judgment. Counselors make these automatically, and there would probably not be a great deal of disagreement about the criteria on which they rest. We assume that it is better for the person to make the decision himself than for others to make it for him. As was said in the previous section, the selection between alternative possibilities must be made, in one way or another. A person who does not or cannot choose for himself must live with the choices circumstances impose upon him. And we feel, though probably we cannot prove, that a person who *decides* is better able to cope with life than a person who *drifts*.

Counselors also tend to agree that knowing what you are doing and being aware of the factors entering into a decision you make is to be preferred to being propelled entirely by unconscious motives. Furthermore, we consider that somehow the positive kinds of motivation, such as values, goals, and plans, are superior to the negative ones, such as fear and self-disparagement. Thus counselors try to create interview situations in which motives of all kinds can be expressed and their relevance to choices and decisions that face the person recognized.

With such standards to guide him as to the sort of decision he wishes to facilitate, the counselor participates in the lives of many of his clients primarily through helping them choose. But he also plays an important part in the other process that is involved in self-actualization, the learning process. Choices must be consolidated through new learning. Sometimes it is skills that must be acquired, such as typing and shorthand for the would-be secretary and dancing for the boy who has decided to widen his social contacts. Sometimes it is knowledge of facts and principles that must be built up, as when a young man decides to enter the medical profession. Sometimes learning involves clarification of confused ideas—differentiation, synthesis, and organization. What a counselor is most likely to contribute to learning in any of these varieties is the initial planning of situations where it can occur. This again is a traditional part of the educational and vocational counselor's role. Counseling is not really completed until the client has taken the first steps of the learning process. Plans for education or for vocational training follow immediately upon decisions that are reached.

Facilitating decisions and planning learning situations are the most common ways in which counselors affect development, but they have other roles to play in some cases. For certain individuals, some *revision of limits* is necessary before decision is possible. If an analysis of the limiting factors shows that the person has no promising alternatives around which his future development can be organized, it is necessary to take another look at the limiting factors themselves, searching for weak spots in the walls that have been constructed. One examines first the circumstances that appear to close the person in. Are there any of them that are less absolute than has been assumed? Sources of financial aid can be explored. Responsibilities a man has for the support of a family can perhaps be temporarily taken over by his wife. A student can perhaps leave the little country town where educational opportunities are limited and live with an aunt and uncle in a nearby city.

The second kind of limitation, that based on relatively permanent characteristics of the person, is probably least subject to revision, but it is always possible to re-examine the judgment as to how permanent one of these qualities is in an individual case. Sex, race, and age cannot be modified, but physical handicaps may be overcome by prostheses, and intellectual and temperamental characteristics may be subject to some modification through learning.

The limits based on past learning experiences and on attitudes are most likely to be modifiable. It is possible to return to a previous stage and master some developmental task that was not handled adequately at the time the person first faced it. It may be something as concrete as learning the multiplication tables or learning to drive a car that must be accomplished if he is to enlarge his scope. It may be something as general as learning to trust people and to differentiate between those who can and cannot be trusted. It is also possible, though not easy, for a person to revise deep-seated attitudes about himself and his capacities so that he sees more possibilities for constructive action.

In dealing with such overlimited clients, the counselor works in two ways. One of his resources is the counseling relationship itself. It constitutes the most promising means of changing self-limiting attitudes. As indicated in previous research summaries, changes in self-concepts are the most convincingly demonstrated effects of therapeutic counseling. His other resource is learning situations outside of the interview itself, participation in which can be planned during counseling. When a client has been helped to see clearly what it is he must learn and has been put in touch with the persons or situations that can direct the learning process, the counselor can leave the rest to him.

All of the separate processes we have been considering— analyzing limits, choosing, learning, revising limits—go on in life whether or not counseling occurs. The counselor's role is to stimulate and facilitate the natural developmental processes—to enable them to operate more efficiently than they do by themselves—in the same way that a gardener encourages the growth of the plants in his care.

In each counseling interaction, it is up to the counselor to decide where he should concentrate his efforts. In the case of a highly intelligent 18-year-old, avid for life and experience, who would like to be a scientist, artist, and statesman all rolled into one, the search for valid limits may be the counselor's principal concern. Unless such a person can find some unusual life plan, in which elements of all these talents and interests are combined and make a distinctive pattern, he must accept the fact that it will be necessary for him to give up several of the possibilities he now sees in order to realize one of them. In the case of a 45-year-old patient who has just suffered a severe heart attack, some revision of the limits as he now sees them may be the paramount consideration. In the case of a widow of 35 with three young children and a 10,000-dollar insurance policy, the planning of learning experience that will permit some previously abandoned potentiality to be actualized may be the counselor's chief responsibility.

If the counselor keeps this purpose of facilitating development in the forefront of his mind, he can utilize his own time to best advantage and avoid wasteful and pointless activities. Much energy has been utilized in trying to overcome limitations that need never have been overcome. If we accept the fact that for a finite human being limits are *necessary*, there is no need to try to raise all IQ's, to provide remedial work for all academic deficiencies, or to prove to all disabled persons that they can do everything the non-disabled can. The counselor's first strategy, to be used wherever possible, should be to accept the existing limits and explore alternative possibilities within them. Only when this strategy appears unpromising need the other strategies directed toward more drastic change be adopted.

LIMITS AND COMMUNICATION

To many persons the emphasis on limitations in the preceding discussion is disturbing or at least distasteful. Americans are an expansive people and like to believe that all things are possible for everybody. What we sometimes fail to see is that superficiality and uncertainty about our own identities are the price we pay for failing to accept the basic fact of the finiteness of any one individual life. Depth, solidity, and individuality depend upon self-limitation.

The one way in which individual limits can be transcended is through communication. Each of us can live only one life, but he can grasp imaginatively the special quality of experience that characterizes each of an unlimited number of others. The dramatist and the actor, the novelist and the artist, open up for us the personal worlds of other individual human beings. Conversation, when it is open and free from barriers, can bring understanding of those to whom we are related by bonds of family or friendship. Counseling itself typifies this communication by means of which we experience vicariously lives we cannot live.

This is one of the things participants in a counseling experience learn, although it is never explained in words. For the counselor, the principal reward of his work is this everwidening human horizon, this grasp of what it would be like to live many other lives which are different from his own. For the client, it is this realization that it is not necessary to experience everything in one's own person in order to know what it is like which enables him to accept with good grace the increasing limitations that maturity, responsibility, and the inevitable vicissitudes of age bring with them. Whatever else counseling accomplishes, this communication is a clear gain. It is for this reason that perceptiveness and responsiveness on the part of the counselor have been so frequently emphasized in previous sections of this book. From a good counselor a client learns many things. Most important of all he learns that "no man is an island." Through bonds of understanding, the one life he lives can be linked to all the other human lives in which he participates.

Appendix A

Date_____19_____

UNIVERSITY COUNSELING CENTER

University of Oregon

Individual Record Form

By answering the questions in this blank you will enable your counselor to learn much that may help in assisting you. If vocational counseling is desired, you will have a preliminary conference during which tests will be selected according to your individual needs, after the test scores are compiled, you and your counselor will together try to fit all the facts into a consistent pattern. It is the intent in all the counseling to assist you in achieving more intelligent and better informed self-direction, rather than to relieve you of the necessity of making your own decisions.

NAME_____ _____ _____SEX_____
      Last   First   Middle

Present Address _____ Phone_____

Home Address _____

Age_____ Date of Birth_____ Place of Birth_____

Religious Preference_____

FAMILY: Marital Status:

Single____Married____Separated____Divorced____Widowed_____

Indicate all members of your family, including parents, husband or wife, brothers, sisters, and children.

Relationship	Age	Occupation	Marital Status	Years of Education

EDUCATION:

Name of High or Preparatory School_____ City_____
Date of Graduation_____
Colleges or special schools attended (including present attendance) and special training in art, music, stenography, etc.

Name of School or College	Dates	Course or Major	Average Grade	Degree

Subjects Taken   Prep Decile_____   *Subjects Taken*   G.P.A._____
in High School   *in College*
English
Mathematics
Social Studies
Languages
Others

Indicate the subjects you liked best above with X and least-liked subjects with O. Also mark those in which you made the highest grades with H and lowest with L.

Have you been handicapped in school because you were a slow _____ or poor _____ reader? Do you consider that your study habits are (efficient, average, or inefficient) for college achievement? (Underline the best phrase.)

Indicate extracurricular activities and offices you have held:

In High School	In College	Years of Participation	Of Much or Little Value?
_____	_____	_____	_____
_____	_____	_____	_____

If you expect to attend some other school in the future, name the school, when you will enter, and what course you plan to take: _____

If you are now in school, how many hours of study do you put in during the week (on the average)? _____ Are you engaged in any outside work? _____ If so, what is the work and how much of your time does it take? _____

While in college, will you be entirely supported by your family? _____ Or will partial or total self-support be necessary? _____ What other aid do you have? _____

How does your family feel about college work? Opposed? _____ Indifferent? _____ Wants you to go? _____ Comments: __

WORK EXPERIENCE:

List in chronological order all your work or employment experiences to date, including part-time or summer jobs and service experience (if any).

Employer	From To (Month & Year)	Nature of Work Performed:	Salary (per month)
_____	_____	_____	_____
_____	_____	_____	_____

In what ways have these work experiences been of most value to you?

PRESENT ACTIVITIES:

What recreational and social activities do you engage in? _____

To what clubs, organizations, or groups do you belong? _____

What are your special interests or hobbies? _____

_____

How well do you like to read? _____ What types of books or articles interest you most? _____

_____

What magazines do you read most frequently? _____

_____

OCCUPATIONAL PLANS:

List the careers which you have considered seriously and those which appeal to you most now:

Occupation	*Reasons for Interest in the Occupation*
_____	_____
_____	_____
_____	_____
_____	_____
_____	_____

What is your present vocational choice? _____ When did you decide? _____ What seem to be the most important reasons for this choice? _____

_____

Does your health or physical condition limit you in planning for a vocation? _____

_____

Are your reasons for coming to the Counseling Center: choice of vocation _____; difficulty with studies _____; difficulty with reading _____; need for personal counseling _____? Describe more in detail, if you wish, the nature of the problem. If there are other matters you would like to talk over with a counselor, you may mention them here too: _____

_____

_____

Appendix B

BRIEF CASE SUMMARIES FOLLOWING
VOCATIONAL COUNSELING

February 26, 19___.

The problem is one of high ability in so many fields that the narrowing of choice to one becomes difficult. Taking everything into consideration, interests and personal characteristics as well as abilities, three main avenues seem to be open: (1) law, leading to a political or judicial position; (2) journalism, with an attempt to get into a foreign correspondent's position; and (3) graduate work leading to college teaching. We discussed these thoroughly. The disadvantage of law is its somewhat narrow field of subject-matter, not corresponding to his variety of interests. The disadvantage of journalism is that a person might have to be satisfied with a regular beat of no particular interest for a number of years. The possibilities in the foreign service were also taken up briefly, with the reminder that the higher ones require independent means. The college teaching still appeals to him most favorably. The most attractive majors in his case are history, philosophy, and the new Pacific Basin curriculum. I tended to emphasize the philosophy, in spite of the fact that he had not yet taken any, because of the breadth of its scope. This choice was, however, left indeterminate. I urged him to become familiar with as many fields of human knowledge as possible, particularly that he get some more physical science courses or do some reading on these subjects.

This boy should go far.

May 10, 19___.

I went through the test scores in some detail summing up the sort of picture they gave. We discussed art occupations and nursing. The former she does not consider because she feels that whatever talent for art she showed in junior high school has never been developed. The nursing appeals to her more, but she holds back from as definite a profession as this because of personal reasons. She is engaged to a medical student in Chicago. They are planning to be married when he finishes in about three years. She would like to take what interests her, expanding her outlook and improving her total background without too much emphasis on a degree. We planned tentatively a course which would do that which could easily be shifted to a degree course with a biology major if circumstances warranted. She anticipates some difficulty with her parents. Her mother is understanding, but her father is a practical business man with an exaggerated idea of her talents. She seems clear in her own thinking and summed up for my approval what she will try to tell them. I invited her to come in any time she wished to talk it over some more.

INTERVIEW NOTES. SEVENTH INTERVIEW WITH A PERSONAL COUNSELING CLIENT

October 18, 19___.

Launched immediately into talking about his mother. Constant criticism—always putting him in the wrong whatever he did. Unreliability and exaggeration of things. Moods. Illnesses.

Father should have left her.

Children died because she did not take care of them. Having his teeth pulled instead of filled. Failure to do anything about his blood poisoning.

Money he sent home during navy years, $2,500, foolishly spent. Always trying to get more out of him.

Always in a fog about what people meant. Sayings like "Not if I see you first," for instance. Same in the Navy, people always saying things that escaped him.

English again. Reference to what Dr. T. had said about his decile not being high enough for graduate work. How bad his English papers are, even for Eng. K. Rejection of my suggestion of the possibility of tutoring.

Work at bakery satisfying in some ways. Gets along well with the girls. Boss has raised him to $1.25 an hour when he threatened to quit. "Scuffling" with girls. Bruises on their arms. One girl especially he is concerned about who has 9 decile—cake decorator for 90¢ an hour. Takes work too seriously.

Determination today to go on—not drop the English course even when I indicated that some satisfying job might be located without college graduation. Plea to go with the counseling.

References

ABELES, N., 1958. A study of the characteristics of counselor trainees. *Dissertation Abstr.*, 18, 2204-2205.

ABRAHAMSON, A. C., 1954. Counseling during a three-year period. *J. higher Educ.*, 25, 384-388.

ADAMS, R. C., 1932. The personal interview and scholastic achievement. *Voc. Guid. Magazine*, 10, 358-360.

ALDRICH, M. G., 1942. An exploratory study of social guidance at the college level. *Educ. psychol. Measmt.*, 2, 209-216.

ALDRICH, M. G., 1949. A follow-up study of social guidance at the college level. *J. appl. Psychol.*, 33, 258-264.

ALLEN, E. P., 1932. Vocational guidance: the Birmingham experiment. *Human Factor*, London, 6, 170-173.

American Association for Adult Education, 1935. *The adjustment service: a report of an experiment in adult guidance.* Adjustment Service Report, No. 1. New York: Author.

American Personnel and Guidance Association, 1957. *The use of multifactor tests in guidance.* Washington: Author.

American Psychological Association, 1950. *Training of psychological counselors.* Ann Arbor: Univer. of Michigan Press.

American Psychological Association, 1952. Recommended standards for training counseling psychologists to the doctorate level. *Amer. Psychol.*, 7, 175-181.

American Psychological Association, 1953. *Ethical standards of psychologists.* Washington: Author.

American Psychological Association, 1954. Technical recommendations for psychological tests and diagnostic techniques. Supplement to *Psychol. Bull.*, 51, No. 2.

American Psychological Association, 1959. Ethical standards of psychologists. *Amer. Psychologist*, 14, 279-282.

ANDERSON, R. G., 1949. Reported and demonstrated values of vocational counseling. *J. appl. Psychol.*, 33, 460-473.

ARBUCKLE, D. S., 1956. Client peception of counselor personality. *J. counsel. Psychol.*, 3, 93-96.

ARBUCKLE, D. S., 1956. Client perception of counselor personality. ment for the measurement of counseling perceptions. *J. counsel. Psychol.*, 4, 304-310.

ASHBY, J. D., FORD, D. H., GUERNEY, B. G., Jr., & GUERNEY, L. F., 1957. Effects on clients of a reflective and a leading type of psychotherapy. *Psychol. Monogr.*, 71, No. 24 (Whole No. 453).

BAER, M. F., & ROEBER, E. C., 1958. *Occupational information.* (2nd ed.) Chicago: Science Research Associates.

BAKER, E., 1960. The differential effects of two psychotherapeutic approaches on client perceptions. *J. counsel. Psychol.*, 7, 46-50.

BALLER, W. R., 1944. Characteristics of college students who demonstrate interest in counseling services. *J. educ. Psychol.*, 35, 302-308.

BARAHAL, G. D., 1950. *Converting a veterans guidance center.* Stanford, Calif.: Stanford Univer. Press.

BARAHAL, G. D., BRAMMER, L. M., & SHOSTROM, E. L., 1950. A client-centered approach to vocational counseling. *J. consult. Psychol.*, 14, 256-260.

BARNETTE, W. L., Jr., 1950. Reactions of veterans to counseling. *J. appl. Psychol.*, 34, 399-405.

BARTLETT, M. R., 1950. A six-month follow-up of the effects of personal adjustment counseling of veterans. *J. consult. Psychol.*, 14, 393-394.

BAYMUR, F. B., & PATTERSON, C. H., 1960. A comparison of three methods of assisting underachieving high school students. *J. counsel. Psychol.*, 7, 83-90.

BECKER, H. S., & CARPER, J. W., 1956. The development of identification with an occupation. *Am. J. Sociol.*, 61, 289-298.

BERDIE, R. F., 1954. Changes in self-ratings as a method of evaluating counseling. *J. counsel. Psychol.*, 1, 49-54.

BERDIE, R. F., 1955. Aptitude, achievement, interest, and personality tests: a longitudinal comparison. *J. appl. Psychol.*, 39, 103-114.

BERDIE, R. F., 1958. A program of counseling interview research. *Educ. psychol. Measmt.*, 18, 255-274.

BERDIE, R. F., & LAYTON, W. L., 1960. Research on the Minnesota Counseling Inventory. *J. counsel. Psychol.*, 7, 218-224.

BLACKWELL, E. B., 1946. An evaluation of the immediate effectiveness of the testing and guidance bureau of the University of Texas. *J. educ. Res.*, 40, 302-308.

BLAU, P. M., GUSTAD, J. W., JESSOR, R., PARNES, H. S., & WILCOCK, R. C., 1956. Occupational choice: a conceptual framework. *Indust. and Labor Relat. Rev.*, 9, 531-543.

BLOOM, B. S., 1942. Test reliability for what? *J. educ. Psychol.*, 33, 517-526.

BLOOM, W., 1952. How good was Air Force counseling? *Personnel Guid. J.*, 31, 96-98.

BLUM, L. P., & SULLIVAN, B. A., 1953. What do college students think of counseling? *J. higher Educ.*, 24, 262-264.

Borow, H., 1960. Research programs in career development. *J. counsel. Psychol.*, 7, 62-70.

Brams, J. M., 1957. The relationship between personal characteristics of counseling trainees and effective communication in counseling. *Dissertation Abstr.*, 17, 1510-1511.

Brayfield, A. H. (Ed.), 1950. *Readings in modern methods of counseling.* New York: Appleton-Century-Crofts.

Brayfield, A. H., & Mickelson, G. T., 1951. Disparities in occupational information coverage. *Occupations*, 29, 506-508.

Brayfield, A. H., & Reed, P. A., 1950. How readable are occupational information booklets? *J. appl. Psychol.*, 34, 325-328.

Broedel, J., Ohlsen, M., & Proff, F., 1960. The effects of group counseling on gifted adolescent underachievers. *J. counsel. Psychol.*, 7, 163-170.

Brophy, A. L., 1959. Self, role, and satisfaction. *Genet. Psychol. Monogr.*, 59, 263-308.

Brown, M. T., 1948. The veterans report two years later. *Occupations*, 26, 364-366.

Bynner, W., 1944. *The way of life according to Laotzu.* New York: Day.

Calhoun, S. R., 1956. The effect of counseling on a group of underachievers. *Sch. Rev.*, 64, 312-316.

Callis, R., Polmantier, P. C., & Roeber, E. C., 1957. Five years of research on counseling. *J. counsel Psychol.*, 4, 119-123.

Campbell, R. K., 1945. A study of interviewing techniques. *Applied Psychology Panel*, NPRC, Project 116a, Memorandum No. 3.

Cantoni, L. J., 1955. Long-term effects of the Flint, Michigan, Guidance Experiment. *Psychol. Rep.*, 1, 359-362.

Caplan, S. W., 1957. The effect of group counseling in junior high school boys' concepts of themselves in school. *J. counsel. Psychol.*, 4, 124-128.

Caravello, S. J., 1958. Effectiveness of high school guidance services. *Personnel Guid. J.*, 36, 323-325.

Cardenal, C., & Granada, A., 1933. L'eficacia del consell orientador. *Rev. de psicol. i. ped.*, 1, 68-76. (*Psychol. Abstr.*, 1933, 7, 508.)

Carlson, H. B., & Vandever, M., 1951. The effectiveness of directive and nondirective counseling in vocational problems as measured by the TAT test. *Educ. Psychol. Measmt.*, 11, 212-223.

Carnes, E. F., & Robinson, F. P., 1948. The role of client talk in the counseling interview. *Educ. Psychol. Measmt.*, 8, 635-644.

Cartwright, D. S., 1957. Annotated bibliography of research and theory construction in client-centered therapy. *J. counsel. Psychol.*, 4, 82-100.

CARTWRIGHT, D. S., & ROTH, I., 1957. Success and satisfaction in psychotherapy. *J. clin. Psychol.*, 13, 20-26.

CARTWRIGHT, R. D., 1957. Effects of psychotherapy on self-consistency, *J. counsel. Psychol.*, 4, 15-22.

CARTWRIGHT, R. D., & VOGEL, J. L., 1960. A comparison of changes in psychoneurotic patients during matched periods of therapy and no therapy. *J. consult. Psychol.*, 24, 121-127.

CASS, J. C., & TIEDEMAN, D. V., 1960. Vocational development and the election of a high school curriculum. *Personnel Guid. J.*, 38, 538-545.

COBURN, H. H., 1954. An experimental comparison of relationship-centered and problem-centered counseling. *Dissertation Abstr.*, 14, 2123.

COLE, R. C., 1939. Evaluating a boys' club guidance program. *Occupations*, 17, 705-708.

CONDON, M. E., 1947. A follow-up study of one hundred veterans counseled at the City College Veterans Administration Vocational Advisement Unit. *J. Rehabilit.*, 13(6), 37-31, 36.

COTTLE, W. C., 1953. Personal characteristics of counselors: I. a review of the literature. *Personnel Guid. J.*, 31, 445-450.

COTTLE, W. C., & LEWIS, W. W., Jr., 1954. Personality characteristics of counselors: II. male counselor responses to the MMPI and GZTS. *J. counsel. Psychol.*, 1, 27-30.

COTTLE, W. C., LEWIS, W. W., & PENNEY, M. M., 1954. Personal characteristics of counselors. III. an Experimental Attitude Scale. *J. counsel. Psychol.*, 1, 74-77.

COTTLE, W. C., POWNALL, J. E., & STEIMEL, R. J., 1955. Counselors and teachers take the Experimental Attitude Scale. *Personnel Guid. J.*, 33, 374-378.

COTTLE, W. C., & WANDS, H. O., 1955. High school counselors and teachers take the Experimental Attitude Scale. *J. counsel. Psychol.*, 2, 28-31.

COWEN, E. L., & COMBS, A. W., 1950. Follow-up study of 32 cases treated by non-directive psychotherapy. *J. abnorm. soc. Psychol.*, 45, 232-258.

COWLEY, W. H., 1933. An experiment in freshman counseling. *J. higher Educ.*, 4, 245-248.

DANSKIN, D. G., 1955. Roles played by counselors in their interviews. *J. counsel. Psychol.*, 2, 22-27.

DANSKIN, D. G., 1957a. A role-ing counselor gathers no moss. *J. counsel. Psychol.*, 4, 41-43.

DANSKIN, D. G., 1957b. Studies on the sociological aspects of specific occupations. *Personnel Guid. J.*, 36, 104-111.

DANSKIN, D. G., & ROBINSON, F. P., 1954. Differences in "degree of lead" among experienced counselors. *J. counsel. Psychol.*, 1, 78-83.

DARLEY, J. G., & WILLIAMS, C. T., 1939. Clinical records of individual student problems. In *Report on problems and progress of the General College.* Minneapolis: General College, Univer. of Minnesota.

DAVIS, D. A., 1959. Effect of group guidance and individual counseling on citizenship behavior. *Personnel Guid. J.*, 38, 142-145.

DAVIS, F. B., 1947. *Utilizing human talent.* Washington: American Council on Education.

DAVIS, S. E., 1958. An investigation of client characteristics shown in interview behavior. *Dissertation Abstr.*, 18, 1855-1858.

DAVIS, S. E., & ROBINSON, F. P., 1949. A study of the use of certain techniques for reducing resistance during the counseling interview. *Educ. psychol. Measmt.*, 9, 297-306.

DEMENT, A. L., 1957. Good students want counseling too. *J. counsel. Psychol.*, 4, 113-118.

DIPBOYE, W. J., 1954. Analysis of counselor style by discussion units. *J. counsel. Psychol.*, 1, 21-26.

DITTMAN, A. T., 1952. The interpersonal process in psychotherapy: development of a research method. *J. abnorm. soc. Psychol.*, 47, 236-244.

Division of Counseling Psychology, Committee on Definition, 1956. Counseling psychology as a specialty. *Amer. Psychologist*, 11, 282-285.

DRAKE, L. E., & OETTING, E. R., 1957. An MMPI pattern and a suppressor variable predictive of academic achievement. *J. counsel. Psychol.*, 4, 245-247.

DRAKE, L. E., & OETTING, E. R., 1959. *An MMPI codebook for counselors.* Minneapolis: Univer. of Minnesota Press.

DRESSEL, P. L., & MATTESON, R. W., 1950. The effect of client participation in test interpretation. *Educ. psychol. Measmt.*, 10, 693-706.

DVORAK, B. J., 1935. *Differential occupational ability patterns.* Minneapolis: Univer. of Minnesota Press.

EARLE, F. M., 1931. *Methods of choosing a career.* London: Harrap.

ELTON, C. F., 1950. A study of client responsibility: counselor technique or interview outcome? *Educ. psychol. Measmt.*, 10, 728-737.

EMBREE, R. B., 1948. The status of college students in terms of IQ's determined during childhood. *Amer. Psychologist*, 3, 259.

ERIKSON, E. H., 1950. *Childhood and society.* New York: Norton.

EWING, T. N., 1954. Changes in attitude during counseling. *J. counsel. Psychol.*, 1, 232-239.

EYSENCK, H. J., 1952. The effects of psychotherapy: an evaluation. *J. consult. Psychol.*, 16, 319-324.

FARIES, M., 1955. Short-term counseling at the college level. *J. counsel. Psychol.*, 2, 182-184.

FEINGOLD, S. N. *Scholarships, fellowships, and loans.* Cambridge: Bellman. (Various editions.)

FEINTUCH, A., 1954. A study of the effectiveness of an integrated program of vocational counseling, casework, and a sheltered workshop in increasing the employability and modifying attitudes correlated with the employability of "difficult-to-place" persons. *Dissertation Abstr.*, 14, 1794-1795.

FERN, A. H., 1954. An experimental investigation of the meanings of understanding in the counseling relationship. *Dissertation Abstr.*, 14, 2123-2124.

FIEDLER, F. E., 1950a. The concept of an ideal therapeutic relationship. *J. consult. Psychol.*, 14, 239-245.

FIEDLER, F. E., 1950b. A comparison of therapeutic relationships in psychoanalytic, nondirective, and Adlerian therapy. *J. consult. Psychol.*, 14, 436-445.

FINE, B. *Fine's American college counselor and guide.* Englewood Cliffs, N. J.: Prentice-Hall. (Various editions.)

FINE, S. A., 1955. The structure of worker functions. *Personnel Guid. J.*, 34, 66-73.

FINE, S. A., & HEINZ, C. A., 1957. The estimates of worker trait requirements for 4000 jobs. *Personnel Guid. J.*, 36, 168-174.

FINE, S. A., & HEINZ, C. A., 1958. The functional occupational classification structure. *Personnel Guid. J.*, 37, 180-192.

FISHER, J., 1959. The twisted pear and prediction of behavior. *J. consult. Psychol.*, 23, 400-405.

FORGY, E. W., & BLACK, J. D., 1954. A follow-up after three years of clients counseled by two methods. *J. counsel. Psychol.*, 1, 1-8.

FORM, A. L., 1953. Measurement of student attitudes toward counseling services. *Personnel Guid. J.*, 32, 84-87.

FREEMAN, H. J., & JONES, L., 1933. Final report of the long-time effect of counseling low percentile freshmen. *Sch. and Soc.*, 38, 382-384.

FROEHLICH, C. P., 1949. Toward more adequate criteria of counseling effectiveness. *Educ. psychol. Measmt.*, 9, 255-267.

FROEHLICH, C. P., 1951. The evaluation of counseling. *Studies in Higher Education*, Purdue Univ., No. 76, 21-31.

FROEHLICH, C. P., 1957. A criterion for counseling. *Psychol. Monogr.*, 71, No. 15 (Whole No. 444).

FROEHLICH, C. P., & MOSER, W. E., 1954. Do counselees remember test scores? *J. counsel. Psychol.*, 1, 149-152.

GAUDET, F. J., CARLI, A. R., & DENNEGAR, L. S., 1950. Attitudes of veterans toward vocational guidance services. *J. appl. Psychol.*, 34, 347-350.

GAW, F., RAMSEY, L., SMITH, M., & SPIELMAN, W., 1926. *A study in vocational guidance.* Industrial Fatigue Research Board Report, No. 33. London: H. M. Stationery Office.

GELLMAN, W., GENDEL, H., GLASER, N. M., FRIEDMAN, S. B., & NEFF, W. S., 1956. *Adjusting people to work.* Chicago: Jewish Vocational Service and Employment Center.

GHISELLI, E. E., 1955. *The Measurement of Occupational Aptitude.* Berkeley: Univer. of California Press.

GIBSON, R. L., SNYDER, W. U., & RAY, W. S., 1955. A factor analysis of measures of change following client-centered therapy. *J. counsel. Psychol.*, 2, 83-90.

GINSBURG, S. W., 1948. Troubled people. *Ment. Hyg.*, N. Y., 32, 4-14.

GINZBERG, E., GINSBURG, S. W., AXELRAD, S., & HERMA, J. L., 1951. *Occupational choice.* New York: Columbia Univer. Press.

GLAZER, S. H., & ENGLAND, A. O., 1949. How veterans feel about vocational advisement. *Educ. psychol. Measmt.*, 9, 717-725.

GOODENOUGH, F. L., & TYLER, L. E., 1959. *Developmental psychology.* New York: Appleton-Century-Crofts.

GOODSTEIN, L. D., & CRITES, J. O. Vocational and educational counseling with low-ability college students (In press).

GOODSTEIN, L. D., CRITES, J. O., HEILBRUN, A. B., Jr., & REMPEL, P. P., 1961. The use of the California Psychological Inventory in a university counseling service. *J. counsel. Psychol.*, 8, 147-153.

GRANT, C. W., 1954a. How students perceive the counselor's role. *Personnel Guid. J.*, 32, 386-388.

GRANT, C. W., 1954b. The counselor's role. *Personnel Guid. J.*, 33, 74-77.

GRIBBONS, W. D., 1960. Evaluation of an eighth grade group guidance program. *Personnel Guid. J.*, 38, 740-745.

GRIGG, A. E., 1959. Childhood experience with parental attitudes: a test of Roe's hypothesis. *J. counsel. Psychol.*, 6, 153-155.

GRIGG, A. E., & GOODSTEIN, L. D., 1957. The use of clients as judges of the counselor's performance. *J. counsel. Psychol.*, 4, 31-36.

GUSTAD, J. W., & TUMA, A. H., 1957. The effects of different methods of test introduction and interpretation on client learning in counseling. *J. counsel. Psychol.*, 4, 313-317.

GUTHRIE, G. M., & O'NEILL, H. W., 1953. Effects of dormitory counseling on academic achievement. *Personnel Guid. J.*, 31, 307-309.

HABBE, S., 1939. Some characteristics of clients who seek guidance. *Amer. J. Orthopsychiat.*, 9, 802-806.

HACKETT, H. R., 1955. Evaluation of a program of counseling students on probation. *Personnel Guid. J.*, 33, 513-516.

HAGEN, D., 1960. Careers and family atmospheres. *J. counsel. Psychol.*, 7, 251-256.

HAIMOWITZ, N. R., & HAIMOWITZ, M. L., 1952. Personality changes in client-centered therapy. In W. Wolff and J. A. Precker (Eds.), *Success in psychotherapy*. New York: Grune and Stratton.

HARDER, D. F., 1959. Differentiation of curricular groups based upon responses to unique items of the MMPI. *J. counsel. Psychol.*, 6, 28-34.

HAVIGHURST, R. J., 1953. *Human development and education*. New York: Longmans.

HAWKINS, L. S., & FIALKIN, H. N., 1935. *Clients' opinions of the Adjustment Service*. Adjustment Service Report, No. 12. New York: American Association for Adult Education.

HEILFRON, M., 1960. The function of counseling as perceived by high school students. *Personnel Guid. J.*, 39, 133-136.

HEIST, P. A., 1956. An experiment utilizing group psychotherapy in a self-analytic procedure for counselors in training. *Dissertation Abstr.*, 16, 2383.

HOEHN, A. J., & SALTZ, E., 1956. Effect of teacher-student interviews on classroom achievement. *J. educ. Psychol.*, 47, 424-435.

HOFFMAN, A. E., 1959. An analysis of counselor sub-roles. *J. counsel. Psychol.*, 6, 61-67.

HOLADAY, P. W., 1929. The long-time effect of freshman counseling. *School and Soc.*, 29, 234-236.

HOOD-WILLIAMS, J., 1960. The result of psychotherapy with children: a revaluation. *J. consult. Psychol.*, 24, 84-88.

HOPKE, W. E., 1955. The measurement of counselor attitudes. *J. counsel. Psychol.*, 2, 212-216.

HOYT, D. P., 1954. Differential outcomes of counseling with college men. *Dissertation Abstr.*, 14, 2126.

HOYT, D. P., 1955. An evaluation of group and individual programs in vocational guidance. *J. appl. Psychol.*, 39, 26-30.

HOYT, D. P., & KENNEDY, C. E., 1958. Interest and personality correlates of career-motivated and homemaking-motivated college women. *J. counsel. Psychol.*, 5, 44-49.

HUNT, E. P., 1943. The Birmingham experiments in vocational selection and guidance. *Occup. Psychol.*, London, 17, 53-63.

HUNT, E. P., & SMITH, P., 1944. *Scientific vocational guidance and its value to the choice of employment work of a local education authority*. Report of Research, City of Birmingham Education Committee, Birmingham, England.

HUNT, E. P., & SMITH, P., 1945. Vocational psychology and choice of employment. *Occup. Psychol.*, London, 19, 109-116.

HUTSON, P. W., & WEBSTER, A. D., 1943. An experiment in the educational and vocational guidance of tenth-grade pupils. *Educ. psychol. Measmt.*, 3, 3-22.

JAQUES, M. E., 1960. *Critical counseling behavior in rehabilitation settings.* Iowa City: Coll. of Education, State Univer. of Iowa.

JENNINGS, J. R., & STOTT, M. B., 1936. A fourth follow-up of vocationally advised cases. *Human Factor*, London, 10, 165-174.

JENSEN, V. H., 1958. Influence of personality traits on academic success. *Personnel Guid. J.*, 36, 497-500.

JENSON, R. E., 1955. Student feeling about counseling help. *Personnel Guid. J.*, 33, 498-503.

JESNESS, C. F., 1955. The effects of counseling on the self-perceptions of college men. *Dissertation Abstr.*, 15, 1553.

JOHNSON, D. G., 1953. Effect of vocational counseling on self-knowledge. *Educ. psychol. Measmt.*, 13, 330-338.

KACZKOWSKI, H. R., & ROTHNEY, J. W. M., 1956. Discriminant analysis in evaluation of counseling. *Personnel Guid. J.*, 35, 231-235.

KAESS, W., & LONG, L., 1954. An investigation of the effectiveness of vocational guidance. *Educ. psychol. Measmt.*, 14, 423-433.

KAMM, R. B., & WRENN, C. G., 1950. Client acceptance of self-information in counseling. *Educ. psychol. Measmt.*, 10, 32-42.

KEET, C. D., 1948. Two verbal techniques in a miniature counseling situation. *Psychol. Monogr.*, 62 (7).

KEFAUVER, G. N., & HAND, H. C., 1933. An appraisal of guidance. *Occupations*, 12, 53-58.

KELLY, E. L., & FISKE, D. W., 1951. *The prediction of performance in clinical psychology.* Ann Arbor: Univer. of Michigan Press.

KING, P. T., & MATTESON, R. W., 1959. Student perception of counseling center services. *Personal Guid. J.*, 37, 358-364.

KIRCHHEIMER, B. A., AXELROD, D. W., & HICKERSON, G. X., Jr., 1949. An objective evaluation of counseling. *J. appl. Psychol.*, 33, 249-257.

KIRK, B. A., 1955. Counseling Phi Beta Kappas. *J. counsel. Psychol.*, 2, 304-307.

KIRK, B. A., 1956. Evaluation of in-service counselor training. *Educ. psychol. Measmt.*, 16, 527-535.

KIRK, B. A., 1959. Counseling graduate students. *J. counsel. Psychol.*, 6, 284-287.

KIRK, B. A., & HEADLEY, R. R., 1950. Factors related to voluntary discontinuance of contact during counseling. *J. consult. Psychol.*, 14, 386-392.

KIR-STIMON, W., 1956. A follow-up study of counseling with anxiety neurotics. *Personnel Guid. J.*, 34, 474-480.

KLEINMUNTZ, B., 1960. Identification of maladjusted college students. *J. counsel. Psychol.*, 7, 209-211.

KLINGELHOFER, E. L., 1954. The relationship of academic advisement to the scholastic performance of failing college students. *J. counsel. Psychol.*, 1, 125-131.

KOESTER, G. A., 1954. A study of the diagnostic process. *Educ. psychol. Measmt.*, 14, 473-486.

KOILE, E. A., & BIRD, D. J., 1956. Preferences for counselor help on freshman problems. *J. counsel. Psychol.*, 3, 97-106.

KREMEN, B. G., 1951. Counselor-certification in the United States. *Occupations*, 29, 584-586.

KULICK, W., 1953. Personality traits and academic standing of probationary engineering students before and after counseling: an evaluation of the effectiveness of non-directive counseling by means of the Rorschach test. *Dissertation Abstr.*, 13, 584-585.

LATHAM, A. J., 1951. Job appropriateness: a one-year follow-up of high school graduates. *J. soc. Psychol.*, 34, 55-68.

LEVITT, E. E., 1957. The results of psychotherapy with children: an evaluation. *J. consult. Psychol.*, 21, 189-196.

LEVITT, E. E., 1960. Reply to Hood-Williams. *J. consult. Psychol.*, 24, 89-91.

LIFTON, M. M., 1958. The role of empathy and aesthetic sensitivity in counseling. *J. counsel. Psychol.*, 5, 267-274.

LIPSETT, L., & SMITH, L. F., 1948. The Rochester Veterans' Guidance Center takes stock. *Amer. Psychologist*, 3, 12-15.

LONG, L., & HILL, J., 1947. A follow-up of veterans receiving vocational advisement. *J. consult. Psychol.*, 11, 88-92.

LORIMER, M., 1944. An appraisal of vocational guidance. *J. higher Educ.*, 15, 260-267.

LOVE, J. W., Jr., 1958. A study of personality changes attending personal adjustment counseling. *Dissertation Abstr.*, 18, 1107-1108.

LOVEJOY, C. E. *Lovejoy's College Guide.* New York: Simon and Schuster. (Various editions.)

LOVEJOY, C. E. *Lovejoy's Vocational School Guide.* New York: Simon and Schuster. (Various editions.)

LUND, S. E. T., 1931. The personal interview in high school guidance. *Sch. Rev.*, 39, 196-207.

MACRAE, A., 1932. A second follow-up of vocationally advised cases. *Human Factor*, London, 6, 42-52.

MACRAE, A., 1937. A Borstal experiment in vocational guidance: a critical notice. *Human Factor*, London, 11, 187-189.

MARTINSON, W. D., 1955. Utilization of the Role Construct Repertory Test in the counseling process. *Dissertation Abstr.*, 15, 2102-2103.

MCARTHUR, C., 1954. Analyzing the clinical process. *J. counsel. Psychol.*, 1, 203-207.

McKinney, F., 1945. Four years of a college adjustment clinic. *J. consult. Psychol.*, 9, 203-217.

McLaughlin, E. F., 1956. A study of the effectiveness of personal counseling with seventh grade pupils. *Dissertation Abstr.*, 16, 2089.

Meehl, P. E., 1954. *Clinical versus statistical prediction*. Minneapolis: Univer. of Minnesota Press.

Merenda, P. F., & Rothney, J. W. M., 1958. Evaluating the effects of counseling—eight years after. *J. counsel. Psychol.*, 5, 163-168.

Merrill, R. M., 1952. On Keet's study, "two verbal techniques in a miniature counseling situation." *J. abnorm. soc. Psychol.*, 47, 722.

Merrill, R. M., & Murphy, D. T., 1959. Personality factors and academic achievement in college. *J. counsel. Psychol.*, 6, 207-210.

Merwin, J. C., & Di Vesta, F. J., 1959. A study of need theory and career choice. *J. counsel. Psychol.*, 6, 302-308.

Miller, C. H., 1956. Occupational choice and values. *Personnel Guid. J.*, 35, 244-246.

Miller, F. W., 1952. Evaluating a counseling procedure. *J. educ. Res.*, 46, 61-69.

Minor, C. A., & Neel, R. G., 1958. The relationship between achievement motive and occupational preference. *J. counsel. Psychol.*, 5, 39-43.

Mirk, M., 1931. Report on some results of vocational guidance given by the Australian Institute of Industrial Psychology. *Aust. J. Psychol.*, 9, 144-150. (*Psychol. Abstr.*, 1933, 7, 736.)

Moore, M. R., & Popham, W. J., 1960. Effects of two interview techniques on academic achievement. *J. counsel. Psychol.*, 7, 176-179.

Munger, P. F., & Johnson, C. A., 1960. Changes in attitudes associated with an NDEA counseling and guidance institute. *Personnel Guid. J.*, 38, 751-753.

Myers, C. S., 1932. Recent evidence of the value of vocational guidance. *Human Factor*, London, 6, 438-450.

National Vocational Guidance Association, 1939. Distinguishing marks of a good occupational monograph. *Occupations*, 18, 129-130.

Nelson, A. G., 1956. Vocational maturity and client satisfaction. *J. counsel. Psychol.*, 3, 254-256.

Newland, T. E., & Ackley, W. E., 1936. An experimental study of the effect of educational guidance on a selected group of high school sophomores. *J. exp. Educ.*, 5, 23-25.

Oakley, C. A., 1937. A first follow-up of Scottish vocationally advised cases. *Human Factor*, London, 11, 27-31.

O'Hara, R. P., & Tiedeman, D. V., 1959. Vocational self-concept in adolescence. *J. counsel. Psychol.*, 6, 292-301.

PARKER, C. A., 1958. As a clinician thinks. . . . *J. counsel. Psychol.*, 5, 253-261.

PARKER, H. J., 1957. A study of immediate recall, delayed recall, and distortion of objective test data in counseling. *Dissertation Abstr.*, 17, 305-306.

PATERSON, D. G., & CLARK, K. E., 1943. Students' judgments of counseling. *J. higher Educ.*, 14, 140-142.

PATTERSON, C. H., 1957. A comparison of counseled and non-counseled industrial school students. *J. appl. Psychol.*, 41, 240-242.

PATTERSON, R. L., & FOTIU, P. G., 1953. The effectiveness of guidance center counseling. *J. educ. Res.*, 46, 359-363.

PEPINSKY, H. B., 1948. The selection and use of diagnostic categories in clinical counseling. *Appl. Psychol. Monogr.*, No. 15.

PEPINSKY, H. B., 1955. *Cogito, ergo*. . . . *J. counsel. Psychol.*, 2, 285-289.

PERRY, W. G., Jr., 1955. The findings of the commission in counseling and guidance. *Ann. N. Y. Acad. Sci.*, 63, 396-407.

POHLMAN, E., & ROBINSON, F. P., 1960. Client reaction to some aspects of the counseling situation. *Personnel Guid. J.*, 38, 546-551.

POLANSKY, N., & KOUNIN, J. S., 1956. Clients' reactions to initial interviews. *Hum. Relat.*, 9, 237-264.

POOLE, A., 1957. Counsel judgment and counseling evaluation. *J. counsel. Psychol.*, 4, 37-40.

PORTER, E. H., Jr., 1949. A simple measure of counseling attitudes. In E. G. Williamson (Ed.), *Student Personnel Work*. Minneapolis: Univer. of Minnesota Press.

PORTER, E. H., Jr., 1957. Clients' evaluations of services at the University of Chicago Counseling Center. *J. counsel. Psychol.*, 4, 274-281.

RAPLUS, H. E., 1956. Evaluating the services of a high school guidance program and a university counseling clinic. *Dissertation Abstr.*, 16, 2352.

REID, D. K., & SNYDER, W. U., 1947. Experiment on "recognition of feeling" in non-directive therapy. *J. clin. Psychol.*, 3, 128-135.

REIK, T., 1949. *Listening with the third ear*. New York: Farrar, Straus and Cudahy.

REMMERS, H. H., & WHISLER, L. D., 1938. The effects of a guidance program on vocational attitudes. *Studies in Higher Education*, Purdue Univ., No. 34, 68-82.

RICHARDSON, L. H., & PERRY, J., 1956. Counseling for academic recovery. *J. counsel. Psychol.*, 3, 136-139.

ROBERTSON, M. H., 1960. Test scores and self-estimates of two curricular groups. *Personnel Guid. J.*, 38, 746-750.

ROBINSON, F. P., 1950. *Principles and procedures in student counseling*. New York: Harper.

RODGER, T. A., 1937. A follow-up of vocationally advised cases. *Human Factor*, London, 11, 16-26.

ROE, A., 1956. *The psychology of occupations.* New York: Wiley.

ROE, A., 1957. Early determinants of vocational choice. *J. counsel. Psychol.*, 4, 212-217.

ROGERS, C. R., 1951. *Client centered therapy.* New York: Houghton Mifflin.

ROGERS, C. R., and DYMOND, R. F. (Eds.), 1954. *Psychotherapy and personality change.* Chicago: Univer. of Chicago Press.

ROGERS, L. B., 1954. A comparison of two kinds of test interpretation interviews. *J. counsel. Psychol.*, 1, 224-231.

ROSENMAN, S., 1955. Changes in the representations of self, other, and interrelationships in client-centered therapy. *J. counsel. Psychol.*, 2, 271-277.

ROSS, C. C., & BOYD, P. P., 1936. An experiment in group counseling for freshmen. *Kentucky Personnel Bull.*, No. 16.

ROTHNEY, J. W. M., 1958. *Guidance practices and results.* New York: Harper.

ROTHNEY, J. W. M., & ROENS, B. A., 1950. *Guidance of American youth.* Cambridge, Mass.: Harvard Univer. Press.

RUBINSTEIN, E. A., & PARLOFF, M. B. (Eds.), 1959. *Research in psychotherapy.* Washington: American Psychological Association.

SAGESER, H. W., 1951. Counseling in their colleges. *Occupations*, 29, 348-349.

SARBIN, T. R., 1943. A contribution to the study of actuarial and individual methods of prediction. *Amer. J. Sociol.*, 48, 593-602.

SCARBOROUGH, B. B., and WRIGHT, J. C., 1957. The assessment of an educational guidance clinic. *J. counsel. Psychol.*, 4, 283-286.

SCHAFFER, R. H., 1953. Job satisfaction as related to need satisfaction in work. *Psychol. Monogr.*, No. 364.

SCHNEIDLER, G. G., & BERDIE, R. F., 1942. Representativeness of college students who receive counseling services. *J. educ. Psychol.*, 33, 545-551.

SCHWEBEL, M., KARR, L., & SLOTKIN, H., 1959. Counselor relationship competence: a unifying concept. *Edu. psychol. Measmt.*, 19, 515-537.

SEEMAN, J., 1948a. A study of preliminary interview methods in vocational counseling. *J. consult. Psychol.*, 12, 321-330.

SEEMAN, J., 1948b. A study of client self-selection of tests in vocational counseling. *Educ. psychol. Measmt.*, 8, 327-346.

SEEMAN, J., 1949. An investigation of client reactions to vocational counseling. *J. consult. Psychol.*, 13, 95-104.

SEIPP, E., 1935. *A study of one hundred clients of the adjustment service.* Adjustment Service Report, No. 11. New York: American Association for Adult Education.

SERENE, M. F., 1953. An experiment in motivational counseling. *Personnel Guid. J.*, 31, 319-324.

SHARTLE, C. L., 1959. *Occupational information: its development and application.* (3rd ed.) Englewood Cliffs, N. J.: Prentice-Hall.

SHERRIFFS, A. C., 1949. Modification of academic performance through personal interview. *J. appl. Psychol.*, 33, 339-351.

SIEGELMAN, M., & PECK, R. F., 1960. Personality patterns related to occupational roles. *Genet. Psychol. Monogr.*, 61, 291-349.

SILVANIA, K. C., 1956. Test usage in counseling centers. *Personnel Guid. J.*, 34, 559-564.

SINGER, S. L., & STEFFLRE, B., 1954. Analysis of the self-estimate in the evaluation of counseling. *J. counsel. Psychol.*, 1, 252-255.

SINNETT, E. R., 1956. Some determinants of agreement between measured and expressed interests. *Educ. psychol. Measmt.*, 16, 110-118.

SKYNE, A. W., 1960. Former clients evaluate a youth service program. *Children*, 7, 175-179.

SLOAN, T. J., & PIERCE-JONES, J., 1958. The Bordin-Pepinsky Diagnostic Categories: counselor agreement and MMPI comparisons. *J. counsel. Psychol.*, 5, 189-193.

SMALL, LEONARD, et al., 1955. *Personality needs as a determinant of vocational choice and their relationship to school and work achievement.* New York: Vocational Advisory Service.

SMIGEL, E. O., 1954. Occupational sociology. *Personnel Guid. J.*, 32, 536-539.

SMITH, P., 1951. Twenty-five years of research in vocational guidance. *Occup. Psychol.*, London, 25, 35-43.

SNYDER, W. U., 1957. The psychotherapy research program at the Pennsylvania State University. *J. counsel. Psychol.*, 4, 9-14.

SONNE, T. R., & GOLDMAN, L., 1957. Preferences of authoritarian and equalitarian personalities for client-centered and eclectic counseling. *J. counsel. Psychol.*, 4, 129-135.

SPEER, G. S., & JASKER, L., 1949. The influence of occupational information on occupational goals. *Occupations*, 28, 15-17.

STASEK, E. D., 1955. The effects of specialized educational counseling with selected groups of underachievers at the secondary school level. *Dissertation Abstr.*, 15, 2107.

STEPHENSON, R. M., 1957. Realism of vocational choice: a critique and an example. *Personnel Guid. J.*, 35, 482-488.

STONE, C. H., 1948. Are vocational orientation courses worth their salt? *Educ. psychol. Measmt.*, 8, 161-181.

STONE, C. H., & SIMOS, I., 1948. A follow-up study of personal counseling versus counseling by letter. *J. appl. Psychol.*, 32, 408-414.

STONE, W. L., 1955. Informal observations in guidance: observations in counseling by a sociologist. *Personnel Guid. J.*, 34, 229-231.

STOTSKY, B. A., 1956a. How important is psychotherapy to the hospitalized psychiatric patient? *J. clin. Psychol.*, 12, 32-36.

STOTSKY, B. A., 1956b. Vocational tests as measures of performance of schizophrenics in two rehabilitation activities. *J. clin. Psychol.*, 12, 236-242.

STOTSKY, B. A., DASTON, P. G., & VARDOCK, N., 1955. An evaluation of the counseling of chronic schizophrenics. *J. counsel. Psychol.*, 2, 248-255.

STOTSKY, B. A., and WEINBERG, H., 1956. The prediction of the psychiatric patient's work adjustment. *J. counsel. Psychol.*, 3, 3-7.

STOTT, M. B., 1943. The appraisal of vocational guidance. *Occup. Psychol.*, London, 17, 6-16.

STRONG, E. K., Jr., 1955. *Vocational interests 18 years after college.* Minneapolis: Univer. of Minnesota Press.

STRUPP, H. H., 1955. An objective comparison of Rogerian and psychoanalytic techniques. *J. consult. Psychol.*, 19, 1-7.

STRUPP, H. H., 1958. The performance of psychoanalytic and client-centered therapists in an initial interview. *J. consult. Psychol.*, 22, 265-274.

STUMP, N. F., 1942. What counseling services do college freshmen expect to receive? *Sch. and Soc.*, 56, 83-84.

SUPER, D. E., 1956. Vocational development: the process of compromise or synthesis. *J. counsel. Psychol.*, 4, 249-253.

SUPER, D. E., 1957. *The psychology of careers.* New York: Harper.

SUPER, D. E., & BACHRACH, P. B., 1957. *Scientific careers and vocational development.* New York: Teachers Coll., Columbia Univer., Bureau of Publications.

SUPER, D. E., CRITES, J. O., HUMMEL, R. C., MOSER, H. P., OVERSTREET, P. L., & WARNATH, C. F., 1957. *Vocational development: a framework for research.* New York: Teachers Coll., Columbia Univer., Bureau of Publications.

SUPER, D. E., & OVERSTREET, P. L., 1960. *The vocational maturity of ninth grade boys.* New York: Teachers Coll., Columbia University, Bureau of Publications.

SWAN, R. J., 1957. Using the MMPI in marriage counseling. *J. counsel. Psychol.*, 4, 239-244.

THOMAS, E., POLANSKY, N., & KOUNIN, J., 1955. The expected behavior of a potentially helpful person. *Hum. Relat.*, 8, 165-174.

THORNDIKE, E. L., *et al.*, 1934. *Prediction of vocational success.* New York: The Commonwealth Fund.

THORNDIKE, R. L., & HAGEN, E., 1959. *10,000 careers.* New York: Wiley.

THRUSH, R. S., 1957. An agency in transition: the case study of a counseling center. *J. counsel. Psychol.*, 4, 183-189.

TINDALL, R. H., & ROBINSON, F. P., 1947. The use of silence as a technique in counseling. *J. clin. Psychol.*, 3, 136-141.

TOVEN, J. R., 1945. Appraising a counseling program at the college level. *Occupations*, 23, 459-466.

TRAVERS, R. M. W., 1949. A critical review of techniques for evaluating guidance. *Edu. psychol. Measmt.*, 9, 211-225.

TRAXLER, A. E., 1956. *Techniques of guidance.* (Rev. ed.) New York: Harper.

TUMA, A. H., & GUSTAD, J. W., 1957. The effects of client and counselor personality characteristics on client learning in counseling. *J. counsel. Psychol.*, 4, 136-143.

TURNEY, A. H., & MOREHEAD, C. G., 1954. An experimental evaluation of a small high school counseling program. *Univer. of Kansas Bull. of Educ.*, 8, 74-77.

TYLER, L. E., 1960. *The national defense counseling and guidance training institutes program. A report of the first fifty institutes.* Washington: U. S. Government Printing Office.

U. S. Bureau of Employment Security, Department of Labor, 1956. *Estimates of worker trait requirements for 4000 jobs as defined in the Dictionary of Occupational Titles.* Washington: U. S. Government Printing Office.

U. S. Bureau of Labor Statistics, Department of Labor, 1959. *Occupational outlook handbook.* Washington: U. S. Government Printing Office.

U. S. Employment Service, Department of Labor, 1944. *Dictionary of occupational titles, entry occupational classification*, Part IV. Washington: U. S. Government Printing Office.

U. S. Employment Service, Department of Labor, 1949. *Dictionary of occupational titles*, Vols. I & II. Washington: U. S. Government Printing Office.

University of Pittsburgh, 1959. *The story of Project TALENT.* Project TALENT Office, Bulletin No. 1.

UTTON, A. C., 1960. Recalled parent-child relations as Determinants of vocational choice. D.Ed. dissertation, Teachers Coll., Columbia Univer.

VAN DOREN, M. (Ed.), 1928. *An anthology of world poetry.* New York: Albert and Charles Boni.

VITELES, M. S., 1929. Validating the clinical method in vocational guidance. *Psychol. Clin.*, 18, 69-77.

WALKER, J. L., 1955. Counselors' judgments in the prediction of the occupational and educational performance of former high school students. *J. educ. Res.*, 49, 81-91.

WALSH, R.. P, 1959. The effect of needs on responses to job duties. *J. counsel. Psychol.*, 6, 194-198.

WALTER, V. A., & JONES, A. W., 1956. An incomplete sentences test and the attitudes of manual arts therapy patients. *J. counsel. Psychol.*, 3, 140-144.

WALTHER, R. H., 1960. The Functional Occupational Classification Project: a critical appraisal. *Personnel Guid. J.*, 1960, 38, 698-706.

WALTHERS, J. E., 1932. Measuring effectiveness of personnel counseling. *Person. J.*, 11, 227-236.

WARD, C. E., 1951. Evaluating counseling in the Vocational Rehabilitation Program, administered by the Veterans Administration. *Educ. psychol. Measmt.*, 11, 409-418.

WARD, J. R., 1948. *An evaluation of the Veterans Administration Counseling Program at the University of Oregon.* Unpublished master's thesis, Univer. of Oregon.

WARMAN, R. E., 1960. Differential perceptions of counseling role. *J. counsel. Psychol.*, 7, 269-274.

WATSON, D. E., RUNDQUIST, R. M., & COTTLE, W. C., 1959. What's wrong with occupational materials? *J. counsel. Psychol.*, 6, 288-291.

WATT, G. D., 1949. An evaluation of non-directive counseling in the treatment of delinquents. *J. educ. Res.*, 42, 343-352.

WEBSTER, E. C., 1942. A follow-up on vocational guidance. *J. appl. Psychol.*, 26, 285-295.

WEEKS, J. S., 1957. Level of affect in the counseling responses of high school senior boys. *J. counsel. Psychol.*, 4, 297-303.

WHITE, B. J., 1959. The relationship of self-concept and parental identification to women's vocational interests. *J. counsel. Psychol.*, 6, 202-206.

WIENER, M., 1955. The effects of two experimental counseling techniques on performances impaired by induced stress. *J. abnorm. soc. Psychol.*, 51, 565-572.

WILLIAMSON, E. G., 1936. The role of faculty counseling in scholastic motivation. *J. appl. Psychol.*, 20, 314-324.

WILLIAMSON, E. G., & BORDIN, E. S., 1940. Evaluating counseling by means of a control-group experiment. *Sch. and Soc.*, 52, 434-440.

WILLIAMSON, E. G., & BORDIN, E. S., 1941a. The evaluation of vocational and educational counseling: a critique of the methodology of experiments. *Educ. psychol. Measmt.*, 1, 5-24.

WILLIAMSON, E. G., & BORDIN, E. S., 1941b. A statistical evaluation of clinical counseling. *Educ. psychol. Measmt.*, 1, 117-132.

WILLIAMSON, E. G., & BORDIN, E. S., 1941c. An analytical description of student counseling. *Educ. psychol. Measmt.*, 1, 341-354.

WISKOFF, M., 1960. Ethical standards and divided loyalties. *Amer. Psychol.*, 15, 656-660.

WORBOIS, G. M., 1947. Effect of guidance program on emotional development. *J. Appl. Psychol.*, 31, 169-181.

WRENN, C. G., 1949. Potential research talent in the sciences based on Intelligence Quotients of Ph.D.'s. *Educ. Rec.*, 30, 5-22.

WRENN, R. L., 1960. Counselor orientation: theoretical or situational. *J. counsel. Psychol.*, 7, 40-45.

YATES, J. W., 1951. An evaluation follow-up of clients of the University of Missouri Counseling Bureau. *Microfilm Abstr.*, 11, 949-950.

YOUNG, F. C., 1955. Evaluation of a college counseling program. *Personnel Guid. J.*, 33, 282-286.

ZAX, M., & KLEIN, A., 1960. Measurement of personality and behavior changes following psychotherapy. *Psychol. Bull.*, 57, 435-448.

ZILLER, R. C., 1957. Vocational choice and utility for risk. *J. counsel. Psychol.*, 4, 61-64.

Index

Abeles, 256, 303
Abilities, patterns of, 119
Abrahamson, 20, 303
Acceptance
    of information about self, 150
    in interviews, 24-27
Achievements, effects of counseling
    on, 268-272
Ackley, 270, 313
Adams, 270, 303
Adjustment
    personal, 211-238, 277-279
    vocational, 273-277
Advice contrasted with information,
    178-181
Aldrich, 278, 303
Allen, 116, 303
Anderson, 266, 303
Aptitude tests based on factor anal-
    ysis, 120
Arbuckle, 256, 257, 303
Arnold, 6
Ashby, 283, 303
Autobiographies, 91-92
Axelrad, 309
Axelrod, 269, 311

Bachrach, 207, 314
Baer, 155, 304
Baker, 283, 304
Baller, 19, 304
Barahal, 281, 282, 304
Barnette, 266, 304
Bartlett, 234, 304
Baymur, 272, 280, 304
Becker, 172, 304
Beers, 11
Berdie, 19, 37, 119, 122, 147, 148,
    278, 304, 315

Bird, 21, 312
Bixler, 125
Black, 282, 308
Blackwell, 268, 304
Blau, 207, 304
Bloom, B. S., 115, 304
Bloom, W., 267, 304
Blum, 267, 304
Bordin, 19, 39, 125, 261, 268, 319,
    320
Borow, 208, 305
Boyd, 271, 315
Brammer, 281, 304
Brams, 256, 305
Brayfield, 125, 170, 305
Broedel, 272, 279, 280, 305
Brophy, 172, 305
Brown, 269, 305
Bynner, 41, 305

Calhoun, 272, 305
Callis, 38, 305
Campbell, 34, 305
Cantoni, 266, 305
Caplan, 279, 280, 305
Caravello, 265, 305
Cardenal, 117, 305
Carli, 266, 308
Carlson, 281, 305
Carnes, 35, 305
Carper, 172, 304
Cartwright, D. S., 236, 305, 306
Cartwright, R. D., 236, 306
Case records, see Records
Case summaries, examples of, 301-
    302
Cass, 208, 306
Certainties, loss of, 6-8
Chappell, 38

Characteristics of counselor, 255-257
Childhood related to occupational choice, 174-175
Clarification in minimum - change therapy, 221-223
Clark, 266, 314
Client
attitudes toward counseling, 266-268
communicating test results to, 140-146
communication problems with, 184-188
confidence of, 14-15
expectations from counseling, 45-50
Client-centered approach, 16-17
effectiveness of, 281-283
effects of, in counseling, 149-151
Coburn, 306
Cole, 264, 306
College counseling, 20-21
Combs, 34, 235, 306
Communication
of information to client, 184-188
in interviews, 29-33
for vicarious experience, 296
with other workers, 253-255
Concurrent validity of tests, 110, 111
Condon, 269, 306
Confidence of client, 14-15, 229
Confidentiality of records, 97-101
Construct validity of tests, 110, 111
Content validity of tests, 110-111
Controls in research, 262-263
Cottle, 171, 255, 306, 319
Counseling
definition of, 1
in development, place of, 292-295
effectiveness of, 260-286
essentials of, 14-17
informal, 8-9
need for, 18-20
psychotherapy distinguished from, 12-14
tests integrated with, 124-152

Counselor
characteristics of, 255-257
as a person, 239-259
professional responsibilities of, 250-251
role of, 21-22
selection of, 245-250
training of, 240-245, 257
Counselor-client relationship
attitudes of counselor in, 50-53
continuation of, 64-71
expectations in, client's, 45-50
use of, as therapy, 229-233
Cowen, 34, 235, 306
Cowley, 270, 306
Crites, 121, 271, 309, 317

Danskin, 37, 172, 306
Darley, 20, 307
Daston, 279, 317
Davis, D. A., 281, 307
Davis, F. B., 205, 307
Davis, S. E., 35, 36, 37, 307
Decision-making interviews, 189-210
Dement, 19, 307
Dennegar, 266, 308
Developmental process, 287-295
Diagnosis
categories of, 78-79
as comprehensive picture, 63-64
decisions in, concerning
continuation of relationship, 64-71
necessity of consultation, 78
treatment, types of, 71-77
in initial stages, 59-81
mental process in, 80-81
objection to, as central concept, 61-63
points of view about, 59-61
Dictionary of Occupational Titles, 157, 159-160
Dipboye, 38, 307
Discrepancies in case data, 137-138
Dittman, 237, 307
DiVesta, 173, 313

Downgrading, 161-162
Drake, 121, 307
Dressel, 307
Dvorak, 119, 307
Dymond, 235, 315

Earle, 116, 307
Educational counseling, use of tests
    in, 102-152
Elton, 35, 36, 307
Embree, 104, 307
England, 266, 309
Equipotentiality, 198
Erikson, 288, 307
Ethics, professional, 258-259
Evaluation research, 260-286
Ewing, 236, 307
Exploration of resources, 213, 215-
    221
Eyseneck, 233, 307

Factor analysis, 111, 120
Faries, 269, 308
Feingold, 177, 308
Feintuch, 280, 308
Fern, 308
Fialkin, 266, 310
Fiedler, 236, 308
Fine, B., 177, 183, 308
Fine, S. A., 171, 308
Fisher, 120, 308
Fiske, 206, 311
Ford, 304
Forgy, 282, 308
Form, 21, 308
Fotiu, 274, 314
Freeman, 271, 308
Friedman, 309
Froehlich, 146, 147, 261, 263, 308

Gaudet, 266, 308
Gaw, 116, 309
Gellman, 280, 309
Gendel, 309

Ghiselli, 105, 119, 309
Gibson, 236, 309
Ginsburg, 18, 309
Ginzberg, 207, 309
Glasser, 309
Glazer, 266, 309
Goldman, 284, 316
Goodenough, 288, 309
Goodstein, 121, 271, 284, 309
Granada, 117, 305
Grant, 22, 309
Gribbons, 266, 280, 309
Grigg, 174, 284, 309
Group *vs.* individual methods, 281
Guerney, 304
Guidance programs, 264-266
Gustad, 149, 304, 309, 318
Guthrie, 270, 309

Habbe, 38, 309
Hackett, 272, 309
Hagen, D., 175, 310
Hagen, E., 118, 119, 275, 318
Haimowitz, 235, 310
Hand, 264, 311
Harder, 310
Havighurst, 288, 310
Hawkes, 274
Hawkins, 266, 310
Headley, 39, 311
Heilbrun, 121, 309
Heilfron, 23, 310
Heinz, 171, 308
Heist, 258, 310
Herma, 309
Hickerson, 269, 311
Hill, 269, 312
Hoehn, 270, 310
Hoffman, 37, 310
Holaday, 271, 310
Hood-Williams, 234, 310
Hopke, 257, 310
Hoyt, 175, 281, 283, 310
Hummel, 317
Hunt, 116, 117, 310
Hutson, 264, 310

Indecision, 197-200
  vs. indecisiveness, 201-202
Individual
  vs. group methods, 281
  limits of, 295-296
  record form, 297-300
  and society, 4-6
Information
  advice contrasted with, 178-181
  essential characteristics of, 181-184
  filed, see Records
  occupational, see Occupational information
  use of, general, 177-188
Interviews
  acceptance in, 24-27
  aspects most important in, 34-37
  attitudes of counselor in, 50-53
  communicating test information in, 140-146
  communication in, 29-33
  decision-making, 189-210
  essential qualities of, 24-39
  initial, 40-58
  notes during, written, 94-95, 302
  procedural differences in, 37-38
  silent intervals in, 32-34
  taping of, 92-94
  understanding in, 28-29

Jaques, 258, 311
Jasker, 170, 316
Jeffers, 7
Jennings, 116, 311
Jensen, 120, 311
Jenson, 21, 311
Jesness, 277, 311
Jessor, 304
Job suitability index, 188
Johnson, C. A., 257, 313
Johnson, D. G., 148, 311
Jones, A. W., 123, 319
Jones, L., 271, 308

Kaczkowski, 265, 311
Kaess, 275, 311

Kamm, 311
Karr, 257, 315
Keet, 237, 311
Kefauver, 264, 311
Kelly, 206, 311
Kennedy, 175, 310
King, 22, 311
Kirchheimer, 269, 311
Kirk, 19, 39, 257, 311
Kir-Stimon, 280, 311
Klein, 236, 320
Kleinmuntz, 121, 311
Klingelhofer, 272, 312
Koester, 80, 312
Koile, 21, 312
Kounin, 36, 314, 317
Kremen, 243, 312
Kulick, 272, 312

Laotzu, 41
Latham, 118, 275, 312
Layton, 122, 304
Legal status of counselor, 97
Lemon, 271
Levitt, 234, 312
Lewis, 255, 306
Lifton, 257, 312
Limits of individual, 295-296
Lipsett, 269, 312
Long, 269, 275, 311, 312
Lorimer, 274, 312
Love, 277, 312
Lovejoy, 177, 183, 312
Lund, 270, 312

Macrae, 116, 117, 312
Martinson, 277, 312
Matteson, 22, 307, 311
McArthur, 80, 312
McGowan, 38
McKinney, 20, 313
McLaughlin, 279, 313
Meehl, 62, 205, 313
Mental health movement, 11-12
Merenda, 265, 313
Merrill, 122, 238, 313

Merwin, 173, 313
Mickelson, 170, 305
Miller, C. H., 209, 313
Miller, F. W., 267, 313
Minimum-change therapy, 213-224
Minor, 174, 313
Mirk, 267, 313
Moore, 270, 313
Morehead, 266, 318
Moser, H. P., 317
Moser, W. E., 147, 308
Munger, 257, 313
Murphy, 122, 313
Myers, 116, 313

Neel, 174, 313
Neff, 309
Nelson, 267, 313
Newland, 270, 313
Norms of tests, 112-114
Note-taking in interviews, 94-95, 302

Oakley, 116, 313
Occupation
    adjustment to, 273-277
    childhood related to, 174-175
    choice of, 206-209
    classification of, functional, 171
    personality differences in, 173-174
    social roles related to, 172
    women's attitudes of, 175-176
Occupational information
    importance of, 153-155
    integration with counseling, 166-
        169
    kinds of, 158-165
    purposes of, 155-158
    use of, in counseling, 153-176
Occupational Outlook Handbook,
    163
Oetting, 121, 307
O'Hara, 207, 313
Ohlsen, 272, 279, 280, 305
O'Neill, 270, 309
Overstreet, 207, 317

Parker, C. A., 80, 314
Parker, H. J., 148, 314
Parloff, 236, 315
Parnes, 304
Parsons, 9
Paterson, 266, 314
Patterson, C. H., 271, 272, 280, 304,
    314
Patterson, R. L., 274, 314
Peck, 172, 316
Penney, 255, 306
Pepinsky, 78, 81, 314
Perry, J., 272, 314
Perry, W. G., 21, 314
Personal adjustment, 211-238, 277-
    279
Personality
    changes in therapy, 235-236
    counseling limits, 224-229
    occupational differences in, 173-
        174
    tests, 107-109, 120-122
Pierce-Jones, 79, 316
Pohlman, 36, 314
Polansky, 36, 314, 317
Polmantier, 305
Poole, 79, 314
Popham, 270, 313
Porter, 257, 267, 314, 317
Potentialities into actualities, 290-
    291
Pownall, 255, 306
Predictive validity of tests, 110, 111
Professional
    ethics, 258-259
    responsibilities, 250-251
Proff, 38, 272, 279, 280, 305
Prognoses, 205-206
Psychotherapy, 12-14

Ramsey, 309
Raplus, 267, 314
Ray, 236, 309
Recording interviews, 92-94
Records, case
    confidentiality of, 97-101
    cumulative, 95-97

Records, case—(*Continued*)
    information for, 90-95
    initial form for, 297-300
    nature of, 82
    objections to, 82-86
    studying of, 87-90
    values of, 86-87
Reed, 170, 305
Referred *vs.* voluntary cases, 39-40
Rehabilitation, 279-280
Reid, 35, 314
Reik, 44, 314
Reinforcement in minimum-change
        therapy, 223-224
Relationship
    to other workers, 251-255
    See also Counselor-client relation-
        ship
Remmers, 264, 314
Rempel, 121, 309
Research, evaluation, 260-286
    difficulties in, 261-264
    implications of, 284-286
Resources, exploration of, 213, 215-
        221
Responsibilities, professional, of
        counselor, 250-251
Richardson, 272, 314
Robertson, 147, 314
Robinson, 35, 36, 37, 305, 307, 314,
        318
Rodger, 116, 315
Roe, 173, 315
Roeber, 155, 304, 305
Roens, 265, 315
Rogers, C. R., 51, 235, 315
Rogers, L. B., 149, 315
Rosenman, 236, 315
Ross, 271, 315
Roth, 236, 306
Rothney, 265, 311, 313, 315
Rubinstein, 236, 315
Rundquist, 171, 319

Sageser, 18, 315
Saltz, 270, 310
Sarbin, 205, 275, 315

Scarborough, 270, 315
Schaffer, 173, 315
Schneidler, 19, 315
Schwebel, 257, 315
Seeman, 34, 36, 315
Seipp, 316
Selection of counselors, 245-250
Self-knowledge, 146-149
Serene, 272, 316
Sexes, attitudes toward, 47-49
Shartle, 155, 316
Sherriffs, 270, 316
Shostrom, 281, 304
Siegelman, 172, 316
Silvania, 122, 316
Simos, 275, 317
Singer, 148, 316
Sinnett, 208, 316
Skyne, 267, 316
Sloan, 79, 316
Slotkin, 257, 315
Small, 173, 316
Smigel, 172, 316
Smith, L. F., 269, 312
Smith, M., 309
Smith, P., 116, 117, 310, 316
Snyder, 35, 236, 283, 309, 314, 316
Social roles and occupations, 172
Socialization, 289-290
Society and the individual, 4-6
Sonne, 284, 316
Speer, 170, 316
Spielman, 309
Stasek, 272, 316
Stefflre, 148, 316
Steimel, 255, 306
Stephenson, 209, 316
Stone, C. H., 170, 275, 276, 316, 317
Stone, W. L., 20, 317
Stotsky, 123, 279, 317
Stott, 116, 311, 317
Strong, 119, 317
Strupp, 237, 317
Stump, 18, 317
Sullivan, 267, 304
Super, 160, 207, 208, 266, 317
Swan, 121, 317

Taping interviews, 92-94
Tests
  aptitude batteries of, 120
  client-centered use of, 149-151
  communicating results of, 140-146
  counseling uses of, 106-107
  integration with counseling, 124-152
  norms, 112-114
  organization of information from, 131-140
  personality, 107-109, 120-122
  planning of, 124-131
  purposes served by, 102-104
  reliability concepts of, 114-115
  self-knowledge from, 146-149
  types of, principal, 107
  usefulness of, 116-117
  validity concepts of, 109-112
  vocational predicting by, 118-120
Therapy
  effectiveness of, 233-235
  minimum-change, 213-224
  personality changes from, 235-236
  relationship used as, 229-233
  theoretical systems of, 236-238
Thomas, 317
Thorndike, E. L., 118, 275, 318
Thorndike, R. L., 118, 119, 275, 318
Thrush, 22, 318
Tiedeman, 207, 208, 306, 313
Tindall, 35, 318
Toven, 270, 318
Training of counselors, 240-245, 257
Travers, 261, 318
Traxler, 90, 318
Tuma, 149, 309, 318
Turney, 266, 318
Tyler, 257, 288, 318

Understanding in interviews, 28-29
Utton, 174, 318

Validity concepts of tests, 109-112
Vandever, 281, 305
Van Doren, 6, 7, 318
Vardock, 279, 317

Viteles, 273, 319
Vocation
  adjustment to, 273-277
  choice of, 206-209
  See also Occupation
Vocational counseling
  historical origins of, 9-11
  occupational information in, 153-176
  tests in, 102-152
Vogel, 306
Voluntary *vs.* referred cases, 39-40

Walker, 206, 275, 319
Walsh, 174, 319
Walter, 123, 319
Walther, 171, 319
Walthers, 270, 319
Wands, 306
Ward, 266, 269, 319
Warman, 22, 319
Warnath, 317
Watson, 171, 319
Watt, 235, 319
Webster, A. D., 264, 310
Webster, E. C., 274, 319
Weeks, 38, 319
Weinberg, 123, 317
Whisler, 264, 314
White, 175, 319
Wicas, 257
Wiener, 238, 319
Wilcock, 304
Williams, 20, 307
Williamson, 19, 39, 261, 268, 269, 319, 320
Wiskoff, 258, 320
Worbois, 265, 320
Wrenn, C. G., 104, 311, 320
Wrenn, R. L., 283, 320
Wright, 270, 315

Yates, 277, 320
Young, 147, 320

Zax, 236, 320
Ziller, 209, 320